LEARNING
FROM
THINGS

LEARNING
FROM
THINGS

Method and Theory of
Material Culture Studies

EDITED BY W. DAVID KINGERY

SMITHSONIAN INSTITUTION PRESS
WASHINGTON AND LONDON

Copy Editor: Karin Kaufman
Production Editor: Duke Johns
Designer: Linda McKnight

Library of Congress Cataloging-in-Publication Data
Learning from things : method and theory of material
    culture studies / edited by W. David Kingery.
        p.   cm.
    Includes bibliographical references.
    ISBN 1-56098-607-7 (alk. paper)
    1. Material culture. 2. Technology and civilization.
    3. Archaeology and history.
    GN406.L43   1995
    306—dc20   95-11673

British Library Cataloguing-in-Publication Data is available

Manufactured in the United States of America
02 01 00 99 98 97 96   5 4 3 2 1

For permission to reproduce illustrations appearing in this
book, please correspond directly with the owners of the
works, as listed in the individual captions. The Smithsonian
Institution Press does not retain reproduction rights for these
illustrations individually, or maintain a file of addresses for
photo sources.

Contents

ix   Preface

1   1. Introduction
       W. DAVID KINGERY

       Part One. Paradigms for Material
       Culture Studies

19   2. Material/Culture: Can the Farmer and the
       Cowman Still Be Friends?
       JULES D. PROWN

       Part Two. Material Culture in the History
       of Technology

31   3. Learning from Technological Things
       STEVEN LUBAR

35   4. Object Lessons/Object Myths? What Historians
       of Technology Learn from Things
       JOSEPH J. CORN

55   5. Object/ions: Technology, Culture, and Gender
       RUTH OLDENZIEL

Part Three. Formation Processes

73   6. Formation Processes of the Historical and
      Archaeological Records
      MICHAEL BRIAN SCHIFFER

81   7. Pathways to the Present: In Search of Shirt-Pocket
      Radios with Subminiature Tubes
      MICHAEL BRIAN SCHIFFER

89   8. The Destruction of the Archaeological Heritage
      and the Formation of Museum Collections:
      The Case of Denmark
      KRISTIAN KRISTIANSEN

102   9. Passionate Possession: The Formation
      of Private Collections
      MARJORIE AKIN

129   10. Formation Processes of Ethnographic
      Collections: Examples from the Great Basin of
      Western North America
      CATHERINE S. FOWLER AND DON D. FOWLER

145   11. The Formation of Anthropological Archival Records
      NANCY J. PAREZO

Part Four. Materials Science in Material
Culture Studies

175   12. A Role for Materials Science
      W. DAVID KINGERY

181   13. Materials Science and Material Culture
      W. DAVID KINGERY

204   14. Optical and Electron Microscopy in Material
      Culture Studies
      DAVID KILLICK

231   15. Dating, Provenance, and Usage in Material
       Culture Studies
       MICHAEL S. TITE

261   Contributors

Preface

W. DAVID KINGERY

As its predecessor volume, *History from Things: Essays on Material Culture* (Steven Lubar and W. David Kingery, eds., Smithsonian Institution Press, 1993), this collection of essays results from a conference on material culture held at the Smithsonian Institution. At the heart of the conference was the conviction that the things humankind makes and uses at any particular time and place are probably the truest representation we have of values and meaning within a society. The study of things, material culture, is thus capable of piercing interdisciplinary boundaries and bringing forward meaningful discussions and interactions among scholars in many disparate fields. This volume is intended as a beginning discussion, an introduction to the methods and theories common to material cultural studies in a variety of specialist fields.

In general, material culture studies require connecting a characterization of inanimate artifacts—attributes, frequency, associations, distribution—with the human activities associated with materials selection, processing, design, and realization on the one hand and use, function, and performance effectiveness on the other. Object characterization can usually be specified and detailed with some precision. Developing credible inferences about human activities from that characterization is a much more subjective and qualitative process; it differs from one field to another and occasionally has led to emotional controversies. It is my hope that discussions about how these endeavors can be effected more successfully in different disciplines will lead to even more piercing of boundaries, more widespread scholarly interactions, and more productive material culture studies.

In organizing the Smithsonian conference, Jules Prown made most of the arrangements for a session on the "Role of Material Culture Studies in Art History." Steven Lubar made most of the arrangements for a session on the "Role of Material Culture Studies in the History of Technology," and Michael Schiffer made most of the arrangements for a session on the "Role of Formation Processes in Material Culture Studies." The organization of the conference and the arrangements at the Smithsonian Institution were supported and enhanced by Robert Hoffmann, Assistant Director for Research; his associate, Ruth Selig; Steven Lubar; and Betsy Burstein, whose contributions are much appreciated.

Most of the manuscript preparation was done by Dorothyanne Peltz; a completed volume would have been impossible without her.

I

Introduction

W. DAVID KINGERY

Things have been the accoutrements of human culture and society throughout history and prehistory. No one denies the importance of things, but learning from them requires rather more attention than reading texts. The grammar of things is related to, but more complex and difficult to decipher than, the grammar of words. Artifacts are tools as well as signals, signs, and symbols. Their use and functions are multiple and intertwined. Much of their meaning is subliminal and unconscious. Some authors have talked about reading objects as texts, but objects must also be read as myths and as poetry. We are ambitious in hoping to bring together the sensibilities and sensitivities of craftspersons, engineers, artists, poets, men, women, societies, and cultures.

It is our hope and it has been our experience that approaching the method and theory of learning from things as a common enterprise establishes us as material culturists, participants in a relatively new and distinct discipline. That is important because our American culture has deeply embedded within it ideals about individual enterprise, individual freedom, and individual accomplishment. We are led to excel within narrow peer groups of scholarly colleagues. We often write for, communicate with, and value the opinions and judgments of a slender slice of humanity. We, as anthropologists, archaeologists, scholars of American studies, historians of technology, art historians, folklorists, cultural geographers, and others, all do learn from things. This common bond has led us to pierce the boundaries between otherwise disparate endeavors and provides a strong motivation for enhancing that capability, the principle driving force for this volume.

The book is divided in four parts. The first focuses on material culture studies in art history. Jules Prown established the paradigm of object analysis in his precedent-setting article "Mind in Matter" (*Winterthur Portfolio* 18, no. 1 [Spring 1982]: 1–19). Here, he examines the bifurcation between "hard" and "soft" material culture studies, an opposition that extends far beyond art history. In Part Two, Steven Lubar, Joseph Corn, and Ruth Oldenziel examine applications of material culture studies, and the lack and difficulties therewith, to the history of technology. In Part Three, Michael Schiffer and others examine the formation processes that lead to object collections and render them available for study. Understanding formation processes is critical for anyone who intends to learn from any object or object collection. In Part Four, we examine the ways in which materials science contributes to material culture studies. It is convenient to take as the beginning of this development 1949, the year Willard Libby announced his invention of radiocarbon (C-14) dating. Over the next decade the implications of laboratory methods expanded into the consciousness of archaeologists and other material culture scholars. Perhaps typically, this has also led to the invention of new narrow specialties, such as archaeometry, archaeomaterials, archaeometallurgy, and so forth. In any event, there has developed in the last two decades an increasing sophistication for the measurement and interpretation of the internal structures and the properties of artifacts. These new data for object analysis must become a familiar part of every material culturist's intellectual tool kit.

Archaeologists are the peer group for whom the object—its attributes, frequency, distribution, associations—is unfettered by textual evidence and for whom material culture interpretations are most difficult. The difficulty of interpretation is evidenced by the increasing growth of ethnoarchaeology, in which the study of hopefully analogous contemporaneous cultures is undertaken to explain the behavior of those now disappeared. A century ago, antiquarians were first faced with the task of ordering the extensive material remains of prehistory in some sort of believable narrative. With the development of science-based dating techniques within which to site diachronic and synchronic episodes, archaeology took on hermeneutic responsibilities. Thirty years ago, the "new" archaeology developed as what was said to be an explicitly "science-based" endeavor, whatever that means. Following historical archaeology and the new archaeology, we have seen develop functional, structural, processual, behavioral, cognitive, evolutionary, symbolic, postprocessual, and poststructuralist method and theory, among others. Unfortunately, the protagonists of these different viewpoints often see their approaches as mutually exclusive and confrontational. Nonparticipants see none of these approaches as exclusionary. They seem to be different ways of seeing, interpreting, and explaining artifacts as indicators of and data for inferences about social and cultural history. Integrating the wide range of perceptions as to the meanings of artifacts justifies a lot of effort aimed at harmonizing these different world views within the shared discipline of material culture studies.

One heritage from Aristotle is the continuing belief that idle speculation by aristocratic literati is at a higher level and superior to material accomplishment. Aristotle thought one might admire, analyze, and value a sculpture without necessarily admiring or placing much value on the sculptor; *mens* over and above *manus*. This framework has been passed on to our modern technological world, where Francis Bacon's paradigm of science inevitably leading to applied science, technology, manufacturing, and the common welfare has led to scientists being honored while engineers are held in rather low regard. In this volume's first chapter, Jules Prown takes it for granted that "lofty, intellectual, abstract" things are inherently superior to "base, pragmatic" things. He comments that the history of Western civilization is a narrative of mind over matter.

Prown sets out what became the key metaphor of informal discussions at the conference: the idea that material culturists can be categorized as either "farmers," who are "hard" systematic scholars interested in diachronic events and behavior and focused on object attributes consciously introduced by the maker, or "cowboys," who are "soft" humanists concerned with aesthetics and cultural belief systems that are often unconsciously introduced by the maker (objects as metaphors). Because Prown's materialists and culturists are focusing on objects as evidence to be interpreted, material culture would seem to provide a unique opportunity to bring together on common ground these two very different sets of scholars. Indeed, it turned out that face-to-face discussion among archaeologists, historians, materials scientists, anthropologists, sociologists, and others led to rising above disciplinary boundaries. Recognizing their differences, members participated and interacted because, as Prown says, "we want to be together to find common ground."

Communication specialists have found that more than 50 percent of the emotion, passion, and sentiment of speech is indicated not in words but in body language and intonation—factors not available to textual analysis. Prown is concerned not so much with the reading of artifacts as texts expressing the overt intent of the maker but rather with understanding objects as metaphors expressing underlying and often subliminal reflections of the cultural belief structure of the object's creator. To a large extent metaphors are culture-specific; as a result, contrary to Lévi-Strauss, some knowledge of referents, always imperfect, is necessary for interpretation. As Fowler and Fowler point out, object interpretation in a completely foreign culture requires establishment of contexts (Chap. 8). But Prown suggests that the potency of objects in providing an entrée into cultural beliefs lies in the universality of many human experiences— life/death, male/female, stasis/change, giving/receiving—which can be expressed in language of formal oppositions—smooth/rough, hot/cold, clean/dirty—that allow us to begin an analysis in a structural mode. In the end, reality rests in the vision seen through the culturally conditioned eyes of the analyst. Neither the objective reality of the "hard" material culturists nor the subjective reality of the "soft" material culturists is antagonistic to the other; they are just different. The sum of both may be greater than the separate parts.

One result of the mind-set that intellectual abstract speculation is inherently superior to pragmatic accomplishment is that the history of technology, an offshoot of the history of science, has been held in the same low esteem as the engineers and craftspersons it studies. In *American Genesis* (New York: Viking Penguin Press, 1989), Thomas P. Hughes has come out of the closet; he proposes that the story of technological system building is "mainstream American history[,] an exploration of the American nation involved in its most characteristic activity," that "inventors, industrial scientists, engineers and system builders have been the makers of modern America. The values of order, system, and control that they embedded in machines, devices, processes, and systems have become the values of modern technological culture. These values are embedded in the artifacts, or hardware." Since the Renaissance, things— how they are made, how they are used, what they signify—have been central to the culture and social history of the Western world. One could well argue with Hughes that material culture should be our central focus in understanding the Western world's experience. Better, we might accept that the warm emotional and aesthetic content of objects should share the spotlight with their cold practical and cognitive aspects in a holistic approach to material culture.

Technological things—machines, objects, and devices that are primarily utilitarian tools—might well be seen as mainly embodying the nature of technological knowledge, technological change, technological achievement. Although often construed this way, Steven Lubar suggests that historians of technology must also see larger issues embedded in the technology: culture change, social change, class, ethnicity, gender, race. These are what he calls the "big questions of American history." He suggests that technologies and technological artifacts be seen as cultural phenomena, constructs embodying both conscious and unconscious reflections of their makers and users. In this effort, as with that of Jules Prown for decorative art objects, the objects themselves are often the best evidence for the unstated significations of their makers and users.

A contrarian view of material objects in this history of technology is presented by Joseph Corn, who, admitting that he himself has not studied objects, acknowledges his field's public rhetoric asserting the primacy of material evidence. However, an empirical study, a survey of the field's primary journal, *History and Culture,* shows that only some 30 percent of the scholarly papers demonstrate any evidence of the actual study of artifacts, and only 13 percent explicitly discuss or cite objects. Most of the authors who studied objects were concerned with ancient, medieval, or early modern technology (my survey shows that 76 percent of the 1985–92 articles in *Technology and Culture* deal with mid-nineteenth- to twentieth-century technology). Some rhetoric to the contrary, the great majority of historians of modern technology are not committed to object study. Further analysis of what historians of technology actually do in learning from things includes looking at, examining, and thinking about objects as well as occasional detailed scientific studies of artifact attributes. Examples were also found of scholars utilizing simulation and of use testing. But historians are much more likely to study what engineers and others who have worked with objects say and *write* about their experiences. Historians of technology place most reliance on the secondary evidence of persons whom they consider more technically competent than themselves.

Corn goes on to suggest a more indirect and subtle role for artifacts in the study of history. He proposes that many historians of technology are influenced by objects in their very decision to enter the field, their choice of subjects, and their interpretation of documents. He cites a number of examples in which an author's personal interactions with artifacts clearly led to a good deal of learning from things, yet no trace of these encounters were left in the published record. He suggests that the process of professional training "teaches the budding scholar to privilege the cognitive, the theorized, and the abstract over the experiential, the ordinary, and the personally particularized," that "knowledge derived from personal experience, whether tactile, visual, or experiential is not likely to be taken seriously," and that "being 'objective' paradoxically may require suppressing experience with actual objects"—strong evidence that material culture studies remain in rather poor regard for many scholars!

Ruth Oldenziel brings a feminist perspective to technology studies, a viewpoint introduced with the formation of the group Women in Technological History in 1976 and widely experienced a decade ago in Ruth Schwartz Cowan's *More Work for Mother* (New York: Basic Books, 1983). Oldenziel suggests that the rise of material artifacts and devices to the forefront of technological histories is a result of social and cultural trends of the nineteenth and early twentieth centuries in which machines and engineers became the dominant metaphor for technology as a symbol of male power. Production and manufacturing became the focus of taxonomies and studies that were unwittingly gender-oriented and male-dominated. More recently, Thomas Hughes's insistence on technology as a network in which artifacts, institutions, and people are all interrelated components has widened our vision, as have proposals that technology is a social construct. It is now possible to imagine the role of consumers as active participants rather than passive customers in the fashioning of technology. When production and consumption constitute each other, the role of women as "active players in the creation of technical artifacts" becomes evident. Oldenziel suggests that the development of information systems and "cyberspace" (in which black-box artifacts are only a small part of the overall technology) may force us to reevaluate the bounds between material and immaterial. She suggests that a postmodern paradigm is developing in which the status of matter is profoundly changed. Technology should be viewed as a "configuration of knowledge, things, organizations and people" in which things are of diminishing importance.

All history is fiction; we can never "know" the past. However, there are certain bounds on the stories we tell, in some cases loose and in others rather stringent. Formation processes are defined as the ways in which evidence of past behavior, beliefs, cultures, and organizations can be addressed by us in the here and now. Formation processes are the ways by which material entities—documents, artifacts, monuments, oral histories, geographical features—are able to survive the ravages of time and become evidence. Historians and archaeologists alike need to find and validate their evidence before the process of analysis and explanation can commence.

Michael Schiffer has been a leading force in the analysis of archaeological formation processes. He has segregated cultural formation processes (C-transforms), which involve human agency, from noncultural formation processes (N-transforms), which involve chemical (e.g., corrosion), physical (e.g., earthquakes, fires), and biological (e.g., bacteria, bugs) agency. Cultural and noncultural processes act together and/or separately to determine or block the pathways toward survival. Further, Schiffer divides evidence of the past into either the historical record (articles used and conserved by societies, such as archives and public and private collections) or the archaeological record (articles that have been lost, abandoned, or discarded and subsequently discovered). These distinctions allow generalizations to be made about formation of the historical and archaeological records and sound strategies to be developed for discovering and interpreting evidence of the past. In Schiffer's view, one problem with current scholarship is the extreme specialization and division of labor among scholars with diverse research traditions who have privileged particular traces of the past. Understanding formation processes for a variety of sources allows a wider range of evidence to be focused on a particular research problem. In the example he selects to demonstrate this point, shirt-pocket radios with subminiature tubes, we find a number of different sources and evidences, including the radios themselves.

In areas of extended human occupation, such as Denmark, there were remnant barrows and other ancient monuments that filled the landscape at the beginning of the nineteenth century in a way that is hard for us to now imagine. Kristian Kristiansen provides an enormously informative description of the different ways in which these relics were collected and found their way into collections from 1800 to the present, beginning with the rapid destruction of thousands of archaeological monuments. During the first period, 1800 to 1860, surface features were excavated by amateur antiquarians for private collections and then for the National Museum, which was founded in 1807. From 1850 on, as provincial museums began to be founded, there was an increased market for archaeological artifacts. The period of greatest recovery of unprofessionally excavated barrows was 1840 to 1890. As more and more of the Danish countryside was tilled by modern farmers with modern machines, surface material was gradually obliterated and subsurface sites were uncovered. The decline of obvious surface features occurred at the same time as the beginning of professional archaeology. The period of most professionally excavated sites was 1890 to 1940, also the period of founding for most culture-historical museums. Although the excavation of barrows has slowed since 1950, there has been an increase in professional archaeologists, rescue excavations, and historical/archaeological monument registrations. A new perception—that these objects are a cultural heritage that must be preserved—has developed. Protection and control of excavations and monuments has become a national cultural responsibility. Kristiansen suggests that the historical process by which archaeological collections are formed is "essential for understanding the context and the representicity of both the archaeological record preserved in museums and the archaeological record preserved in the landscape."

Private collections are different in kind from public collections. They are often less well catalogued, provenanced, and referenced and more difficult for the scholar to gain access to and use—at least until they are donated and become part of a public collection. Indeed, for archaeologists the ethics of having anything to do with material they deem looted, or at least destructively collected, creates an often unbridgeable chasm between collector and scholar. How and why private collectors have assembled and kept their treasured things and then how these collections are subsequently dispersed and reformed is the topic of Margie Akin's essay.

The formation processes of small private collections have not been so well studied as museum, archival, and other institutional assemblages. Indeed, the differentiation between user/collector is often diffuse. Central to explaining collection behavior is the "widespread desire to connect oneself to the past through the ownership of material culture" and "the very human urge to put the universe in order, to categorize and name things." These compulsions lead people to collect in ways that satisfy personal aesthetics, impart a sense of control or completion, establish connections with the past, and sometimes lead to profit as well as the "thrill of the chase." These drives shape collections. Akin points out that the process of collecting is one of decontextualizing objects from their original culture associations. The collection process, private and public, changes the primary original and intended function of an object into a new social-ideological function taking place in a new cultural context. The association of objects in a new form can tell us a lot about the conscious and unconscious beliefs of the collector and his or her cultural context. Most of the chapters in this volume are concerned with the study of men, women, and children individually and collectively through what they make and use. The study of humankind through what they *collect* and how they use it, the associations and transformations involved, offers a new and fascinating perspective.

Among the reasons archaeologists and some other serious scholars abjure private collections as a source of data are deep-rooted ethical concerns. It is thought that working with, authenticating, using, and giving public exposure to looted or destructively collected objects will tend to reward and encourage looting and other site-destructive sources of material. Professional scholars tend to see themselves as the anointed excavators and preservers of culturally significant material, and there is strong peer pressure not to work with improperly excavated and docu- mented materials. In a somewhat self-serving way, many collectors see themselves playing a positive role in rescuing and conserving material that would otherwise be discarded or destined for neglect in basement storage. The net effect of these differing world views has often been hostility and a loss of data having great intrinsic value for material culture studies. Although Akin does not foresee resolution to this conflict, she suggests we might consider "salvage" data recovery from private collec- tions as analogous to "salvage" archaeology from private sites about to be destroyed. Well worth considering!

Two essays consider different aspects of the formation processes of ethnographic or anthropological collections. Catherine and Don Fowler explore the formation processes for the collections themselves; Nancy Parezo discusses the production and fate of records necessary to effectively use and fully interpret these collections.

Ethnographic collections relate to living or folk groups and are held in natural science or anthropological museums. In the present context they are collections related to Native Americans, which began to be systematically collected about 1870. These must be understood in the institutional context of their formation—funded and organized primarily by museums and also, perhaps surprisingly, by international fairs and exhibits featuring displays related to native peoples. The ideological framework encompassed a model of the vanishing savage, either regretted or anticipated, and also the idea of an "ethnographic present," that is, the native unacculturated state just prior to Anglo-European contact. Somewhat later, when professional anthropologists came on the scene, there were intentional efforts to focus collections on cultural units, that is, a single people, or cultural areas, that is, groups of peoples, as well as typological collections related to morphology or function.

Like other collections, ethnographic assemblages are not a random statistical representation of the theoretical universe of material culture. What is selected and retained depends on explicit or unacknowledged sampling procedures. In order to sort out these institutional, personal, and ideological biases, it is necessary to have some collection history and documentation. Formation processes continue when a collection arrives at the museum depository. By and large, museums have greater ease in funding collections than funding curation and conservation—and many freight cars full of material culture were transferred from the exhibitions of international fairs into the custody of museums. Late nineteenth-century collections have not fared well in this process; collections acquired in the last half-century are doing better.

Fowler and Fowler recount the field collection practices and museum curation and conservation for several collections dating from the 1870s to the recent past. The Powell (1867–80) and Powers (1875) Collections reflect Anglo-European perceptions and rather casual museum behavior at a time of cultural transition. The Lowie (1912–14) and Barrett (1900–1915) Collections were formed by academically trained museum professionals. Curation and conservation of these materials have been effective, but there is a lot of confusion in some of the cataloguing. These collections are valuable for trained scholars, but few of the objects have risen from museum storage rooms to public display. Isabel Kelly (1932–33) and Willard Park (1933–40) were professional ethnographers with rather clear concepts of the purpose of their collection within the framework of sponsors' desire for representative assemblages. More recently, state museums (1930–70) have built collections that tend to focus on comparative culture areas, largely through donations with much less documentation. At the present time, there are a number of new tribal museums centered on contemporary culture and defining a new vision of the "ethnographic present."

Good documentation is essential if there is to be full anthropological study of ethnographic collections. Material objects from a completely foreign culture need analysis in terms of their principle of operation, either as tools or signs, much of which is not decipherable from the object alone. Important documents consist of (1) photographs that show how the object is used in its natural environment; (2) fieldnotes that describe the artifact and recount the time and method of acquisition, along with observations of methods of production and use and auxiliary artifact and environment measurements; (3) accession and catalogue information as well as conservation activities; (4) correspondence records; and (5) research documents, such as project reports and analyses relating the object to a larger body of anthropological knowledge.

For students of material culture, Parezo points out that it is important to recognize that the formation processes for documentation of ethnographic collections and the objects contained in ethnographic collections are very different. Historically, researchers have considered that artifacts are institutionally owned but fieldnotes, and often photographs, are personal possessions. As a result, the formation paths of documentation and artifacts into museums or archival collections are different, and it is rare for them to end up at the same place. For personal records, there is a wide range of retention practice among different scholars. In museums, curators are trained to work with objects and often have not considered documentation to be an integral part of the "collection" and hence not their responsibility. Thus, some large fraction of original documentation is lost, and the records that do accompany collections are made by people far removed from the makers, users, and collectors of the artifacts.

These concerns apply to all museum material culture collections but are particularly difficult for anthropological records because anthropology is such an eclectic discipline, having a wide variety of different sorts of records. The picture is further complicated by the fact that the assemblage of ethnographic collections is often done by avocational anthropologists whose records are even slower to find their way into repositories. The overall result is that the documentation of ethnographic collections is often spotty, frequently discarded, and usually dispersed in a variety of sites difficult to unearth or rationalize. Although the use of archival material in the study and interpretation of material culture collections seems to be increasing, it remains pretty much a hit or miss effort.

The fourth section of this volume discusses contributions and possible contributions of materials science in material culture studies. Many materials scientists have good intentions and are willing to contribute. Every other year the Material Research Society organizes a symposium and publishes *Material Issues in Art and Archaeology;* the 1992 edition ran to more than eighty articles and comprised 1,101 pages. The 1992 volume of *Art and Archaeological Technical Abstracts* contained more than three thousand abstracts. Anthropologists, art historians, and others have difficulty coping with the sheer mass of this material; they see few memorable cultural accomplishments and tend to throw up their hands in despair. At the same time, they recognize that carbon-isotope (C-14) age determination, thermoluminescent dating, X-ray radiography, and trace-element analysis are techniques that must become part of the intellectual tool kit of every material culturist. The output data of these techniques—object age, internal visual structure, and "fingerprinting" of provenance—are useful, even necessary for material culture investigations. History has shown that the naïve acceptance of these results for particular cases is fraught with danger.

Kingery presents a paradigm for materials science and engineering in terms of material structure and properties providing a bridge between performance effectiveness and production activities. He suggests that this same paradigm determines the behavior of craftspersons, artists, and modern and ancient industries. Hence, materials science—particularly concerned with the internal structure of artifacts and with their properties—is the scientific discipline best prepared to participate in any science/anthropology/art/ humanities dialogue. Often easily quantified, inclusion of internal structure—attributes of shape and form, surface texture, color, design, style, typology—can strengthen the credibility of inferences. Properties—mechanical, electrical, thermal, optical, chemical—affect the performance of artifacts in utilitarian, social, and ideological uses and functions, as tools and as signals, signs, and symbols. These data can be applied to explanations of the human activities of design, creation, and manufacture on the one hand and use, function, signification on the other. Kingery presents a number of examples to illustrate ways in which materials science can enhance the effectiveness of the "hard" (objective, material) side of the picture, data that is, he urges, a prerequisite for effective "soft" (aesthetic, cultural, subjective) analyses and interpretations.

The principle technique for the elucidation of internal structure in materials science studies comes from direct observation with optical and electron microscopes, which are each year becoming more effective and easier to use. David Killick discusses the use of low-power microscopy (5–50×), which is easy for anyone to use, and intermediate- (50–1,500×)

and high-magnification ($1,500$–1M$\times$) techniques, which require specialist sample preparation, sophisticated equipment, and techniques. Of increasing importance is the development of quantitative microscopy and image processing, which can be applied to statistical analyses that in previous times required much drudgery.

Killick focuses most of his attention on a realm of human experience, which is poorly recorded in written texts: the development and growth of technology, the processing of raw materials, and the production of material artifacts. Written descriptions of weapons, building crafts, bridges, and mining are meager, but the descriptions of illiterate practitioners at work are at least based on direct observation. Chemical and metallurgical processes are not so visible to nonparticipants. Uncovering the methods, knowledge, and skill of undocumented technologies is based on the recovery, dating, and study of authentic material remains using all the available tools of materials science, often combined with experimental testing and replication of any proposed process. In this endeavor, microscopy is essential in tracing innovations of technology and their diffusion, and in determining the level of knowledge or skill inherent in a given technology and the development of craft specialization and standardization.

In the use of microscopic techniques, it is important to begin with careful visual ($1\times$) examination of an object and then increase the levels of magnification in a systematic way. This implies the need for a truly interdisciplinary effort, a team approach, to integrate the information available from the different levels of structure as they apply to questions posed. Much information is available from surface features observed at low magnification, which does not require specialist apparatus and should be a part of every material culture investigation. Kingery gives examples related to ceramics, machine tools, prehistoric stone working, and cut marks on bones in which examination of surface structures supports inferences about processing methods. Higher-magnification studies have revolutionized ceramic, glass, and glaze investigations and play a continuing primary role in the study of metals.

In addition to materials processing and artifact production, materials science techniques have been critical for dating artifacts, for determining the source of raw materials and tracing trade in exchange patterns, and for finding how artifacts were actually used. Michael Tite shows how dating methods have revolutionized archaeology, providing something like a worldwide absolute chronology from two million years ago to modern times. Of a dozen methods used for special purposes, it is radioactive carbon dating (C-14) for organic materials and thermoluminescent methods for inorganic materials that have proved most important. Metals and glasses have been most difficult to date. The development of accelerator mass spectroscopy, which allows dating with milligram-sized samples has extended the application of radiocarbon dating to art objects, organic residues, and even individual seeds. Three separate laboratories were able to date small snippets of the Turin Shroud to A.D. 1260–1398. Thermoluminescent dating has wider confidence bounds but has been particularly useful for authentication of art and archaeological ceramics. In one example, forty-eight of sixty-six supposed "Hacilar" ceramics, more than two-thirds, were found to be modern forgeries!

Provenance studies are more difficult than dating. Chemical analysis, optical petrology, neutron activation analysis, and stable-isotope analysis have all been useful. Metals are difficult because they are chemically modified during processing and smelting. However, Tite recounts the success of stable lead isotopes in identifying the source of copper ingots in the Mediterranean region and their subsequent distribution along trade and exchange networks. In the last few years, new techniques for analysis of traces of organic residues have made it possible to determine use patterns of tools and cooking vessels. Combined with microscopic observation of these trace materials and wear patterns on tools, we now have a basis for developing and testing models for past human behavior. Tite concludes with the thought that these new methods provide data that can only be fully interpreted in close cooperation with archaeologists evaluating the complete system, from raw material selection through use, function, and discard. Interpretation of data about technology, provenance and usage is only meaningful within an overall historical, cultural, sociological, and economic context.

One common theme in many of these essays on theory and method is the need for applying a variety of methods in order to reach a confident interpretation of material culture. Careful visual examination and a substantial physical analysis of the materials contained, the ways in which various parts of an object are fabricated and joined, composition, surface texture, internal structure, sources of raw materials, and other appropriate measurements are necessary to enhance a primary visual examination. All objects are to some extent art and thus require consideration of both form and content. Subsequent analysis can take many roads, objective and subjective, and must be guided by some purpose, some objective, some problem. It will almost always call for breaking out of narrow disciplinary bounds if truly important insights are to be gained.

Michael Polanyi (*Personal Knowledge* [Chicago: University of Chicago Press, 1962], 328) proposed that understanding any device requires a knowledge of its *operational principle,* "how its characteristic parts . . . fulfill their special function in combining to an overall operation" to achieve some purpose, that is, how it works. This is a major component of what Walter Vincenti (*What Engineers Know and How They Know It* [Baltimore: Johns Hopkins University Press, 1990], 208) describes as fundamental design concepts for engineers. Polanyi goes on to argue that understanding the operational principle requires special tacit knowledge and can never be inferred solely from the device itself standing alone. We can properly extend this idea from Polanyi's utilitarian focus to devices serving as signals, signs, and symbols. Even when use can be inferred with some credibility, the function of an object or device is culture-specific. Fowler and Fowler (Chap. 10 in this volume) insist on the absolute necessity for documentation to accompany ethnographic collections of "foreign" cultures. All other and past cultures are foreign to some extent. The relationship of documentation—written and oral—to objects in the method and theory of material culture studies is an aspect of our discourse we need to expand.

A motif that appears in several chapters relates to the disadvantages of extreme specialization. In America, from the first or second grade onward, we are indoctrinated with the cultural imperative of individual competence, individual performance, individual freedom, individual rewards. In our scholarly endeavors this leads to restricted specialties in which a high degree of competition and achievement is reached in narrower and narrower peer groups. Schiffer (Chap. 6 in this volume) says, "Among archaeologists, the study of retrieved objects is now endlessly partitioned among diverse specialists who examine only one kind of material." The same might be said of historians of technology; Oldenziel (Chap. 5) decries the tyranny of taxonomies. In materials science and archaeology (Chap. 12) Kingery castigates specialists who use only one kind of measurement technique. Both historians and archaeologists often specialize in highly constrained space and time. It is hoped that material culture studies can bring together performance and production, consumers and creators, men and women, diachronic and synchronic, tools and signs, practicality and aesthetics, societies and cultures in a way that enlightens a wide, multidisciplinary audience.

Part One

Paradigms for
Material Culture Studies

2

Material/Culture
Can the Farmer and the Cowman Still Be Friends?

JULES D. PROWN

The term that describes our area of shared interest, *material culture,* links two words that carry very different implications.[1] In my 1982 article "Mind in Matter," I noted that "despite its concision and aptness, the term *material culture* seems self contradictory. *Material* is a word we associate with base and pragmatic things; *culture* is a word we associate with lofty, intellectual, abstract things." Our daily experience of earth and sky "provides a powerful and pervasive metaphor for the distinctions we make between such elemental polarities as material and spiritual, concrete and abstract, finite and infinite, real and ideal. . . . Material things . . . break, get dirty, wear out; abstract ideas remain pristine, free from such worldly debilities."[2]

The history of Western civilization has been a narrative of the progressive mastery of mind over matter. As a result, we have been inculcated with a mode of hierarchical ordering in the way in which we evaluate human activities and experiences, privileging that which is cerebral and abstract over that which is manual and material. Our professional terminological connection of base *material* and lofty *culture* is not simply a verbal matter of seemingly incompatible terms. Among scholars who come from different disciplines yet share an interest in material culture, there is a real division between those who are primarily interested in material and those who are primarily interested in culture. This division marks fundamental differences in focus and approach between the practitioners of "hard" and "soft" material culture, or, more graphically, between the "farmers" and the "cowmen."

The farmers are hard material culturists, focussed, systematic scholars who gather and order information. They are often interested in science and technology, but virtually all curators, regardless of specialization, are farmers. Historians or anthropologists who are farmers tend toward the "social" side of their fields, interested in events and actions, and concentrate on diachronic developments and influences. They concentrate on those characteristics of objects that are consciously put there by the makers. The process is frequently deductive.

The cowmen, soft material culturists often coming from the social sciences or the humanities, tend to range more widely away from the material facts of the artifacts they study. They gravitate toward the "cultural" side of history or anthropology and are more interested in synchronic conditions of belief than in deeds and happenings and their effect over time. They explore aspects of objects that inadvertently express underlying patterns of belief through structure, and they consider what is excluded as well as what is present. The process is frequently inductive.

In brief, farmers are more interested in material and cowmen are more interested in culture. The differences in scholarly interest and modes of investigation get papered over when we assemble, encouraged by broad-minded gurus like David Kingery, to find common ground in our shared interest in the structure of things, internal and external. Although we are aware that the schizophrenic nature of material culture poses a continuous threat of rupture to the enterprise, we gather together because we *want* to be together, to find common ground, and we bend over backward, as we should, to be polite.

I began my academic career as a farmer, producing a standard life and works of the artist John Singleton Copley in which I recorded biographical facts; made attributions to winnow out the copies, fakes, and misattributions; sorted out the chronological relationship of drawings and oil studies to finished works; and created and analyzed a database of information on 240 sitters using a number of variables.[3] Later, as a curator, I became increasingly interested in the cultural dimensions of the decorative arts and over the years have gravitated toward the soft, or cultural, aspect of material culture.

In my introductory graduate seminar at Yale on material culture, called "American Art and Artifacts: The Interpretation of Objects," we examine a series of artifacts week by week, moving from the most aesthetic (painting and the decorative arts) through architecture and clothing to the most utilitarian (tools, instruments, implements), folding in as we proceed an introduction to methodologies such as formalism, structuralism, deconstruction, and semiotics, which are more oriented toward soft interpretation than hard facts. I make it clear at the start that outside of the arts I cannot impart the kind of expertise that is required to do hard material culture, but we do touch on methodologies such as quantification, technical analysis, iconography, and Marxist analysis that relate, at least in part, to the material side of material culture. The emphasis, however, is on culture.

The important point is that neither approach—hard or soft, farmer or cowman—is inherently superior. They are simply different. As Aunt Eller quotes in *Oklahoma!* on behalf of the farmers, "I don't say I'm no better than anybody else, but I'll be dammed if I ain't jist as good."[4]

Material culture is the study of material, raw or processed, transformed by human action as expressions of culture. In order for the object-based study of culture to have validity, the primary datum, the artifact, must be authentic; it must be what we think it is. And in order for the interpretation of culture to have richness, complexity, and significance, we need to know as much about the artifact as possible. That is the essential, fundamental work and focus of the hard material culturists. If the material is not authentic, the cultural interpretation will necessarily be wrong; if the material evidence is thin, the cultural interpretation will be shaky.

The hard material culturist focuses on the reality of the object itself, its material, configuration, articulation all the way down to the molecular level, color, and texture, and then proceeds to a primary level of abstraction by not only absorbing but also producing information in the form of words and numbers. On the intake side, there may be inscriptions, touch marks, labels, and so forth on the object, and there may be external data in the form of written records that provide information about both the artifact and its geographical and chronological context. Language and numbers, although abstractions, are acceptable as evidence to the hard material culturists because they are conscious, intentional expressions relating to the artifact and its world. On the output side, investigators produce writing and statistics, charts and graphs, abstract expressions of understanding and interpretation that are similarly conscious and intentional.

The soft material culturist reads the artifact as part of a language through which culture speaks its mind. The quest is not to gather information about the object itself and the activities and practices of the society that produced it, but rather to discover underlying cultural beliefs. The language of objects, like the language of words, employs a second level of abstraction analogous to figures of speech, including metonymy (one thing representing another), synecdoche (a part representing a whole), and simile.

Although some metaphors are culture-specific, many can be understood transculturally because of the commonality of the human neurophysiological apparatus through which we experience the physical world—our experience of gravity, for example, and of innumerable binary oppositions: day/night, open/closed, wet/dry, etc.[5] In addition to shared perception of the phenomenal world, fundamental life experiences common to all cultures—birth, illness, death, laughter, pain, sexual intercourse, losing, finding, breast feeding—provide another basis for universality. Anthropomorphizing at an appropriate point in object analysis becomes therefore not a logical error but a way of gaining insight.

Metaphors embody and express information about how individuals in a culture feel about their relationship to other people, to things, and to themselves (their sense of identity). Structural metaphors express similarity to something experienced in the physical world.[6] For example, one of my students working on a 1928 candlestick telephone likened the mouthpiece to an ear—you speak into the ear of the other person while grasping the shaft of the phone firmly as if holding your auditor by the throat, having intruded uninvited into their world with an insistent ring.[7] Issues of privacy, communication, and power are involved. Textual metaphors express emotional similarity to something experienced in the inner world of feeling[8]—a squat teapot perceived as "cheerful, comfortable, and grandmotherly," for example.[9]

Over the years I have tried to understand, with only limited success, those factors that suggest to me prior to analysis, often quite strongly, whether or not an artifact will convey significant cultural evidence. Potency seems to depend on a linkage—formal, iconographic, or functional—between the object and one or more of those universal human experiences noted earlier such as engagement with the physical world, interaction with other individuals, sense of self (often expressed anthropomorphically), common emotions, or significant life events. The most persistent object metaphors expressive of belief, based on the evidence of work done by my students over the years, seem to relate to polarities such as life and death (mortality), male and female, privacy and communication, seeing and being seen, power and lack of control, acceptance and rejection, security and danger (fear), truth (reality) and deception (illusion), the natural and the artificial, stasis (permanence) and change (transience), pain and comfort, desire and frustration, protection and vulnerability, freedom and constraint, health and disability, and giving and receiving.[10] These are expressed in a vocabulary of formal oppositions, including:

smooth/rough	stability/instability
shiny/dull	forward/backward
hot/cold	vertical/horizontal
soft/hard	straight/crooked
light/dark	light/heavy
transparent/opaque	thin/thick
up/down	clean/dirty
in/out	

Metaphors in material culture analysis can relate directly to the artifact or to some part or aspect of it (the mouthpiece as ear), or they can arise as figures of speech in articulating responses to the object (the teapot as grandmotherly). Roland Fletcher characterizes artifacts as a mode of nonverbal communication, akin to body language—proxemics. Nonverbal modes of communication have a subliminal dimension—what is betrayed by body language is often not intentional—and can express and provide a way for the analyst to penetrate the ambiguity that is characteristic of human social life.[11] Subtleties are expressed through linguistic disguises—saying one thing but meaning or implying another, that is, through metaphorical language. Soft material culture analysis, like the explication of poetry, is the process of bringing these half-hidden, metaphorical aspects of the language of forms to the surface by articulating them, making that which is felt explicit.

It has long troubled me, as a believer in the power of objects and the authenticity of their language, that in examining an artifact, be it a telephone or a building or a painting, it is necessary to convert vision into words, to say what you see, even if only to yourself, in order actually to see it. A painting or a room exposes itself to your view all at once when you encounter it, but in practice you only see it bit by bit as you become conscious of the details. Interpretation of artifacts is a process, not a revelation, analogous to the comprehension of language—it takes time to complete a sentence or a thought. The necessity of saying you see something in order to see it—ratcheting perception up to conception—is a necessary step in the hermeneutic process, enabling one first to interpret the object and then to convey that interpretation to others. I continue to believe, however, that an object itself can function subliminally as a sign, as a reified metaphor, without requiring the mediation of words. A river coming from an unknown source and flowing toward an unseen destination may function subliminally in all times and all places as a felt metaphor for human existence—we do not know where we came from or where we are going—even when that interpretation is not raised to the level of conceptual awareness. The fact that an unnoticed quotidian event, encounter, or incident can resurface in a dream, often in an altered form, attests to the existence of a fundamental human process of subliminal registration and metaphorical transformation.

Both hard and soft material culturists seek truth or reality. The division between them boils down to a conviction of where reality resides. For farmers, reality lies in facts—in the artifact itself as surviving historical event, in written records and comments, in experimental proof, in statistical data. The enterprise is scientific; interpretations are verified by physical or verbal or statistical data. For soft material culturists, the cowmen, reality resides in neither the physical object nor contextual data, but in the underlying belief structure of the culture that produced the object. To unmask this, the investigator becomes a creator, in some sense superseding the original maker of the object. This is necessary because the pattern of cultural belief embedded in the artifact was not consciously put there by its creator for whom it was a subconscious cultural given, accepted without thought or attention. Reality thereby resides in the interpretation, in the mind of the analyst, and interpretation is conditioned by, indeed limited by, the interpreter's own cultural givens. Over time, the facts of the object may remain the same, but readings will vary. Because art is long and life is short, a constant stream of new interpreters provides a stream of new interpretations.

A substantial problem arises here in the gap between the cultural perspective of the analyst and that of the culture being analyzed. Lévi-Strauss tried to bridge it by defining structural anthropology—the discovery of the underlying belief structures of a culture by analyzing its verbal, ritualistic, and artifactual languages—as a hard science. To defend this position, he adopted a self-denying ordinance, asserting that we are too complicit with Western structures, present or past, to arrive at scientific analysis of them, and therefore can only discover the underlying cultural structures of non-Western societies.[12] Many subsequent investigators have been unwilling to accept this limitation and have creatively explicated Western as well as non-Western, and contemporary as well as historic, artifacts.

In semiotic terms, metaphors are signs that are located between signals, which orient human action (a red traffic light), and symbols, the meanings of which are clearly understood (a cross or the Star of David).[13] In material culture terms, signals convey factual information of interest to curators, social historians, social anthropologists, or psychologists interested in behavior, whereas symbols as intentional expressions of concept interest intellectual historians or, in the form of iconography, art historians. The meaning of the sign, or metaphor, however, is felt but not fully conceptualized. The artifact as sign, as material metaphor, is useful for the study of belief—cultural history, cultural anthropology, psychology, or cultural art history. These second-level metaphorical expressions are no less real than the first-level abstraction of words and numbers, but they are for the most part culturally specific, a language of artifactual metaphor selected out of a universe of possibilities, rather than universally true and verifiable like the abstractions of science. In physics, for example, abstract formulae can, sooner or later, be tested experimentally; an abstract equation can become the reality of an atomic bomb. In astronomy, big bang equations describing the dispersion of matter call out for empirical verification through observation by sophisticated instrumentation. In the cultural interpretation of material metaphors there is rarely supporting documentary proof in hand—if there were, the cultural interpretation would not be necessary—but there is speculation and hypothesizing, which indicates paths that, investigated further, may eventually supply convincing quantitative or verbal reinforcement.

An artifact is the product of a particular historical context—of particular makers using particular tools in a particular place at a particular time. Absent a time machine, it is impossible for the analyst to retrieve that historical context in its totality, its affective as well as factual dimensions. Thus history in the sense of recapturing as well as recording the past is necessarily false.[14] Or, as Christopher Tilley puts it, history is myth. It is not that the past did not exist. It is that it is irretrievable, a strange, alien place and time. We read the evidence, artifactual or otherwise, to construct a story consistent with our explanation of an evolutionary development leading to the present. This is not to say that history lacks meaning or value. Through our interpretations of history we construct our present and shape our future.[15] The soft material culturist, however, is not trying to illuminate our condition, but rather to use our particular cultural perspective to uncover the deeper, unarticulated structures of belief of other cultures—other people, other times, other places—even the culture of ourselves as we were yesterday. History may be myth, but artifacts, which are historical events, are not myth; they are reality—signifieds—that become myth as we interpret them with words—signifiers.

The resolution of the problem, bridging the gap between hard and soft material culturists, may lie in the mutual realization that reality probably resides neither solely in the artifact and its contextual data as the farmers would have it nor only in the culturally conditioned mind of the perceiver as the cowmen are inclined to believe, but in the relationship between perceiver, whether farmer or cowman, and artifact. This suggests the value of striving toward mutual or joint undertakings by hard and soft material culturists, following the model of the sciences in which theoreticians and experimenters collaborate—experimentation to corroborate theory and theory to explain laboratory results. Joint publication would seem a logical concomitant. I hope that we will discuss further, with light rather than heat, the farmer and cowman dichotomy in our shared discipline of material culture and in our specialized fields in order to understand it more fully, and consider models of investigation that might be applicable and helpful.

NOTES

1. The subtitle of this chapter is a paraphrase drawn from the lyrics of "The Farmer and the Cowman," Oscar Hammerstein II, Book and Lyrics, *Oklahoma: A Musical Play by Richard Rogers and Oscar Hammerstein II, Based on Lynn Riggs "Green Grow the Lilacs"* (New York: Random House, [1943]), 85.

2. Jules D. Prown, "Mind in Matter: An Introduction to Material Culture Theory and Method," *Winterthur Portfolio* 17, no. 1 (Spring 1982): 2.

3. *John Singleton Copley*, 2 vols. (Cambridge: Harvard University Press, 1966).

4. Oscar Hammerstein, *Oklahoma*, 89.

5. Jules David Prown, "Style as Evidence," *Winterthur Portfolio* 15, no. 3 (Autumn 1980): 208; Christopher Tilley, "Interpreting Material Culture," in *The Meaning of Things: Material Culture and Symbolic Expression,* ed. Ian Hodder (London: Unwin Hyman, 1989), 187, citing Claude Lévi-Strauss.

6. James Fernandez, "The Mission of Metaphor in Expressive Culture," *Current Anthropology* 15, no. 2 (June 1974): 120.

7. Kenneth Haltman, "Reaching Out to Touch Someone? Reflections on a 1923 Candlestick Telephone," *Technology in Society* 12 (1990): esp. 342–43.

8. Fernandez, "Mission of Metaphor," 120, 123.

9. See my article "The Truth of Material Culture: History or Fiction?" in *History from Things: Essays on Material Culture,* ed. Steven Lubar and W. Kingery (Washington, D.C.: Smithsonian Institution Press, 1993), 9–10.

10. Students in the "American Art and Artifacts" course analyze closely a single object following the procedure spelled out in Prown, "Mind in Matter."

11. Roland Fletcher, "The Messages of Material Behaviour: A Preliminary Discussion of Non-Verbal Meaning," in Hodder, *Meanings of Things,* 33–40.

12. As summarized by Christopher Tilley, "Claude Lévi-Strauss: Structuralism and Beyond," in *Reading Material Culture: Structuralism, Hermeneutics, and Post-Structuralism,* ed. Christopher Tilley (London: Basil Blackwell, 1990), 42–43.

13. Fernandez, "Mission of Metaphor," 120.

14. Prown, "Truth of Material Culture," 6.

15. Tilley, "Claude Lévi-Strauss," 76–77.

Part Two

Material Culture in the History of Technology

3

Learning from Technological Things

STEVEN LUBAR

As a curator of engineering and industry at the National Museum of American History, I spend a lot of time with technological artifacts—moving them around, evaluating them, deciding whether to accept them for the collections, trying to figure out what they are, how they work, how people interacted with them. In my role as curator, I focus on the machines. But I am not only a curator; I have another job as well—or, more accurately, another aspect of that same job. As a historian of American culture, as one responsible for using artifacts to teach American history to a public audience, I spend a lot of time thinking about the ways in which technological things connect with history, connect with culture.

Indeed, for me, understanding how machines work and the details of technological change are merely a means to an end. The end is to better understand some bigger issue, whether it be, on the one hand, cultural change, social change, class, ethnicity, gender, race—the big questions of American history, or, on the other hand, the nature of technological knowledge, the relations of science and technology, or the processes of technological change or technological creativity and design—the key issues of the history of technology.

Historians of technology are not alone in this bifurcated notion of their job. Scholars in many other academic fields have gone through the same divide and have found the change equally difficult. When Clifford

Geertz insisted in 1983 that the job of the anthropologist was to under-stand cultural phenomena "not merely on their own" but also "as signifi-cative systems posing expositive questions," that is, questions about their meaning or intent, many social scientists were alarmed.[1] Richard Fox and Jackson Lears, in their new book *The Power of Culture,* suggest that those who study intellectual history have made this change only in the last decade, and not easily, moving from "arranging the 'great ideas' in proud procession across the centuries" to "considering how all ideas were produced, communicated and received."[2] Historians of technology, too, have begun to accept this idea, though there remain many who think that to understand the technology or, one step further, to understand the changes in technology, is sufficient. This is particularly true of those who work with artifacts and (there is obviously a lot of overlap here) in museums. The weight of the artifacts seems to hold us down, to keep us from asking the bigger and more important questions that these machines can help us answer. (In some cases, the weight is literal; it simply costs too much to move the steam engines and production machinery put in place when rigging was cheaper and museums had more money.) This is too bad, for it is in museums that the general public learns the history of technology; and what they find there, all too often, is the display of technological artifacts in chronological order, the great inventions arranged in proud procession across the exhibit floor.

It is also too bad because, I would like to suggest, it is artifacts that can help us answer the interesting questions. They can do more than display bigger, faster, better. Technological artifacts must be considered in the way we consider other aspects of culture—that is, we should look at technological ideas and objects to see how they were made, communicated, and received, the ways in which they set forth meaning and intent, for both the maker and the user. A technological artifact should be regarded as, to use Geertz's term, a "cultural phenomenon," like any other cultural phenomenon, because it makes for better historical explanation. If we do not consider technology part of culture, if we continue to keep technology separate from culture, if we privilege it, it begins to seem a driving force of history, which leads quickly to a hard technological determinism. The machines seem to come first, to influence rather than reflect society and culture. Machines do, of course, influence society, but this is only a small part of the story they can tell.

The idea that technology is a part of culture is implicit in the school of historiography of technology that holds that technologies are "socially constructed," that is, they are the product not only of economic or scientific or materials forces but also of the social and cultural needs of their makers and users. Technological artifacts might seem to stand outside this view of history. After all, in their size, their power, their very physicality, they provide material proof of the power of technologies. It is hard not to be overwhelmed by the evident power of a giant steam engine or factory machine, the apparently undeniable force by which a bridge or railroad or subway system shapes society. Technological artifacts, perhaps more than any other, possess what might be called "the tyranny of the artifact." They have a presence, a power, that is hard to deny—a presence that, alas, is all too often emphasized in museum exhibits.

But technological artifacts have another sort of power, too—harder to see at first, perhaps, but nonetheless there. Artifacts, more than any other evidence, allow us to understand the ways in which technology is socially constructed. They show us, literally, the ways in which machines reflect culture, in the sense that what we see is the material that has been shaped. It is here that artifacts are important, perhaps primary, evidence, playing a major role in allowing us to answer the big questions about technology.

How do technological artifacts answer cultural questions? The key, Fox and Lears suggest, is semiotics. "A semiotic approach," they write, "encourages the historian to recognize that cultural meaning can be carried by a variety of vehicles—that political pageants and advertisements as well as sermons and speeches are texts to be deciphered." Even census rolls, they propose, have an "inescapable textuality."[3] It seems to me that objects, even technological objects, share something of this textuality. We should add machines and tools and useful objects to the list of texts we must decipher to understand the past. That, in some ways, has been what historians of technology have always done. What we must do differently, though, is to read them not only as technological texts but also as cultural texts, to read them for information about their writers and the others who have read them in the past—in more traditional terms, their makers and users.

The history of technology, when viewed as a part of cultural history, is distinguished, in large part, by its evidence, not its end. What distinguishes historians of technology from other cultural historians are the texts they read. And for historians of technology, objects are among their most important texts.

The chapters in Part Two of this volume set forth some of the ways that understanding technological artifacts serves to answer important questions. Not all of the questions are about cultural history, the ways in which technology and culture overlap and mutually influence each other. Some of them are about the nature of technology itself—the ways in which people think about technology, or the nature of technological choice and change. And some of the questions are about social issues—the ways in which technology influences and is influenced by society. But they have in common that they use as evidence technological things and, in being asked, suggest ways we might learn from technological things.

NOTES

1. Clifford Geertz, *Local Knowledge: Further Essays in Interpretive Anthropology* (New York: Basic Books, 1983), 3.

2. Richard Fox and Jackson Lears, *The Power of Culture: Critical Essays in American History* (Chicago: University of Chicago Press, 1993), 2.

3. Ibid.

4

Object Lessons/Object Myths?
What Historians of Technology Learn from Things

JOSEPH J. CORN

It would seem axiomatic that objects are central to the history of technology. Like archaeologists or historians of art, historians of technology take *things* seriously. They lavish much time, energy, and not a little affection on the documenting and analyzing of things ranging from airplanes to bridges, clocks to drilling rigs, and much more—literally devices or artifacts from A to Z. Additionally, the field's public rhetoric asserts the primacy of material evidence. "The historian of technology must deal with the real article," claims Carroll Pursell, past president of the Society for the History of Technology; objects are our "primary sources."[1] Laurence Gross, a respected scholar of textile industry and technology, stresses "the importance of research outside the library," the hands-on scrutiny of three-dimensional objects.[2] For writer T. E. Leary, the object is not merely a source, it is literally the key to historical meaning, a "sort of Rosetta Stone" that helps us "decipher the language" of industrial sites and other artifacts.[3]

Not surprisingly, many are drawn to the history of technology by their attraction to and interest in technical objects. I suspect my own personal experience is not unusual. As a youngster, I loved cars, trains, planes, and most kinds of machines, and though I somewhat suppressed these interests during college and graduate school, they were rekindled when, as a newly minted Ph.D., I joined the Society for the History of Technology (SHOT). There I met many kindred spirits, people who were not only scholars but also interested in old machines or industrial sites.

Like myself they enjoyed watching trains, attending old car swap meets, or visiting museums filled with old clocks or radios. When I took my first full-time university job in 1980, I found myself offering courses with titles such as "Machines in History," "The Automobile and American Culture," and "Introduction to Material Culture."

I should mention one additional biographical fact, for it complicates the picture of a field seemingly built around learning from things. Despite my lifelong fascination with the machines of transportation, I have never done any systematic research on objects. I have written *about* them, but I have not considered myself to have learned much directly *from* them. To admit this in a book titled *Learning from Things* is somewhat embarrassing, but given the fact that I am not wholly aberrant in my field, my admission raises a key question: What exactly is the place of object study in the history of technology?

To get some sense of what my colleagues in the history of technology have been learning from artifacts, I decided to survey all of the articles published in *Technology and Culture* (*T&C*), the quarterly publication of SHOT, over the last decade.[4] *T&C* is the premier publication of its kind in the United States and enjoys the respect of scholars abroad as well. Although there are a few other journals in which people who consider themselves historians of technology occasionally publish, *T&C* reflects some of the best work done in the field and can give us a bench mark of what practitioners are doing with material culture.[5] Thus I examined every article, research note, and essay on "cover design" with an eye toward determining whether it was primarily about technical artifacts and, if so, the degree to which it drew upon artifactual evidence and made the object a primary source.[6]

My survey revealed first that slightly more than half of the authors publishing in *T&C* did not write about objects at all.[7] Instead of being interested in the development, production, deployment, impact, or even the perception of technical artifacts, these writers were concerned about ideas, institutions, or politics, although such subjects in the history of technology obviously can not easily be wholly divorced from their material contexts. Articles with titles like "The Philosophy of Luddism," "Marx and the Machine," and "Academic Entrepreneurship and Engineering Education: Dugald C. Jackson and the MIT-GE Cooperative Engineering Course, 1907–1932" fall into this category.[8] Scholarship displaying a lack of concern with artifacts has disproportionately influenced historiographical controversies within the history of technology, however, and has contributed significantly to the field's professionalization, especially relative to its older sister specialty, the history of science.[9] The second conclusion of my survey is that, of the authors writing in *T&C* who did focus on the history of technical artifacts, slightly more than 70 percent relied exclusively on traditional written or published sources, occasionally supplemented by oral interviews.[10]

These points lead to the third and most important conclusion of my survey: less than 15 percent of the authors publishing in *T&C* employed *any* material evidence.[11] Or, to put this most positively, about 30 percent of the scholars writing about objects also derived some of their evidence from actual study of the artifacts. Not surprisingly, these "object persons," as we might term them, were more likely to write on ancient, medieval, or early modern technology, presumably because fewer written documents survive from those periods. Additionally, the group contained a disproportionate number of archaeologists, whose discipline disposes them to object study.[12] Parenthetically, the survey suggests that object persons are no more likely to be based in museums than in universities, and they are no more likely than their academic colleagues to use artifacts as evidence.

Rhetoric to the contrary, then, the history of technology as a field is not deeply committed to learning from things. Claims that artifacts are "primary documents," that they can supplant libraries, or that like the Rosetta stone they can make mute objects speak grossly exaggerate practice. They constitute what I call "object myths" and distort the saliency of real objects in historical work.[13] Nor does there appear to be any strong trend toward object study among historians of technology.[14] This is not to deny, however, that some scholars have gleaned valuable object lessons from artifact study. On the basis of my survey of *T&C*, I have identified five different methods or approaches used by scholars in their learning from things: (1) ordinary looking, (2) technical analysis, (3) simulation, (4) testing through use, and (5) archaeological science. I do not claim this list is comprehensive; I am not even sure the label "method," with all its connotations of rigor and system, is warranted. Furthermore, obviously not every approach works for every artifact. Finally, these methods are not mutually exclusive, and scholars often employ more than one simultaneously, as is true of a number of the examples that follow.[15]

An instance of "ordinary looking" may be found in an essay by Steven Lubar, titled "Culture and Technological Design in the 19th-Century Pin Industry."[16] Lubar focuses on the pin-making machine invented in 1841 by the Reverend John Howe. The device was acquired

in the late nineteenth century by the Smithsonian Institution, and Lubar
became involved with it while curating an exhibition on the industrial
revolution for the National Museum of American History (NMAH). As
part of that work, he oversaw its restoration to operating condition.
Lubar's article seeks to illuminate the design and configuration of Howe's
invention. He assumes that there was no single or obvious way to construct a pin-making machine, and that Howe's device was a cultural
artifact, explicable within specific beliefs and practices. Indeed, Lubar's
study of patent records and other documentation revealed that many
other inventors had also built machines to automate the ancient handcraft
process of making pins, but that none of them resembled Howe's.

Looking at Howe's machine raised for Lubar various questions about
the form and function of its various components. Why, for example, had
Howe decided to have his machine pass partially finished pins from one
work station on the machine to another instead of holding the workpiece
stationary and, like many modern machine tools, bringing a variety of
shaping tools to bear on it? Part of the answer came through traditional
scholarship, through reading. Lubar knew that Howe had observed pins
being made by hand and that he was familiar with the practice, so well
described by Adam Smith in *Wealth of Nations,* whereby each artisan
performed only a single operation, say, extruding the wire, pointing the
pin, or forming the head, and then passed the partially manufactured
pins on to a colleague in the workshop. But a crucial piece of the puzzle,
an answer to his question about the machine's design, came through
looking at the Howe machine in operation.[17] Observing the work table
intermittently rotate and pass a partially made pin to a new station for
pointing, heading, or some other process, Lubar realized that the inventor
had in effect inscribed "the previous structure of the industry" in his
machine.[18] The choice by Howe of rotary motion for his pin-making
machine, although influenced by other factors, dovetailed nicely with
workshop practice and common experience.

The second approach to learning from things, what I call "technical
analysis," is almost antithetical to ordinary looking. Walter J. Vincenti's
article, "Technological Knowledge without Science: The Innovation of
Flush Riveting in American Airplanes, ca. 1930–ca. 1950," provides a
good example of this method.[19] To anyone familiar with this widely cited
article, my inclusion of it here might seem puzzling, for Vincenti did not
himself analyze rivets as part of his research. Unlike Lubar, who as a
museum curator lives in what might be called a culture of material culture,

Vincenti, as an academic engineer turned historian, had no particular stake in humanistic learning from things. His primary interest, in fact, was not really rivets at all. Rather, as the title of his article suggests, he was interested in the processes whereby technological knowledge was created and the ways in which it differed from scientific knowledge. Most broadly, his work sought to rebut the widely held belief that technology is merely applied science by demonstrating that technology often operates independently of science. In the context of these larger aims, flush rivets just happened to be a subject that served his intellectual ends; it was the innovation process that concerned him.

Although Vincenti himself did not carry out any technical analyses of rivets in his research, his article rests firmly on object study. He relied greatly on the writings (and recollections) of engineers who, at Lockheed, Douglas, Northrup, and other aircraft plants in the 1930s and 1940s, had conducted extensive analyses while developing the flush-riveting technique. Those men, Vincenti told me in an interview, could "read a rivet like a book." But they also could write, and they left behind a vast corpus of written reports, tables, and manuals bearing on flush riveting design and practice. It was largely by reading what those who "read" rivets had themselves written that Vincenti could reconstruct the historical process of invention at the airframe companies some half-century earlier. One doubts that he ever could have acquired so full an understanding of the development of the new aircraft fasteners by studying rivets directly, either as isolated artifacts or in situ in preserved vintage aircraft. The object lessons he sought were enmeshed in and inseparable from the specific processes of design, fabrication, and testing that occurred in the 1930s. What a lawyer would call the "best evidence" as to what those processes consisted of, after the historical moment of their inception had passed, lay not in things but in contemporary accounts about those things, particularly in contemporaneous, written, technical analyses.

No such written analyses exist for technical artifacts from premodern times, so historians of those technologies must rely on other sources and methods. A few scholars have employed "simulation," our third approach to learning from objects. David P. Billington and Robert Mark used several simulations in their article "The Cathedral and the Bridge: Structure and Symbol."[20] Like Vincenti, the authors were interested in issues related to technical knowledge. Specifically, they wanted to know what the builders of cathedrals understood about statics, the branch of physics covering the behavior under stress of various stationary elements in a building or structure, and how that knowledge influenced design. After studying the form and construction techniques of cathedrals, and noting the location of visible stress cracks, they employed their data to build "both small-scale physical models and computer-based mathematical models" of the buildings. They then used the models and contemporary theory to test how specific loads would stress and deform the structure. The stresses predicted by modeling were then compared with the cracking visible in the actual structures. The modeling experiments showed, the authors argued, that the builders of medieval cathedrals had a highly developed knowledge of the principles of statics.[21]

This conclusion then supported a larger argument about the relationship of engineering knowledge to aesthetic form. Art and architectural historians traditionally have held that the "joyous" period of medieval cathedral building ended "when problems of statics and dynamics displaced passion," as Billington and Mark put it. They propose instead that Gothic builders only became capable of "joyous" expression by developing an understanding of statics, which made possible the new, more delicate and soaring structural forms.[22]

Other historians have obtained the kind of knowledge Billington and Mark derived from simulated objects by testing actual (or sometimes replicated) artifacts. "Testing through use," then, is our fourth approach to object study. This method has helped scholars resolve a major scholarly controversy over whether the parts of the muskets made by Eli Whitney were interchangeable. Whitney had long been celebrated as the first arms maker to perfect the practice of interchangeability, but when historians actually tried to interchange lock components from the muskets he manufactured, that is by testing the actual artifacts, they discovered the parts did not fit. Whitney was, as David Hounshell has written, a "publicist of mechanized, interchangeable parts manufacture, not a creator."[23] Many historic technics, however, are not so easily tested as small-arms parts. The owners of many old machines and other devices are often hesitant to let people handle or operate them because use might harm the object, the user, or others nearby. Some historic objects might not operate at all, or their original construction may have been so altered that any current test would provide performance data of dubious historical value. And other artifacts have not survived to be tested. Such factors have encouraged the reproduction of artifacts that have then been used as a source for generating historically relevant information. Considerable knowledge, for example, has been gleaned from the building and use of reproduction sailing and rowing craft, and similar valuable information has been extracted from the replication and use of historical weapons and tools.[24]

Only a few authors in *T&C* have employed data gleaned from historical replication, but one notable example is an essay by Vernard Foley on "Leonardo, the Wheel Lock, and the Milling Process."[25] Foley offers a fresh perspective in an ongoing controversy over whether Leonardo da Vinci ever invented anything original or useful. Siding with advocates of Leonardo's genius, Foley focuses on the wheel lock, which was an early improvement to firearms. Once activated by a trigger, the wheel lock automatically ignited the gunpowder in the pan, leading to the discharge of the weapon. "The wheel lock made it possible for the first time to carry a weapon which was concealable but instantly ready for action," Foley explains. "Hence the pistol now appeared," facilitating the work of assassins, highwaymen, and altering the practice of cavalry and other soldiers. The device, Foley adds, "was by no means a trivial invention."[26]

No dispute exists as to da Vinci's interest in the wheel lock; a page in his notebooks, the *Codex Atlanticus,* features several designs that "everyone agrees are for the wheel lock design." What interests Foley on that page of the *Codex,* however, are some sketches of cutting-edge tools similar to those used to cut screw threads. These sketches, previously unremarked upon, resonated for Foley, who was wondering how Renaissance craftsmen produced the groove in which the wheel of the wheel lock rotated and whether the wheel itself might not have cut its own groove. (This line of speculation might seem arcane, yet as we shall see, Foley pursued it as a means to a larger historiographical end.) Unless "the fit between wheel and pan" were unusually close, Foley figured, the fine-grained gunpowder used in firing pans would have dribbled out when the weapon were holstered or carried on a galloping horse, thereby negating the wheel lock's supposed benefits. Measurements of a number of sixteenth-century firearms showed that in fact the close fits between wheel and pan "approach modern industrial standards and raise the question of how the slot was made." The question became all the more interesting because, as Foley continues, "the wheel can run as thin as 1.8 millimeters, and the pan may embrace up to a third of the circumference of a wheel whose diameter may range from 25 to 40 millimeters. The slot can thus be 5 or 6 millimeters deep and is quite cramped for any kind of hand filing or chiseling." Study of the various parts of historic wheel-lock mechanisms under magnification confirmed that no hand filing had been done on the critical parts.[27]

Foley's evidence supported a radical hypothesis, that "the job was mechanized, with the wheel rim utilized as a cutter to create its own cavity." He believed that the concave shape of the wheel rim, cut by tools such as were illustrated in da Vinci's notebooks, would better enable the wheel to act efficiently as a cutter. Yet the mechanical engineers he consulted as to the capability of such wheels to cut mild steel expressed doubts over his hypothesis. At this point Foley concluded that "nothing would do but to try it," which brings us to his historical replication. He constructed a lock "using traditional hand tools and methods" and tried to use the turning wheel of the wheel lock to cut or mill its own grove. "The results," he writes, "were gratifying." Although the two and a half to five hours it took to cut about 2.5 millimeters into the mild steel pan "seems absurdly slow by modern industrial standards, yet it is several times faster than hand fitting, at least with an amateur's skill," he concluded. Foley's hands-on replication and use of a historic technic provided evidence attainable only from the object and its use (or, more precisely, from its production) and enabled him to make a bold revisionist claim regarding the significance of the wheel lock. "The wheel-lock wheel," Foley asserts in his conclusion, "is thus a rotary metal cutter, the most crucial component of the milling machine." Da Vinci, in other words, contributed not only to firearm technology but also significantly to what Foley terms the "prehistory" of machine tools. Historians, he suggestively adds, may thus have underestimated the influence of firearms on technical development and exaggerated the importance of the clock.[28]

Whereas replication entails the construction of a new artifact, my fifth and final method, what I call "archeological science," can produce important new knowledge from old things. Robert Gordon gives us a fine example of the approach in his essay "Who Turned the Mechanical Ideal into Mechanical Reality?"[29] He is interested in the skill possessed by workers producing goods with machinery. "Documentary sources reveal little about what was required of the artificers engaged in manufacturing in the 19th century," Gordon explains, so "the problem must be approached by archaeological methods. The surviving examples of 19th-century products are a source of information about the work of those who made them; they give us a kind of direct contact with the individual artificers that cannot be attained in any other way. Heretofore there has been little progress in interpreting many of these artifacts, for want of appropriate methods of analysis. But now appropriate methods are available."[30]

Gordon focuses his search for evidence of skill on a study of the gun locks turned by federal and commercial armories during the decades in which precision metal-cutting machinery was introduced into the workplace. His methods include the microscopic analysis of "surficial markings" made by cutting tools, precise measurement of the dimensional variations and eccentricity of tumblers, and metallurgical analysis of their hardness. The evidence Gordon draws from his investigation shows that "by 1850 artificers using hand files had learned to bring rough forged and machined parts of complex shape to final dimensions specified by gages to an accuracy of a few thousandths of an inch" and that "hardening remained a difficult problem for the makers of lock parts long after good dimensional control had been achieved in production."[31] The "mechanical ideal" of interchangeability, Gordon concludes, owed as much to skilled artificers as to improved machine tools. And thus the introduction of technology did not lead to a general deskilling of the armory work force, as so much historiography suggests.

This brief survey of recent scholarship clearly shows that technical things can be valuable and even unique sources of learning for the historian of technology. More important, it demonstrates that the study of material culture can not only provide knowledge about particular artifacts but also contribute to the broader historiographic discourses of concern to scholars. This is certainly the case with articles like Gordon's on the deskilling of work or Vincenti's regarding the nature of technical knowledge. At the same time, however, our review helps explain why, despite the "thingness" of the field, only a minority of its practitioners appear to have studied things firsthand and drawn their evidence from them. One reason for this is that many of the issues that interest historians of technology are not easily studied through artifacts.[32] As noted earlier, historians of technology have shown a strong interest in issues involving the nature of technical knowledge, the role of institutions in stimulating technical innovation, and other issues whose important sources are not objects. Even when one's questions directly concern things, the objects themselves are not always the best evidence on the subject.

Yet we should not conclude this discussion of the place of object study in the history of technology without considering the ways in which writing, seemingly based entirely on written, non-artifactual sources, may still influence a scholar's experience with artifacts. As an example, consider again Walter Vincenti's article about the development of flush riveting. I asked him whether he had learned anything from studying rivets or airplanes firsthand, and he answered no. Yet he quickly volunteered that some fifty years earlier, while a young graduate student, he had "bucked rivets" while working for a summer in a southern California aircraft plant. Clearly he *had* learned something through a firsthand encounter with objects, although the notes of his article acknowledge no learning from things. As a result of that conversation, I found myself wondering to what extent Vincenti's summer job might have influenced his choice of the subject of flush riveting. Seeking a case study in which new technological knowledge had been generated without any dependence on science, and inclined to continue his historical exploration of aeronautical engineering, his former specialty, might not the early rivet work have suggested a topic for investigation? More importantly, might not his experience bucking rivets have helped Vincenti more readily to negotiate the theoretical, engineering-oriented information he unearthed in researching his article?

Definitive answers to such musings are impossible, but I began thinking about the degree to which work in the history of technology might be indebted to personal encounters with objects, experiences authors did not deem part of their research or even relevant to their scholarship yet nevertheless influenced their writing. I suspected that many writers in the field had, like Vincenti, undergone what we might term "artifactual apprenticeships," which provided them with tacit and explicit knowledge that then might influence the history they wrote. I decided to test this hypothesis by talking to a few other *T&C* authors. I chose writers who had written about technological artifacts but whose articles, judged at least by their scholarly apparatus, had not been based on learning from things.

An article by Bernard S. Bachrach, a leading scholar of medieval warfare and military organization, and Rutherford Aris, a chemical engineer and Latin paleographer, typified my requirements. In "Military Technology and Garrison Organization: Some Observations on Anglo-Saxon Military Thinking in Light of the Burghal Hidage," the authors employ some archeological data from secondary sources but largely rely on the traditional written sources of the medieval historian.[33] Nothing in the text or notes of the piece directly acknowledges that the authors themselves had learned from objects, yet their confident and knowing discussion of weaponry, specifically the two-handed ax and long sword, raised the question whether artifact learning contributed to their analysis.[34] When I asked Bachrach to "tell me on what kind of knowledge the passage was based," he emphasized first the importance for his and his coauthor's work of previous publications by scholars who *had* studied objects. He also claimed scholars could learn a great deal about the use of particular hand-to-hand weapons by mathematically modeling the movements and forces involved in wielding them. In response to further questioning, Bachrach admitted that he had handled medieval weapons of the kind he wrote about. He also mentioned that, much earlier while in high school, he had been a fencer, "but that is neither here nor there," he quickly added.[35]

If firsthand familiarity with relevant objects did not figure consciously in Bachrach's historical analysis, they did for Gail Fowler Mohanti, who wrote "Experimentation in Textile Technology, 1788–1790, and Its Impact on Handloom Weaving and Weavers in Rhode Island."[36] Although Mohanti's article similarly betrays no indication of any learning from things, she readily admitted that the handling of the technologies about which she wrote was very important for her. She felt strongly that to learn about a technology, she had "to touch" and use it; only then does a handloom or its parts become "more a part of your own vocabulary," she added.[37]

Perhaps the strongest case for the proposition that historians of technology frequently learn much more from objects than their published work reveals came from my conversation with Larry Lankton, author of "Machine *under* the Garden: Rock Drills Arrive at the Lake Superior Copper Mines, 1868–1883."[38] His article, although citing no firsthand study of mining machinery, showed a keen appreciation of the heft of rock drills, the difficulties one man had in operating them, and the challenges of setting such equipment up on a stope far below the surface. "I didn't learn much from three-dimensional artifacts," he confessed in talking about his mining research, which recently resulted in a book; indeed, he had not seen firsthand most of the equipment about which he wrote. Yet Lankton definitely had held an artifactual apprenticeship of no little significance: years earlier he had been a curator at the Henry Ford Museum. There he was responsible for machinery, although the institution's collections contained little related to mining. But museum experience, he claimed, gave him a general knowledge about mechanical artifacts that could readily be brought to bear on his research about late nineteenth-century mining technology.

Lankton also mentioned two other kinds of object lessons that were valuable surrogates for any direct consultation of nineteenth-century rock drills. One was the visiting of mines, where he observed rock drills in use. What he saw in these mines was obviously not nineteenth-century practice or even "living history" using nineteenth-century machinery. But modern mines nevertheless conveyed information about many aspects of the underground work environment, including noise levels and general ambience, that Lankton felt was somewhat timeless and thus critical to his scholarly reconstruction of past experience. Second, Lankton "went to photographs," as he put it, for evidence. He told me that he looked at literally thousands, many contemporaneous with his period, in researching his subject. Three of these are included as illustrations in his article.[39] Photos enabled Lankton to see miners at their work sites, study how they used their rock drills, and understand the way the rock machines were mounted. Photographic representations are obviously subject to manipulation, and in his article Lankton notes how one image "sanitizes the environment" of the mine, where men "would normally work amid far more dust and have far less light."[40] He argues, however, that photographs served as a corrective to the "sanitized line drawings done for commercial purposes" that were published in mining trade journals. Overall, then, Lankton's artifactual apprenticeship—his handling of other kinds of machinery in the museum and his visits to modern mines—along with his study of photographic representations of the material culture of mining, enabled him to approach nineteenth-century mining artifacts without actually studying them firsthand. As he put it in concluding our interview, he "didn't feel the lack of real-world representations."[41]

In showing that Vincenti and Lankton learned more from things than they acknowledge in their articles, that they in effect possessed some sort of artifactual apprenticeship not admitted in their publications, I in no way aim to discredit these fine historians. I want only to call attention to a scholarly practice that understates what historians of technology learn from objects. As to how many historians have used artifact-derived knowledge to augment the traditional evidence cited in their published writings, and what sort of artifactual apprenticeships they have brought to their work, it is impossible to know without conducting many more interviews. It is much easier to find a reason for this masking or erasure of experience. The process of graduate training quickly teaches the budding scholar to privilege the cognitive, the theorized, and the abstract over the experiential, the ordinary, and the personally particularized. One then readily learns that the opposite of a "professional" publication is a personal account, and that knowledge derived from personal experience, whether tactile, visual, or experiential, is not likely to be taken seriously. Even in an object-centered specialty like the history of technology, being "objective" paradoxically may require suppressing experience with actual objects.

I'm aware of only one article published in *T&C* in which the author alludes to any special knowledge derived from personal encounters with things, but the reference is in the biographical blurb provided by the author.[42] There is, however, a well-known book by a historian of technology that not only alludes to knowledge gleaned from personal experience but uses it to frame the study: *More Work for Mother*, by Ruth Schwartz Cowan.[43] Cowan's book examines the evolution and use of household technology in the United States from the early nineteenth century to the present. It grew out of extensive learning in libraries and archives, but Cowan also explicitly acknowledged what she learned while interacting with the washers, dryers, and other appliances and gadgets in her own home. As a homemaker and mother of little children, as well as a scholar, she observed how the design of her own kitchen created more work for mother. Wanting her little girls to help her set the dining-room table for dinner, for example, she writes how the high location of her kitchen cabinets and their closed doors meant that the children couldn't see, let alone reach, the plates, cups, or other items she asked them to get. Cowan also recounts her experiences living with a washing machine and dryer. The machines enabled her to ensure that her children's clothes sparkled whenever they ventured into public. Yet Cowan describes the moment when, noticing one day that egg had dribbled down the front of her daughter's freshly cleaned dress, she decided the hell with it. The child didn't care, and so Cowan did not undress the child, toss the jumper into the wash, and put her in clean clothes as she usually did in the past, just to keep up appearances among her children's teachers or other mothers. She decided to resist the culturally constructed standards of cleanliness that, facilitated by supposed "labor-saving" devices, imposed unnecessary burdens of work.

Cowan's perspective on domestic technology obviously owed much to feminism. Starting with the publication of Betty Friedan's *Feminine Mystique* in the 1960s, feminist analysis has alerted thousands of women to the ideological and exploitative traps of domesticity. As the personal became the political, as the saying goes, the scholarly study of domestic life took off as a specialty. As a woman, mother, and home laborer, as well as a trained historian of science and technology, Cowan was one of the first to focus on the machinery and material environment of the homemaker. And as a feminist, she saw those objects—the cabinets and washing machines—through different eyes, learning much that others before her never really noticed or deemed historically relevant. Interestingly, however, her own Dexter Prize–winning book relegated the personal and object-based learning to the introduction and postscript, the latter titled "Less Work for Mother." The pressures to suppress personal, experiential learning and to privilege text-based learning, it seems, influenced even Cowan's exemplary monograph.

One wonders what kind of history of technology might be written were authors to follow Cowan's lead and be more self-reflexive, even ethnographic, when they write about technical objects. Exactly how the acknowledgment of such experiences, and a direct engagement with them in the process of historical analysis, might reshape historical narratives remains to be seen. Yet not only feminist scholarship but also work in anthropology, legal studies, and literary criticism increasingly blurs the lines between the personal and the professional in ways that have greatly enriched intellectual discourse.[44] Some of this work may be suggestive for the practice of historians of technology.

Although this is not the place to try and envision what a more self-reflexive scholarship in the history of technology might look like, I'd like at least to gesture toward such an approach by briefly looking back on my first book, *The Winged Gospel,* which I published ten years ago.[45] That study examined the cultural response to aviation in the United States during the first half of this century. It was researched, first as a dissertation, exclusively in libraries and archives, and one would find in its pages no mention of any learning from things. Only as a result of writing this essay did I come to realize that the book was definitely shaped by what I call an artifactual apprenticeship. As a child I spent much time building and flying model airplanes, and as a young adult I received informal flying lessons from pilot friends who let me take over the controls of their small planes. It now seems quite obvious that these encounters with real three-dimensional airplanes, full-sized and models, influenced my choice of subject. More important, learning from aeronautical objects also shaped my interpretations. In a chapter about the dream of an airplane in every garage, for example, I sympathetically interpreted the effort in the 1930s to replace traditional aircraft controls with what was then a new, "simplified control" system, probably because I had experienced firsthand the difficulty of coordinating my hands and feet so as to make a smooth banked turn without losing altitude while using the traditional control system.[46]

In another chapter in the book I discussed aviation's association with youth and education in the 1920s and 1930s.[47] I suggested that changes in the material basis of model building contributed to the heightened "air-mindedness" of the era, especially among children. The shift in the late 1920s to lightweight balsa wood from heavier spruce as the primary model building material, I argued, lent a new and different psychological aura to the hobby. Balsa-framed, tissue-covered model planes, often powered by miniature gasoline engines, simulated real aircraft in ways that earlier models never could. They looked like actual planes and, more important, they dramatically outperformed the spruce-framed, rubber-powered models. As a consequence of these new artifacts of play, I claimed that a youngster's imaginative identification with flying and pilots was deepened and intensified. I believe that these assertions owed as much to memories of my own modeling experiences, to recollections of tactile, sensory, and emotional associations with artifacts, as they did to the documents and periodicals I perused in libraries and archives. If asked today to reconstruct my thought process in writing that chapter, I would say that first the historical study of model building recalled for me the tacit knowledge about what it meant and felt like to cut and shape balsa wood compared to spruce. I then extrapolated that personal experience back into the 1920s and 1930s. A mental procedure somewhat like what I've just described then enabled me speculatively to imagine what it must have been like as youngsters began to shift, at the end of the 1920s, from building models of spruce to working with the much lighter balsa.

I am not arguing here that historians of technology must have personal, hands-on experience. The human mind is a supple and wondrous tool, and I do not for a minute doubt that many historians without any familiarity with building models *might* also have described, even more imaginatively, the shift in practice about which I wrote. But the fact remains that I reached my conclusion regarding the links between model types and youthful aviation enthusiasm by remembering my own experiences and viewing, as it were, historical practice through that experiential lens. In the context of the debate over when and how scholars learn from things, it behooves us to spell out more precisely our debts to objects and to think about how those artifactual apprenticeships, however minor, have shaped our historical questions and interpretations. Even when one believes, as I did for a decade, that one's published work about things was based exclusively on "documents," it pays to think about the artifacts. Sometimes things speak to us in mysterious ways, even when they are not our apparent primary sources. We should listen carefully to what they have been saying.

NOTES

1. Carroll W. Pursell Jr., "The History of Technology and the Study of Material Culture," in *Material Culture: A Research Guide,* ed. Thomas J. Schlereth (Lawrence: University of Kansas Press, 1985), Chap. 5, p. 120. Pursell offers an insightful discussion of other scholars, most notably Brooke Hindle, who have argued for the primacy of artifacts in studying the history of technology.

2. Laurence F. Gross, "The Importance of Research Outside the Library: Watkins Mill, A Case Study," *Industrial Archeology* 7 (1981): 15–26.

3. T. E. Leary, "Industrial Archeology and Industrial Ecology," *Radical History Review* 21 (Fall 1979): 182.

4. My research strategy here obviously owes a debt to John Staudenmaier, S.J. See his *Technology's Storytellers: Reweaving the Human Fabric* (Cambridge, Mass.: MIT Press, 1985).

5. American scholars publishing articles dealing with the history of technology in English have one other journal exclusively devoted to the field, *History and Technology* (Berkshire, England). In addition, contributions to the history of technology regularly appear in various journals specialized by particular technologies, such as *Annals in the History of Computing, Air Power History,* and *Railroad History.*

6. To simplify and focus my analysis, I confine my use of the terms *things, objects,* and *artifacts* to three-dimensional material culture. Articles in *Technology and Culture* that focus on "flat" material culture, such as engineering drawing, or which draw their evidence from such sources, are therefore omitted here from consideration. For excellent examples of articles that are about technical representation, see Sergio Sanabria, "From Gothic to Renaissance Stereotomy: The Design Methods of Philibert de l'Orme and Alonso de Vandelvira," vol. 30, no. 2 (April 1989); and "Harold Belofsky, "Engineering Drawings—A Universal Language in Two Dialects," vol. 32, no. 1 (January 1991): 23–46. For articles about other technical artifacts but using two-dimensional visual sources, see, for example, Lu Gwei-Djen, Joseph Needham, and Phan Chi-Hsing, "The Oldest Representation of a Bombard," vol. 29, no. 3 (July 1988): 594–605; and Andrea Matthies, "Medieval Treadwheels: Artists' Views of Building Construction," vol. 33, no. 3 (April 1992):

510–47. A number of articles employing visual sources have also appeared under *Technology and Culture*'s "cover illustration" department; see, for example, Lettie S. Multhauf, "The Light of Lamp Lanterns: Street Lighting in 17th-Century Amsterdam," vol. 26, no. 2 (April 1985): 236–52; and John White, "Riding in Style: Palace Cars for the Cattle Trade," vol. 31, no. 2 (April 1990): 265–70.

7. During the decade from 1983 to 1992, *Technology and Culture* published 174 essays, of which 80, or 46 percent, were "about" things; 94, or about 54 percent, did not concern themselves with objects.

8. Adrian J. Randall, "The Philosophy of Luddism: The Case of the West of England Woolen Workers, ca. 1790–1809," *Technology and Culture* 27, no. 1 (January 1986): 1–17; Donald MacKenzie, "Marx and the Machine," *Technology and Culture* 25, no. 3 (July 1984): 473–502; W. Bernard Carlson, "Academic Entrepreneurship and Engineering Education: Dugald C. Jackson and the MIT-GE Cooperative Engineering Course, 1907–1932," *Technology and Culture* 29, no. 3 (July 1988): 536–67.

9. This discourse on the similarities and differences between technology and science, and their changing historical relationships, appears to have functioned for academic historians somewhat the same as has the discourse about the primacy of objects in historical research for museum historians.

10. By my count fifty-seven of the eighty articles "about" technical artifacts, or 71 percent, actually credited object study in the text or notes.

11. Twenty-three of 174 articles, or 13 percent, explicitly discussed and/or cited artifacts.

12. One should not overly stress the distinction between object people and idea people. Obviously, nobody learns *wholly* from artifacts, and although many historians of technology seem to learn wholly from printed sources, few would on principle insist that nothing can be learned from things. And as I suggest later in this paper, a number of logocentric scholars whose published work appears wholly based on written sources have, in fact, learned much from things.

13. Writing in a slightly different context, Wilcomb E. Washburn has noted that "the object can become a fetish that, if we merely worship it, impedes our understanding of the object itself and its place in our society." See Washburn, "Collecting Information, Not Objects," *Museum News* 62, no. 3 (February 1984): 5–6, 9–10, 12–15.

14. John M. Staudenmaier does not mention object study, either in his *Technology's Storytellers* or in his "Recent Trends in the History of Technology," *American Historical Review* 95, no. 3 (June 1990): 715–25. Other discussions or assessments of the field similarly ignore object study. See, for example, David Hounshell, "On the Discipline of the History of American Technology," *Journal of American History* 67, no. 4 (March 1981): 854–65.

15. For an example of an article that ably employs many of these

approaches, along with elements of art historical connoisseurship, see John Guilmartin Jr., "Guns of the *Santissimo Sacramento*," *Technology and Culture* 24, no. 4 (October 1983): 559–601.

16. Steven Lubar, "Technological Design in the 19th-Century Pin Industry," *Technology and Culture* 28, no. 2 (April 1987): 253–82. By "ordinary looking," I mean to emphasize the observational practices available to generally educated individuals as opposed to techniques usually requiring specialized schooling or training, such as might be deployed by a trained archaeologist. See, for example, Fred Schroeder, "More 'Small Things Forgotten': Domestic Electrical Plugs and Receptacles, 1881–1931," *Technology and Culture* 27, no. 3 (July 1986): 525–43. Yet archaeological approaches often do not involve sophisticated technical analysis but merely systematic observation. See, for example, Nicholas Adams, "Architecture for Fish: The Sienese Dam on the Bruna River—Structures and Designs, 1468–ca. 1530," *Technology and Culture* 25, no. 4 (October 1984): 768–97; John Daniels and Christian Daniels, "The Origin of the Sugarcane Roller Mill," *Technology and Culture* 29, no. 3 (July 1988): 493–535; and Thomas J. Oertling, "A Suction Pump from an Early 16th-Century Shipwreck," *Technology and Culture* 30, no. 3 (July 1989): 584–95.

17. Interestingly, Lubar said that the machine only operated in a halting and sporadic fashion. The edited video tape of its "operation," however, represents the Howe machine working more continuously than it ever did in the museum shop. Thus watching the taped representation, Lubar said, gave a much better sense of the machine at work than did the real thing.

18. Lubar, "Technological Design," 258.

19. Walter G. Vincenti, "Technological Knowledge without Science: The Innovation of Flush Riveting in American Airplanes, ca. 1930–ca. 1950," *Technology and Culture* 25, no. 3 (July 1984): 540–76. For another article that uses the technical publications of others in support of an analysis of an artifact, see Christine Macleod, "Accident or Design? George Ravenscroft's Patent and the Invention of Lead Crystal Glass," *Technology and Culture* 28, no. 4 (October 1987): 776–803.

20. David P. Billington and Robert Mark, "The Cathedral and the Bridge: Structure and Symbol," *Technology and Culture* 25, no. 1 (January 1984): 37–52; see also the authors' "Structural Imperative and the Origin of New Form," *Technology and Culture* 30, vol. 2 (April 1989): 300–329.

21. Billington and Mark, "Cathedral and the Bridge." Robert Mark pioneered the method of modeling and simulation and has published extensively on it and its various applications. See, for example, his "Structural Archaeology: A New Methodology for the Study of Historical Architecture," *Interdisciplinary Science Reviews* 12, no. 3 (1987): 230–40.

22. Billington and Mark, "Cathedral and the Bridge," 39.

23. David A. Hounshell, *From the American System to Mass Production, 1800–1932* (Baltimore: Johns Hopkins University Press, 1984), 31. See also Robert S. Woodbury, "The Legend of Eli Whitney and Interchangeable Parts," *Technology and Culture* 1, no. 3 (Summer 1960): 235–53.

24. See, for example, William A. Baker, "Sailing Reproductions of Historic Ships," *Sea History* 17 (Summer 1980): 25–26. See also William L. Withuhn, "Testing the John Bull, 1980," in *The John Bull: 150 Years a Locomotive,* by John H. White (Washington, D.C.: Smithsonian Institution Press, 1981), App. A.

25. Vernard Foley, with Steven Rowley, David F. Cassidy, and F. Charles Logan, "Leonardo, the Wheel Lock, and the Milling Process," *Technology and Culture* 24, no. 3 (July 1983): 399–427. See also William Rostoker, Bennet Bronson, and James Dvorak, "The Cast-Iron Bells of China," *Technology and Culture* 25, no. 4 (October 1984): 750–67; and Thomas J. Oertling, "A Suction Pump from an Early 16th-Century Shipwreck," *Technology and Culture* 30, no. 3 (July 1989): 584–95.

26. Ibid., 402.

27. Ibid., 402–3, 409.

28. Ibid., 404, 406.

29. Robert Gordon, "Who Turned the Mechanical Ideal into Mechanical Reality?" *Technology and Culture* 29, no. 4 (October 1988): 744–78; see also Robert Gordon, "Materials for Manufacturing: The Response of the Connecticut Iron Industry to Technological Change and Limited Resources," *Technology and Culture* 24, no. 4 (October 1983): 602–34; and Robert Gordon, "The 'Kelly' Converter," *Technology and Culture* 33, no. 4 (October 1992): 769–79.

30. Gordon, "Mechanical Ideal into Mechanical Reality," 747.

31. Ibid., 766.

32. Historians may intuitively grasp what anthropologist Grant McCracken has noted about material culture, to wit, that it is "severely limited in the number and range of things it can communicate." McCracken, *Culture and Consumption: New Approaches to the Symbolic Character of Consumer Goods and Activities* (Bloomington: University of Indiana Press, 1988), 69. Recently, some scholars have written about technical artifacts from the vantage of the new field of material culture studies, but their articles, although methodologically interesting, do not address issues of interest to historians of technology. See Joel Pfister, "A Garden in the Machine: Reading a Mid-19th-Century, Two-Cylinder Parlor Stove as Cultural Text," *Technology and Culture* 13 (1991): 327–43; and Amy B. Werbel, "The Foley Food Mill," *Technology in Society* 14 (1992): 245–356.

33. Bernard S. Bachrach and Rutherford Aris, "Military Technology and Garrison Organization: Some Observations on Anglo-Saxon Military Thinking

in Light of the Burghal Hidage," *Technology and Culture* 31, no. 1 (January 1990): 1–17.

34. The passage, found on pp. 10–11, is as follows: "When wielded in their normal manner at arms' length with a slashing or hacking stroke they imperiled one's fellow fighting men over at least a radius of 6 feet. Moreover, both weapons were most effectively wielded in concert with vigorous body movements that call for 'stepping into' the enemy either to the side or forward, much in the same way a batter in baseball moves in the batter's box in relation to the movement of the ball. Certainly these weapons cannot have been used in the space of slightly more than 4 feet that was allotted to each defender on the wall of an Anglo-Saxon burg; indeed, the combination of body movement and arm extension renders it impossible to use the long sword and the two-handed ax in a space of less than 10 feet."

35. Telephone interview with author, July 9, 1993.

36. Gail Fowler Mohanti, "Experimentation in Textile Technology, 1788–1790, and Its Impact on Handloom Weaving and Weavers in Rhode Island," *Technology and Culture* 29, no. 1 (January 1988): 1–31.

37. Telephone interview with author, July 9, 1993.

38. Larry Lankton, "Machine *under* the Garden: Rock Drills Arrive at the Lake Superior Copper Mines, 1868–1883," *Technology and Culture* 24, no. 1 (January 1983): 1–37.

39. Lankton, "Machine *under* the Garden," Figs. 1, 2, and 6.

40. Ibid., caption for Fig. 6, p. 30.

41. Telephone interview with author, March 8, 1993.

42. See Joseph O'Connell, "The Fine Tuning of a Golden Ear: High-End Audio and the Evolutionary Model of Technology," *Technology and Culture* 33, no. 1 (January 1992): 1, in which the author in his biographical blurb notes that he "has been an audiophile and amateur designer of audio equipment for several years."

43. Ruth Schwartz Cowan, *More Work for Mother: The Ironies of Household Technology from the Open Hearth to the Microwave* (New York: Basic Books, 1983).

44. For a few examples of writings reflecting on, or exemplary of, the new reflexivity in scholarly writing, see James Clifford and George E. Marcus, eds., *Writing Culture: The Poetics and Politics of Ethnography* (Berkeley and Los Angeles: University of California Press, 1986); and Derrick Bell, *And We Are Not Saved: The Elusive Quest for Racial Justice* (New York: Basic Books, 1987).

45. *The Winged Gospel: America's Romance with Aviation, 1900–1950* (New York: Oxford University Press, 1983).

46. Ibid., Chap. 5.

47. Ibid., Chap. 6.

5

Object/ions
Technology, Culture, and Gender

RUTH OLDENZIEL

Until recently, technology studies have devoted their undivided attention to the material world. To the detriment of other components of technology, the technical artifact, or hardware, continues to assume center stage in Western understanding of what constitutes technology. In popular readings as well, technology is usually understood in its most material appearance.[1] In the words of historian David Noble, "Because of its very concreteness, people tend to confront technology as an irreducible brute fact, a given, a first cause, rather than as hardened history, frozen fragments of human and social endeavor."[2]

Instead of viewing such sentiments skeptically, we need to understand that they represent the material, political, and symbolic formation of the nineteenth and early twentieth centuries. Material notions of technology accurately represent a social and cultural configuration that emerged during the nineteenth century. That hardware is technology's exclusive site is a view that became dominant only after World War I, after a century-long contest about technology's meanings.

How recently this understanding emerged is indicated by the word *technology,* which did not enter American culture as a key word until World War II. If in the early nineteenth century, for example, the domain of inventions could still embrace such diverse subjects as the arts, music, language, literature, and the crafts, by the twentieth century, its domain became almost exclusively limited to the products of engineering, in particular mechanical and civil engineering. Michael Adas has demonstrated how in the nineteenth century machines developed as a measure of human achievement and self-definition for Europeans in their encounters with other cultures over and against other gauges of cross-cultural comparison (such as religion and morality).[3] Machines became the dominant metaphor, model, and material embodiment of its subject matter and, as such, a symbol of male power.[4]

Inventions in particular acquired a special place in this new understanding of technology. More to the point, inventions functioned as the locus for what was to be regarded as technology. Nineteenth-century notions placed inventions—as represented by patent activity—at the center of the technological domain. By 1900, the rate of inventions, and of things mechanical in particular, signified an index of civilization or the prowess of a nation. Not surprisingly, then, governments invested a lot of manpower in counting patents and their country of origin as a means of establishing the relationship between the number of patents and national economic progress.

Such a taxonomy of the material world posed a particular problem for groups excluded from the institutions of inventions. Increasingly, inventiveness and mechanical genius became important arbiters of gender and race differentiation, at times politically employed in the argument over whether women should have the right to vote or used to justify Western domination of other cultures. For example, both advocates and opponents of women's rights employed the absence of women's inventions as the ultimate proof in their arguments.

But even counting patents was not a simple or gender-neutral matter, as the compilation of the United States Patent Office's list in 1892 at the instigation of activist Charlotte Smith shows. Federal clerks were biased against women's mechanical inventions: by reexamining the patents issued for 1876—the year of the centennial exhibition—Autumn Stanley found that the compilers omitted one woman's invention for every four they recorded and that these omissions were not random. Machines turned out to be the largest single category of omitted inventions, compared to categories such as agriculture, chemical, furnishings, health/medicine, heating, cooling, domestic labor-saving devices, and apparel. Mechanical devices omitted were nondomestic, or what might be called nontraditional inventions for women.[5] Thus, despite feminist intervention and the help of well-intentioned clerks, the late nineteenth-century Patent Office's list provides a fascinating instance of how the emerging ideology suppressed the ability to *see* women's mechanical genius. This suppression coincided with the paradigmatic shift to seeing inventions as machine-bound and masculine, as I have argued elsewhere.[6]

This focus on, fascination with, and fetishism of commodities was, of course, closely related to the stage of and adherence to industrial capitalism. After all, machines were for the most part embodiments of products as well as the producers of nineteenth-century industrial capitalism.[7] The concept of the artifact as an object with clear boundaries ran parallel to the understanding of the human body as a bounded object. Compare such views of the material world to the current notion that objects and the body are linguistic or discursive constructs, and it will be clear that the status of matter has undergone a dramatic reversal. Under the aegis of discourse analysis, communication theory, and information technologies, we are entering a new paradigm in which material has become dematerialized and the body disembodied. These new modes of practice and thinking challenge root categories and subvert traditional borders, such as those between nature and culture, object and subject, material and immaterial world, and workplace and home. Instead of fixed and rigid boundaries, current theories portray these borders as areas of exchange, trading, and negotiation, but ultimately as analytically obsolete. Even the body, long considered the temple of nature and antithesis of the technological domain, can no longer escape the close workings of technical means and artifacts. Bodies, women's in particular, have always been modified and shaped by hairdos, perfumes, piercing, and diet practices. The employment of sonar technology in pregnancy monitoring, the routine procedures of filling teeth, the use of the pill in order to control the hormonal economy of the female body, and the replacement of body parts are common practices that have been rhetorically closed and are no longer controversial. But increasingly, these new medical technologies have come to challenge the concept of the body as bounded, inviolable, or inimical to the domain of technology.

As the title of this chapter, "Object/ions," conveys, my discussion seeks to examine the evolving relationship between the material and "other" aspects of technology in order to look at the status of matter. In view of the insights of feminist scholarship, social constructivist's theories, and cultural studies of technology, the question is what indeed can we learn from the paradigmatic shift in the thinking about material as represented in both objects and bodies? In the sections that follow, I discuss three approaches, possibly stages, developing in the field.

OBJECTIONAL OBJECTS AND FROZEN FACTS

Through involvement in a multivolume project that seeks to establish a standard history of Dutch technology in the twentieth century (1890–1970), I have become once more impressed by the obduracy of the technical artifact, the difficulty of escaping the tyranny of things and the continued dominance of existing taxonomies.[8] These are common pitfalls in the writing and research of the history of technology. I would argue that such trappings belong to a paradigm of the culture of production, to borrow the useful terminology of Warren Susman.[9] In contrast to a culture of consumption, this cultural frame stresses hard work rather than leisure, character rather than personality, objects rather than subjects, and products rather than process. In a paradigm of the culture of production, the technical artifact guides, rules, and frames the decisions for case studies, periodization, and definitions. Such a material taxonomy of technology often carries implicit gender codings. In the past, a sizable amount of feminist intellectual scholarship has devoted attention to women's limited access to technological domains. But, as current studies indicate, taxonomies are as much, if not more, decisive in rendering invisible the gender dimension of technology. The reproduction of existing taxonomies loom larger in the reproduction of gendered technologies than do actual barriers to women's participation in the technical world. What counts as true technology is imprisoned by, for example, the designation of patent activities as the real locus of invention, the emphasis on engineering products as technical objects, the preponderance of an ethos of producerism, the priority on capital-intensive technologies, the neglect of users' presence in design, and, on the level of research and museum practices, prevailing preservation policies.

Conceptualization of the multivolume Dutch history of technology took place under the leadership of Harry Lintsen in the Netherlands, in close consultation with Thomas Hughes, the historian and sociologist known for his insistence that technical artifacts be seen as part of a technological system, not in isolation. Using the metaphor of a network, Hughes has argued that artifacts, institutions, and people are all interlocking into a system. In other words, an artifact always has a network attached to it and should be studied as an evolving process. Lintsen and Hughes proposed to slice up the history of technology thus: steel, waterworks, city, electricity, agriculture, transportation, chemical industry, office, and media. In order to give coherence to the history, technical artifacts would serve as case studies.

The project's planning group found its path well paved for such an artifactual approach. In the early 1960s, two venerable men in the history of technology, Melvin Kranzberg and Eugene Ferguson, had chosen a strategy of mapping artifacts when they were faced with the similar task in providing a coherent framework for an American history of technology. Yet they realized their project was hampered rather than helped by the traditional artifactual approach of what they called the "taxonomy of machines." As Ferguson explained: "Because I have been familiar with earlier attempts to classify and anatomize machines, I have been quite skeptical of finding any particular sensible approach since 'machines' can only be anatomized . . . if they are restricted to an assemblage of linkages."[10] Such a genealogy of machines as a means to organize and narrate the history of technology, however, continues to pose a problem because it tends to freeze the taxonomies of artifacts void of histories. And so does the idea that the history of engineering provides an exclusive guide for technological change. From a gender point of view, such a focus is problematic, because engineering has been the most male-dominated profession. Rather than a road map, such a framework unwittingly functions as a mechanism of exclusion in mapping a history of technology.

Among many issues, the plotters of the Dutch history of technology encountered a question that illustrates some of this chapter's points: Under what heading should the telephone be classified? The classification of the telephone symbolizes how an artifact may be gender-coded through ordinary decisions of taxonomy. The question was whether the telephone should go under the heading of transportation, because, in the Dutch case, the telephone resided under the Department of Transportation and Water Works, or under the heading of the office or under household technology—a subject that, significantly, had not been covered at first. Seen from the point of production, conventionally defined, the telephone indeed developed as a means of distribution for business exchange. But considered from the vantage point of the residential user, the telephone served as a means of communication firmly embedded in social life. Lana Rakow, Claude Fischer, Ann Moyal, and other scholars in Britain, Canada, and the Netherlands have uncovered the different frames of meaning of the telephone.[11] Women (especially on the farm) used the telephone to escape their isolation, to sustain social networks, and to build communities. Developed by telegraph men, industry men pushed it as an utilitarian tool for short, useful, efficient, and businesslike conversations with entrepreneurial men in mind. At first they considered women's residential use of the telephone as improper and their telephone conversations as gossip, waste, and subversion. After initial attempts to suppress women's "improper" employment of the telephone, telephone companies changed their marketing strategy and started encouraging, exploiting, and expanding women's telephone habits as a social tool. Casting the telephone in this way, communication companies no longer charged for the connection made but charged, much more profitably, for the duration of the call. Placing the telephone under the heading of transportation, the rich story of meaning-giving practices would have been lost. The case of the telephone also raises the question of whether an artifact continues to be the same materially when it means something different to various groups of users.

The static economic dichotomy between production and consumption that underlay many concepts in the history of technology represents the most stubborn taxonomy of all. It closes off possibilities for understanding the dynamic relationships between the construction of technology and gender, and it fixes gender codings. The tacit adherence to commonplace, not economic, divisions as the basis for technology's classification threatens to freeze out entire domains, such as department stores, amusement parks, mail-order companies, and households outside the range of permissible inquiry. It is erroneous, though perhaps not surprising, that household technology continues to occupy a secondary place in the descriptions of technological processes, because household work remains stigmatized as nonproductive labor and therefore its technology fails to qualify as "real."

As feminist scholars who have mapped the cult of the separate spheres have argued for a decade, these divisions have been propped up and participated in by a gender system of meanings that construct distinctions between productive and nonproductive labor. Such divisions were problematic for the nineteenth century not only because they prescribe more than they describe economic activities, but also because they cannot account for the traffic that goes on between the spheres. Feminist scholars of the history of technology have challenged the rigid separation between the productive and nonproductive, the technical and atechnical, the female and the male world.[12] Elaborating on Hughes's approach, for example, Ruth Schwartz Cowan has shown how household technologies are part and parcel of technical networks of food, clothing, health care, transportation systems, water, gas, and electricity.[13] She demonstrated that households might have been represented as separate from the so-called public sphere, but in practice they were an important substance of the larger economy.

It is not only the rigid distinctions between production and consumption that may carry gender codings. The focus on capital-intensive and large-scale artifacts reinforces the economic thinking embedded in understanding technological processes and tends to exclude low-tech systems, leisure-time and daily use technologies, and the social actors that use them. From a manufacturing point of view, mainframe computers may command a greater authority. They certainly represent the spectacular more than technologies such as the pill and carbon paper. But for users, the majority of whom are women inside and outside the workplace, it could be easily argued that carbon paper radically changed both the nature of information circulating within and outside the office and the way business was conducted. Similarly, the pill was of greater significance than computers, particularly in the Dutch case, as only a few mainframe computers had been introduced before 1970. Emphasis on capital-intensive technology, for instance, renders inexplicable why a contraceptive pill for men has been regarded as an impossibility. Such a pill is not "technically" impossible, but culturally so, because it poses a threat to virility.

BORDERLANDS AND TRADING ZONES

A second approach developing in the field highlights classification systems of technical artifacts by edging the analytical focus to the borders. If conventional economic constructions prevent us from bringing the nineteenth-century history of technology into focus, they are of even less value in understanding the twentieth century in a proper light, because consumer culture has come to dominate economic life and its cultural configurations in profound ways. Consumer goods play an increasingly large role in what counts as economic activity. Although these are familiar insights for scholars of consumer culture, those in technology studies stand to learn a great deal from this emerging body of scholarship if they wish to understand the life trajectory of technical artifacts, from their design to their uses.

Users are neither obedient actors nor passive victims, but active participants in the shaping of technologies, not in the least because consumers produce frames of meanings that are, and of course always have been, crucial to a technology's ultimate application. Using his studies of the irrigation systems in Sri Lanka, Pfaffenberger notes that a technology only exists when the people who use it can use it over and over again.

In other words, technologies are to a large degree constituted through their use. Technology, then, is not technical, but essentially social.[14] This truism applies to both developing countries and Western companies. As companies learn, their investments in sales departments and advertising agencies take up an increasingly large portion of their budgets compared to the actual manufacturing of products. What companies actually aim at with these investments is producing the "proper frame of meaning" for their product. In this context, Carlson offers a compelling interpretation of the history of invention in the motion-picture industry that further challenges easy distinctions between production and consumption. Rather than looking at the point of production, he argues that to better understand the process, one needs to examine inventions at the point of consumption, or better still, at the trading zone between them. "Inventors," Carlson argues, "invent both artifacts and frames of meanings that guide how they manufacture and market their creations" because problems do not simply exist in a vacuum but are first named so by inventors, who then "find" solutions for them. In other words, problems are framed by their solutions. Adhering to a culture of production, Carlson maintains, Edison failed to develop the Kinetoscope for the leisure industry during the 1890s because, not knowing otherwise, he framed his invention and its meaning as a business tool.[15] In analyzing the fate of the early motion-picture technology, Carlson both describes and uses a twentieth-century paradigmatic shift. Consumer culture itself, and the products it generated during the twentieth century, challenge, change, and question the exclusive construction of technical artifacts as products of manufacturing.

Expanding on Carlson's insights from both cultural and technological studies, it becomes possible not only to understand cultural meanings as essential building blocks for technological developments but also to read women back into technological development by edging to the borders of current taxonomies. Opening the trading zone between production and consumption, women appear suddenly present, visible, and alive. Production and consumption are not separate affairs, but constitute each other. Understanding the relationship between production and consumption as an intricate web, women appear as active players in the creation of technical artifacts. Research by Dana Frank, Jackie Dirks, and Jeanne Lawrence point to women's negotiation in the area between production and consumption. In particular, Carolyn Goldstein's research shows how women home economists tried to formalize and professionalize that border zone within corporations during 1930s and 1940s. These women professionals not only mediated but also helped frame the meanings of technical products.[16] They were, therefore, participants in and producers of a culture of consumption. Other studies that focus on the design of technical artifacts evoke a similar trading zone—a going back and forth between designer and user, the designer's projected user and real user, the world inscribed in the object and the world described by its displacement.[17] Still others look at the different employments of technological artifacts and meanings assigned to them once they are in place, circulating, discarded, disassembled, reassembled, and reused.

Taken together, these studies, in fact, redefine the boundaries of objects, economic categories, and notions of creation. In doing so, they question where the technical artifact or product begins or ends, where or whether the divide between production and consumption should be drawn, what constitutes invention, what constitutes use, and whether or not a technical artifact continues to be the same in material terms when the meanings ascribed to it diverge for different social groups. In the end, such studies render the physical and material liquid, leaking, and plastic once again. Sharp divisions dissolve into analytical obsolescence what were once designated as design, production, artifact, technology, or—as their constructed opposites—context, consumption, culture, and factors.

THE POSTMODERN PARADIGM: DISEMBODIED BODIES AND DEMATERIALIZED MATERIAL

In step with contemporary notions in the 1970s, feminist perspectives on technology were caught in a black-box view of technology. Shulamith Firestone's now classic and optimistic view that reproductive technologies would liberate women from their traditional role as mothers represents one side of such technological determinism. According to this assessment, women are imprisoned by their biological ability to bear children. Reproductive technologies, so it was thought, would open the way to liberation and emancipation because women would no longer be exclusively identified by their reproductive organs. At the other end of the spectrum, some feminists dismissed any technological intervention by the medical profession on the grounds that doctors violated the sanctity of the (female) body. Both positions represented the same technological (and biological) determinism.[18] In other words, whether technology was seen in a positive or negative light, both views framed technology as an autonomous and decisive force for social and cultural transformations of gender relations.

More recently, new strands in feminist research in technology studies challenge these black-boxed and technologically determinist views. Feminist technology assessment and postmodern cultural studies both offer new strategies in opening up technological black boxes. Taking technology as a social practice open to intervention as a point of departure, technology assessment, for example, claims a critical approach by which the impact of technological change is identified and evaluated. As part of design decisions, feminist technology assessment calls for an evaluation of a technological design that asks where it comes from, what its trajectory is, what its intended and actual use is, what its relevance for women might be, and how it affects women's status.[19]

Biologist and philosopher Donna Haraway, on the other hand, has proposed a more speculative strategy in her 1985 "Cyborg Manifesto," in which she calls on women to infiltrate the technical domain without naïveté about or technophobia for a technology's design, production, or use. Her pose is purposefully provocative—after all, her call stands in the long tradition of manifesto writing. As with Firestone's, hers is not the first to exude an exuberance that borders on a belief in the technological sublime. But Haraway's theories are grounded in the conviction that feminist intervention is possible, necessary, and desirable.[20] Particularly new in Haraway's approach has been her visionary and enthusiastic, but critical, endorsement of new technologies. Her exuberance and technophilic stance has erased some of the more technophobic expressions in feminist thought but also raised new and high expectations.

The new electronic technologies in particular have raised feminist expectations, such as the possibilities for gender bending, or possibly a genderless society in which the body takes a back seat, vanishing in cyberspace, invisible and irrelevant. In cyberspace—a three-dimensional area generated by electronic technologies in which digital data may be visualized, heard, and even felt—some data may even be people. The possibilities of the new information technologies for new ways of thinking or being seem endlessly exciting. In cyberspace, so the postmodern promise goes, the body, long thought to be the basis for gender identity and women's roadblock to liberation, may vanish.

Roseanne Stone has related an anecdote (whether apocryphal or not) to buttress such a hope for escaping the body. In the 1980s, Julie, a severely disabled elderly woman, successfully projected her personality through the electronic network without the usual hindrance of her impaired body. She quickly won the confidence of many women, who logged on the network finding her advice useful, reassuring, and inspiring. Only later was it discovered that Julie was a middle-aged male psychiatrist. Many women felt betrayed, some even raped in a physical sense.[21] Even though the incident occurred in cyberspace, it reveals how gender distinctions can be subverted, reinforced, and made material electronically. After all, it was important to the network women to assign Julie gender: it guided their behavior and their mode of expression.

This poses the question, What is materiality in cyberspace? Is it not more or less what semioticians have proposed for some time—that things are not existent and meaningless unless a meaning has been ascribed to them through essentially linguistic processes? Are the new information and communication technologies and the cyberspace they create another version of the age-old printed media and its cybernetic imagination? In other words, is the digital Julie the mirror image of George Eliot of the printed age? The answer to these questions is in part affirmative, but the argument that all things should be read as texts denies the place of the material within those linguistic processes. Cultural studies teach us important lessons about how meanings are assigned to and encoded in material objects, and the new information technologies open a window to see how texts, codes, and signals are capable of acquiring materiality.

Katherine Hayles has recently offered analytically useful distinctions, which I believe offer new avenues in thinking about the status of matter in a postmodern paradigm. Hayles argues that bodies and objects may be cultural constructs, as recent studies insist, but the experiences of embodiment individual people within a culture feel and articulate are distinct. Second, she argues that a distinction should be drawn between inscribing and incorporating practices: inscribing practices are textual, whereas incorporating practices are partly material in nature. In the electronic age, the body and objects may seem to disappear into "virtual realities," but, and this is Hayles's third point, the immateriality of information is distinct from the material conditions of production that make that information possible.[22] These analytical reminders may offer possible research strategies for Donna Haraway's more speculative approach. As Haraway has pointed out, dissolving the boundary between the physical and the nonphysical renders it invisible, ubiquitous, seemingly clean and innocuous. But such opaqueness carries its dangers. "Our best machines are made of sunshine," she has suggested in referring to our silicon computers. "They are all light and clean because they are nothing but signals, electromagnetic waves, a section of a spectrum, and these machines are eminently portable, mobile—a matter of immense human pain in Chicago and Singapore. People are nowhere near so fluid, being both material and opaque." But their ubiquity and invisibility is precisely why these sunshine belt machines are so deadly, Haraway warns. They are as hard to see politically as materially.[23]

This leads me back to the beginning of this chapter. Current scholarship proposes viewing technology as a configuration of knowledge, things, organizations, and people. When political scientist Langdon Winner argued that artifacts have politics, he insisted not only that artifacts were politically shaped but also, more forcefully, that objects should be seen as solidified social and political relations.[24] Or, to quote another scholar, they are the "congealed outcome of a set of negotiations, compromises, conflicts, controversies and deals that were put together between opponents in rooms filled with smoke, lathes or computer terminals."[25] But the hardening of history into objects might be increasingly hard to recognize, because objects take on different shapes in this electronic age. Looking back from cyberspace into the material world as we see it, we might want to ask not only how history is hardened into objects but also what our focus on objects tells us about our historical specificity in time and place. In doing so, we should look back to the study of formation processes of material culture studies during the nineteenth century and look forward to the crossing of the materiality of informatics with the immateriality of information currently emerging. Both approaches may give important clues to the genealogy and status of matter in its historical context. We need to map the genealogies of incorporations, embodiments, and locations in order to understand material culture and technical artifacts in their proper historical light. Only then may we see the ways in which gender has been encoded in material objects and how the material objects and technical artifacts have in turn (re)constructed gender relations and representations.

NOTES

1. Popular readings include both popularized versions of academic writings and the pop culture's representations of science and technology. For a fine discussion on this distinction, see George Basalla, "Pop Science: The Depiction of Science in Popular Culture," *Science and Its Public: The Changing Relationship,* ed. Gerald Holton and William A. Blanpied (Dordrecht: D. Reidel, 1976), 261–78.

2. David F. Noble, *Forces of Production: A Social History of Industrial Automation* (New York: Oxford University Press, 1986), xi.

3. Michael Adas, *Machines as the Measure of Men: Science, Technology, and Ideologies of Western Dominance* (Ithaca, N.Y.: Cornell University Press, 1989).

4. See, for example, Adas, *Machines as the Measure of Men.*

5. Autumn Stanley, "The Patent Office as Conjurer: The Vanishing Lady Trick in a Nineteenth-Century Historical Source," in *Women, Work, and Technology: Transformations,* ed. Barbara Wright Drygulski Wright (Ann Arbor: University of Michigan Press, 1985), 118–36.

6. Ruth Oldenziel, "Gender and the Meanings of Technology: Engineering in the U.S., 1880–1945" (Ph.D. diss., Yale University, 1992), Chap. 2. See also Anne L. Macdonald's finely researched book *Feminine Ingenuity: Women and Invention in America* (New York: Ballantine Books, 1992).

7. Robert Friedel has made a beginning in offering a possible chronology for understanding the history of objects. Robert Friedel, "Some Matters of Substance," in *History from Things: Essays on Material Culture,* ed. Steven Lubar and W. David Kingery (Washington, D.C.: Smithsonian Institution Press, 1993), 41–50, 48–49.

8. The project continues the series of nineteenth-century Dutch history of technology currently in progress with Walburg Press, Netherlands, but also seeks to formulate new approaches appropriate for and particular to the twentieth century.

9. On the values of the culture of production and consumption: Warren Susman, *Culture as History: The Transformation of American Society in the Twentieth Century* (New York: Pantheon Books, 1984); Leo Lowenthal, "The Triumph of Mass Idols," *Literature, Popular Culture, and Society* (1961; reprint, Palo Alto, Calif.: Pacific Books, 1985).

10. Letter to author, cited in Oldenziel, "Gender and the Meanings of Technology," Chap. 2.

11. Lana F. Rakow, "Women and the Telephone: The Gendering of a Communications Technology," in *Technology and Women's Voices: Keeping in Touch,* ed. C Kramarae (New York: Routledge, 1988), 207–28; Ann Moyal, "The Gendered Use of the Telephone: An Australian Case Study," *Media, Culture, and Society* 14, no. 1 (January 1992): 51–72; Claude S. Fischer, "'Touch Someone': The Telephone Industry Discovers Sociability," *Technology and Culture* 29, no. 1 (1988): 32–61; and Claude S. Fischer, *American Calling: A Social History of the Telephone to 1940* (Berkeley and Los Angeles: University of California Press, 1992), Chap. 8.

12. See in particular Women in the History of Technology (WITH), a group of women scholars within the Society of the History of Technology (SHOT). For an excellent overview, see Judith A. McGaw, "Review Essay:

Women and the History of American Technology," *Signs* 7, no. 4 (Summer 1982): 798–828; and Judith A. McGaw, "No Passive Victims, No Separate Spheres," in *In Context: The History and the History of Technology,* ed. Stephen H. Cutcliffe and Robert C. Post (Bethlehem, Pa.: Lehigh University Press, 1989), 172–80.

13. Ruth Schwartz Cowan, "The 'Industrial Revolution' in the Home: Household Technology and Social Change in the Twentieth Century," *Technology and Culture* 17 (January 1976): 1–42; Ruth Schwartz Cowan, *More Work for Mother: The Ironies of Household Technology from the Open Hearth to the Microwave* (New York: Basic Books, 1983); and Thomas P. Hughes, *Networks of Power: Electrification in Western Society, 1880–1930* (Baltimore: Johns Hopkins University Press, 1983). See also Thomas P. Hughes, "The Evolution of Large Technological Systems," in *The Social Construction of Technological Systems: New Directions in the Sociology and History of Technology,* ed. Wiebe E. Bijker, Thomas P. Hughes, and Trevor J. Pinch (Cambridge, Mass.: MIT Press, 1987), 58–82.

14. Bryan Pfaffenberger, "Fetishised Objects and Humanised Nature: Toward an Anthropology of Technology," *Man* 23 (June 1988): 241. See also on this point Langdon Winner, "Do Artifacts Have Politics?" *Daedalus* 109, no. 1 (1980): 121–31; and Madeleine Akrich, "The De-Scription of Technical Objects," in *Shaping Technology/Building Society: Studies in Sociotechnical Change,* ed. Wiebe E. Bijker and John Law (Cambridge, Mass.: MIT Press, 1992), 208.

15. W. Bernard Carlson, "Artifacts and Frames of Meaning: Thomas A. Edison, His Managers, and the Cultural Construction of Motion Pictures," in Bijker and Law, *Shaping Technology/Building Society,* 175–200.

16. Carolyn Goldstein, "Mediating Consumption: Home Economics and American Consumers, 1900–1940" (Ph.D. diss., University of Delaware, 1994).

17. Madeleine Akrich, "The De-Scription of Technical Objects," and "User Representations: Practices, Methods and Sociology," in *Managing Technology in Society,* ed. A. Rip, Thomas Misa, and Johan Schot (London: Pinter, 1995), 167–84. See also Bryan Pfaffenberger, "Technological Dramas," *Science, Technology, and Human Values* 17, no. 2 (Summer 1992): 282–312.

18. S. Firestone, *The Dialectic of Sex* (New York: William Morrow, 1970); Judy Wajcman, *Feminism Confronts Technology* (Cambridge, Mass.: Polity Press, 1991).

19. Janine Morgall, *Developing Technology Assessment: A Critical Feminist Approach* (Copenhagen: Stougaard Jensen, 1991).

20. The term *technological sublime* was first used in passing by Leo Marx in his *Machine in the Garden* (New York: Oxford University Press, 1965) and

is treated at great length in David E. Nye, *American Technological Sublime* (Cambridge, Mass.: MIT Press, 1994).

21. Allucquere Roseanne Stone, "Will the Real Body Please Stand Up?: Boundary Stories and Virtual Cultures," in *Cyberspace: First Steps,* ed. Michael Benedikt (Cambridge, Mass.: MIT Press, 1991), 81–118.

22. N. Katherine Hayles, "Materiality of Informatics," *Configurations* 1, no. 1 (Winter 1993): 147–70.

23. Donna Haraway, "A Manifesto for Cyborgs: Science, Technology and Socialist Feminism in the 1980s," *Socialist Review* 15 (March/April 1985): 69.

24. Winner, "Do Artifacts Have Politics?"

25. John Law, "Technology and Heterogenous Engineering: The Case of Portuguese Expansion," in Bijker, Hughes, and Pinch, *Social Construction of Technological Systems,* 111–35.

Part Three

Formation Processes

6

Formation Processes of the Historical and Archaeological Records

MICHAEL BRIAN SCHIFFER

As I observed a number of years ago (Schiffer 1977, 13), "The study of the past is a remarkable pretension. The past no longer exists as part of the phenomenological world, yet we claim to know it." The study of the human past is made possible by the fact that some objects made and used long ago survive into the present and so can serve as evidence for inference (Schiffer 1977, 13; 1987, 3). Only through inference, a scientific process, can we obtain knowledge of what people once did. The soundness of an inference about past human behavior depends upon the weight of relevant evidence and of relevant generalizations marshalled in its support. During recent decades, archaeologists have gained new insights into inference as process and as product (e.g., Schiffer 1976, Chap. 2; Rathje and Schiffer 1982, Chaps. 8 and 9; Sullivan 1978). In this first chapter of Part Three, I present a brief overview of these new understandings, stressing the importance of appreciating the processes by which evidence of the human past comes to be.

Working with the remains of everything from Paleolithic encampments to antebellum plantations to yesterday's lunch, the archaeologist is most comfortable with an expansive definition of evidence. To wit, evidence consists of any material entity that carries traces of past human behavior. Thus, a ceramic roof tile, recovered from excavations at a Roman house site, yields traces of how the tile was formed and fired and, from mortar remnants, how it was positioned in relation to other roof tiles. A radio made in 1924 preserves, for example, traces of electronics assembly and cabinet crafting; the component-buying behavior of the manufacturer; the materials purchasing and manufacturing operations of component-makers; and, in use-alteration traces (sensu Skibo 1992), activities of the radio's users. An automobile advertisement from a 1902 magazine holds traces of paper making and printing as well as of automobile manufacturing and marketing behaviors. An octogenarian has, encoded in biochemical structures, traces of a lifetime's experiences, which investigators probe through oral history. Diverse material phenomena of today, then, retain, in their physical and chemical makeup, traces that can serve as evidence of the human past.

In order for material entities—documents, photographs, the ordinary and extraordinary things of everyday life, even people—to serve as evidence, they must persist over time and be found and studied by investigators. *Formation processes create the pathways leading from past behaviors to evidence of them in the present.* By means of formation processes, material entities, sometimes greatly modified, are able to persist and become potential evidence. A consideration of formation processes, then, is what allows the investigator to locate and assess evidence relevant to a given research question.

FORMATION PROCESSES AND THEIR STUDY

There are two major families of formation processes. The first is *cultural,* and involves human agency. Cultural formation processes are activities that affect or transform artifacts after the latter's initial period of use in a given kind of activity. This post-use life history can include reuse and assembly into collections or deposition and subsequent retrieval by archaeologists; deposited objects may also be disturbed and reclaimed by others. Useful works on cultural formation processes include those by Schiffer (1987; Chaps. 3–6 and 13 provide a general introduction), Binford (1983), Kristiansen (1985), Staski and Sutro (1991), and Cameron and Tomka (1993).

The second major family of formation processes is *noncultural,* or environmental. Noncultural processes encompass the myriad chemical, physical, and biological agents that alter and disturb artifacts and sites— from corrosion and erosion to earthworms and earthquakes. A general introduction to noncultural formation processes is furnished by Schiffer (1987, Chaps. 7–9); more detailed coverage of specific topics is supplied by Binford (1981), Davidson and Shackley (1976), Goodyear (1971), Brain (1981), Shackley (1981), Shipman (1981), Rosen (1986), Nash and Petraglia (1987), Stein (1992), Stein and Farrand (1985), and Waters (1992). Acting simultaneously and sequentially, cultural and noncultural formation processes establish the pathways of material entities from any past activity to the present. It is these diverse processes of people and nature that determine what survives, and in what condition and which location it survives.

Formation processes create two different records of the past, the *historical* record and the archaeological record. The historical record consists of artifacts that have been reused and so remain within a behavioral system. Objects in archives and private collections, for example, survive in the historical record by virtue of secondary use and conservatory processes. The archaeological record, on the other hand, consists of objects that have been culturally deposited—that is, lost, discarded, abandoned, and so on. Some of these items are recovered and enter collections where they are accessible to scholarly inquiry. Obviously, particular objects may alternate between the historical and archaeological records.

The material entities that today can supply evidence for studying a particular past behavior may be widely dispersed among varied collections and deposits in the historical and archaeological records. Traditionally, parts of these records are studied by specialists. Historians, for example, concern themselves with the minute subset of objects called documents. Similarly, other material entities have come to be the province of folklorists and art historians. Surprisingly, most objects in the historical record— from chairs to cars to cameras—rarely attract the mainstream academic scholar. Rather, these artifacts are studied, if at all, by academics on the fringes of various disciplines and by collectors.

In academe we are accustomed to allocating the study of the archaeological record to peculiar scholars called archaeologists. In fact, the artifacts deposited by past peoples are recovered and scrutinized by scholars and nonscholars alike. Amateurs, relic hunters, and professional looters retrieve objects from the archaeological record, contributing to the growth of collections, and art historians, numismatists, and so on study these collections and generate scholarly and quasi-scholarly literatures. Among archaeologists, the study of retrieved objects is now endlessly partitioned among diverse specialists who examine only one kind of material, such as human bone, chipped stone, or ceramics.

The extreme division of labor on materials from the historical and archaeological records enables research by well-trained specialists, but it also militates against the emergence of integrated, unified approaches to the study of the human past. This unfortunate effect comes about because evidence relevant to researching any particular past behavior may be unexamined or split among scholars steeped in separate research traditions who often have scant sympathy for, much less contact with, one another. Inevitably, the behavioral inferences that individual researchers create are based on a small and usually biased sample from a large population of demonstrably relevant evidence. As a result, we face incomplete inferences championed by investigators who have privileged what very well may be fatally limited or fatally biased samples of evidence.

Let us envision another way of organizing inquiry into past human behavior. I suggest that we privilege not the possession of particular bodies of evidence but the systematic effort to answer a research question. Answering research questions requires that we seek relevant evidence wherever it may be, whether its caretakers are members of our own or other academic disciplines, or have no scholarly affiliation at all. The key to avoiding chaos in this endeavor is to formulate explicit and general methods for delineating, locating, and assessing relevant evidence. The study of formation processes enables us to build these general methods and thus helps us to unify the study of the human past (Schiffer 1977).

If formation processes were utterly haphazard in their operation and effects, the study of the past would be nearly hopeless. Systematic research would be precluded because the discovery of relevant evidence would depend upon chance alone. Fortunately, formation processes are highly patterned, enabling us to find and assess the material entities relevant to a specific behavioral question. That environmental processes are patterned and conform to various generalizations is not a controversial assertion. After all, countless textbooks in geology, biology, and so forth provide principles in abundance. Somewhat more contentious, however, is my long-standing claim that cultural formation processes also exhibit marked regularities (Schiffer 1972, 1976, 1987).

Generalizations describing these behavioral regularities vary along the two dimensions of *scale* and *scope,* which together specify a statement's boundary conditions—its precise domain in the universe of human behavior (Schiffer 1978). Scale delineates the unit that manifests a specific behavioral pattern. Common scales or units include individuals, task groups, families, clans, companies, communities, nation-states, and empires. Two examples can illustrate behavioral generalizations at different scales. First, long-lived communities tend to dispose of trash in a small number of specialized dumping locations. Second, nation-states usually conserve objects and monuments that commemorate the rule of prominent leaders. These two simplified examples are fully general: they are thought to apply, respectively, to all communities and to all nation-states. Most behavioral generalizations, however, relate to somewhat more limited domains.

We can characterize variation in this latter dimension by the concept of scope. A generalization's scope may range from broad and fully general to narrow and highly particularistic. To illustrate variation in scope, let us take the reuse behavior of inventors (as a class of individuals). If we think about all inventors who ever lived, we would be hard-pressed to find any commonalities in, for example, their reuse behavior. If, however, the scope of our generalization seeking were narrowed to independent inventors working in capitalist-industrial societies, we might discover that most tended to carefully conserve diaries, notebooks, models, prototypes, and so on (in the expectation of having to demonstrate their claims of priority in court). Generalizations may even describe the behavioral regularities of one person, a scope of ultimate narrowness. In addition to saving invention-related artifacts, for example, Henry Ford conserved vast amounts of personal memorabilia ranging from grocery receipts to car insurance policies (Olson 1963).

Theorists of cultural formation processes strive to include generalizations of broad scope within larger systems of laws and theories (Schiffer 1987). For the practical researcher, however, any behavioral generalization is of value—whether of nomothetic standing or not—if it furnishes guidance in seeking and assessing relevant evidence. For example, the generalization that inventors in capitalist-industrial societies tend to conserve invention-related documents and other artifacts would help us to initiate the search for such artifacts today. Aiding this search would be a host of other behavioral generalizations about reuse processes that pertain to the individual in question, the handling of inventors' estates, the collecting behavior of individuals and institutions, and so on. These generalizations assist in establishing the linkages between a person's inventing behavior in the past and the evidence of that behavior that still exists today, perhaps dispersed among numerous public and private locations. Once relevant evidence is located, the investigator uses generalizations about formation processes along with other behavioral generalizations (e.g., those that inform source criticism) to assess biases in particular lines of evidence.

In assembling the session that gave rise to the chapters that follow,

I asked contributors to prepare essays on the formation processes of collections. Because collections are accumulations of related objects that can be conveniently studied, historians, anthropologists, archaeologists, and other scholars gravitate to them. The chapters that follow introduce some of the diverse processes of people and nature that go into the formation of collections.

Michael Brian Schiffer furnishes a case study on the search for surviving traces of pocket radios with subminiature tubes. He shows the importance of finding the radios themselves and illuminates the kinds of biases that inhere in various lines of evidence. Kristian Kristiansen employs historical information to illuminate the processes by which certain ancient objects come to be included in Danish museum collections. He shows how both the destruction of archaeological sites and the formation of museum collections are responses to social and economic developments of the last two centuries.

Marjorie Akin uses coins to examine the formation processes of small-scale private collections. An understanding of collecting behavior sensitizes investigators to the nature of collections, which affects their suitability to serve as sources of evidence. She demonstrates that private collections, even of mundane objects (the sort that many scholars traditionally eschew), can furnish valuable evidence on past human behavior. Catherine S. Fowler and Don D. Fowler discuss the formation of ethnographic museum collections. Their case study centers on objects collected from Native Americans of the Great Basin. They describe a panoply of diverse processes that need to be understood by scholars seeking to employ in their research objects found in ethnographic collections.

The archival records pertaining to anthropological collections of ethnographic objects is the subject of Nancy J. Parezo's essay. She argues that when such documentation is divorced from the ethnographic collections themselves, the results are dire, for undocumented collections are of limited value in answering many research questions. Drawing upon her own research pertaining to the material culture of Native Americans in the southwestern United States, Parezo illustrates the rich array of processes that can affect the persistence of ethnographic documentation.

The following chapters demonstrate that through the skillful application of generalizations about formation processes, the investigator is able to seek evidence of past behaviors relevant to solving particular research problems. Generalizations expressed at diverse scales and scopes help us to model and understand the pathways that link past activities to their

surviving traces in material entities extant today. Following these pathways, which may lead to museum collections, archives, private collections,
libraries, companies, individuals, and so on, calls attention to an unap-
preciated unity of historical inquiry: all scholars who would use evidence
from the historical and archaeological records to make rigorous inferences
about the human past must develop a sophisticated understanding of
formation processes.

REFERENCES

Binford, Lewis R. 1981. *Bones: Ancient Men and Modern Myths*. New York:
    Academic Press.
Brain, C. K. 1981. *The Hunters or the Hunted? An Introduction to African
    Cave Taphonomy*. Chicago: University of Chicago Press.
Cameron, Catherine, and Steven Tomka, eds. 1993. *Abandonment of Settle-
    ments and Regions*. Cambridge: Cambridge University Press.
Davidson, D. A., and M. L. Shackley, eds. 1976. *Geoarchaeology: Earth Sci-
    ence and the Past*. London: Duckworth.
Goodyear, Frank H. 1971. *Archaeological Site Science*. New York: Elsevier.
Kristiansen, Kristian, ed. 1985. *Archaeological Formation Processes: The Rep-
    resentivity of Archaeological Remains from Danish Prehistory*. Copenha-
    gen: Nationalmuseets Forlag.
Nash, D. T., and M. D. Petraglia, eds. 1987. "Natural Formation Processes
    and the Archaeological Record." *British Archaeological Reports, Interna-
    tional Series*, no. 352. Oxford.
Olson, Sidney. 1963. *Young Henry Ford: A Picture History of the First Forty
    Years*. Detroit: Wayne State University Press.
Rathje, William L., and Michael Brian Schiffer. 1982. *Archaeology*. New
    York: Harcourt Brace Jovanovich.
Rosen, Arlene Miller. 1986. *Cities of Clay: The Geoarchaeology of Tells*. Chi-
    cago: University of Chicago Press.
Schiffer, Michael Brian. 1972. "Archaeological Context and Systemic Con-
    text." *American Antiquity* 37:156–65.
———. 1976. *Behavioral Archeology*. New York: Academic Press.
———. 1977. "Toward a Unified Science of the Cultural Past." In *Research
    Strategies in Historical Archaeology*, edited by S. South, 13–50. New
    York: Academic Press.
———. 1978. "Methodological Issues in Ethnoarchaeology." In *Explorations
    in Ethnoarchaeology*, edited by R. A. Gould, 229–47. Albuquerque: Uni-
    versity of New Mexico Press.

————. 1987. *Formation Processes of the Archaeological Record.* Albuquerque: University of New Mexico Press.

Shackley, Myra. 1981. *Environmental Archaeology.* London: George Allen and Unwin.

Shipman, Pat. 1981. *Life History of a Fossil: An Introduction to Taphonomy and Paleoecology.* Cambridge: Harvard University Press.

Skibo, James M. 1992. *Pottery Function: A Use-Alteration Perspective.* New York: Plenum.

Staski, Edward, and Livingston D. Sutro, eds. 1991. "The Ethnoarchaeology of Refuse Disposal." *Arizona State University, Anthropological Research Papers,* no. 42. Tempe, Arizona.

Stein, Julie K., ed. 1992. *Deciphering a Shell Midden.* Orlando, Fla.: Academic Press.

Stein, Julie K., and William R. Farrand, eds. 1985. *Archaeological Sediments in Context.* Orono: Center for the Study of Early Man, Institute for Quaternary Studies, University of Maine.

Sullivan, Alan P. 1978. "Inference and Evidence: A Discussion of the Conceptual Problems." In *Advances in Archaeological Method and Theory,* vol. 1, edited by M. B. Schiffer, 183–222. New York: Academic Press.

Waters, Michael. 1992. *Principles of Geoarchaeology.* Tucson: University of Arizona Press.

7

Pathways to the Present
In Search of Shirt-Pocket Radios with Subminiature Tubes

MICHAEL BRIAN SCHIFFER

In perusing electronics magazines from the late 1940s, I came across some fascinating ads for vacuum tubes by Raytheon and Sylvania.[1] In full-page displays, both companies promised that their subminiature tubes would make possible new miniaturized products, including radios tiny enough to slip into a shirt pocket. Were pocket radios actually sold to the American public years before the transistor made such products commonplace? Conventional histories (e.g., Braun and MacDonald 1982) of electronics seemed to suggest they were not. Even in the definitive history of the vacuum tube, Stokes (1982) expressed doubt that subminiature tubes had actually been incorporated into home radios. There is no mention of such consumer radios in Gilbert's (1961) volume on electronic miniaturization or in standard historical encyclopedias of electronics and technology. If, contrary to widespread belief, subminiature tubes did give rise to pocket radios in the late 1940s and early 1950s, then it will be necessary to rethink facile notions about the "transistor revolution" that permeate historical discussions of consumer electronic products (e.g., Braun and MacDonald 1982; Dixon 1984).

Knowing that these radios, if they existed, had been a minor genre of commercial radios—a technological dead-end—I made a special effort to track down their traces. Drawing upon my knowledge of formation processes, I delineated pathways and launched a search to find traces of these radios in diverse lines of evidence. It was my hope to learn which companies made these radios, in which years, and which markets they targeted. I also wanted to find out about the consumer response to these sets.

When I began the search, in late 1988, about four decades had elapsed since publication of the tube ads. During these years, purchasers of the radios, participating in varied cultural formation processes, would have initiated pathways leading to the archaeological and historical records of today. Many radio owners, finding after a few years that small radios are difficult and often costly to repair, would have thrown out dead sets. Any such radios would now be entombed in landfills, practically inaccessible to scholarly inquiry. Similarly, owners irritated with the high cost of operating their tiny battery radios might have discarded them after the novelty wore off. Other owners might have given their sets to electronics enthusiasts or to charitable organizations for resale at thrift shops, and many of these would have ended up disassembled and/or discarded. In a small number of cases, people who especially valued their sets, perhaps having received them as gifts, would have retained their radios—even when nonfunctional. Upon the owners' death, retained radios might be inherited by relatives or friends or sold at an estate sale.

Although reuse processes such as inheritance and resale tend to disperse radios, separating them from their original owners, other reuse processes result in their aggregation into collections, where scholars can find them. By the early 1980s, radio collecting was becoming an important pastime for thousands of Americans. Collectors scoured flea markets, thrift shops, yard and estate sales, and so on, and some would have encountered shirt-pocket radios that had reentered the marketplace. Like collectors of most other products, radio enthusiasts have founded dozens of local, state, and regional clubs in order to share information on product histories and to facilitate the buying and selling of sets.

Aware of these reuse processes, I targeted radio collectors as a source of relevant evidence. I wrote to the clubs, asking about the existence of radios with subminiature tubes, and some published my inquiry in their newsletters. I placed advertisements in *Antique Radio Classified*, *Radio Age*, and other hobbyist journals, offering to buy the radios themselves. These tactics paid off. A handful of people wrote with descriptions of such radios in their collections, and some also furnished copies of documentary information; a few even sold me their sets. Clearly, the manufacture of highly miniaturized portable radios had preceded the transistor revolution. Additional lines of evidence helped me flesh out the story of pocket radios with subminiature tubes (Schiffer 1991, Chaps. 12–14; 1992, Chaps. 5–6; 1993). I also wrote to a number of technology museums claiming substantial radio holdings. Not one reported having a pocket radio with subminiature tubes. My search of technology museums, however, was far from exhaustive.

Another pathway I pursued began at Raytheon and Sylvania, the companies that made subminiature tubes. It was my hope that archival materials pertaining to the employment of their tubes in pocket sets would have been conserved. The Sylvania inquiry turned up nothing. However, my letter to Raytheon was passed along to Norman Krim, a retired Raytheon engineer who had developed subminiature tubes before the war and promoted their use in pocket radios afterward. In interviews with Mr. Krim, I learned about Raytheon's efforts to employ subminiature tubes in consumer products. This included the design and sale of the world's first shirt-pocket radio in 1945–46, through a subsidiary, the Belmont Radio Company of Chicago.

Having identified the first pocket radio with subminiature tubes, I followed different pathways that furnished evidence about the other companies that had made them—and when. In the late '40s and '50s, all radio and television service shops subscribed to *Howard W. Sams PhotoFacts*. *PhotoFacts* provided pictures, circuit diagrams, and parts lists for home electronic products. Over the decades, most service shops went out of business, and their *PhotoFacts* were either discarded or transferred to hobbyists and radio collectors. From radio collectors I was able to obtain some of the folders I needed. It goes without saying that a complete set of *Sams Photofacts*—the single most valuable source of evidence on the technologies of postwar consumer electronic products— is held by precious few libraries.

Trade magazines with new-product information and ads furnish another line of evidence. Regrettably, trade magazines are woefully under-represented in university libraries. For example, one of the most important radio trade periodicals, *Radio Retailing,* is very scarce; fortunately, I was able to use the run at the Crerar Library in Chicago—the closest set. In addition, I sample-searched other trade and technical periodicals, such as *Electronic Industries* and *Radio and Television News,* in various libraries. When they can be found in libraries, hobbyist magazines, such as *Popular Science, Radio Craft,* and *Popular Electronics,* also yielded nuggets, especially about the use of subminiature tubes in "home-brew" pocket radios.

Ads, blurbs, and articles in these diverse periodicals also brought to light a number of short-lived companies on the entrepreneurial fringe that had been organized to manufacture and sell shirt-pocket radios, mostly through the mail. When such companies expire, usually in obscurity, their records are not sought by libraries and archives. Unless intercepted by collectors or concerned family members, documents from tiny companies usually end up in landfills. Regrettably, my inquiries turned up no such materials that had fallen into collectors' hands.

Insofar as major companies are concerned, only a few made radios with subminiature tubes. Company records on the manufacture, marketing, and sale of these sets were sought with very few results. Apparently, it is the rare firm that conserves such records for many decades. Among the company records salvaged by radio collectors, I was unable to locate any concerning pocket radios with tubes.

Some of the people involved in the design, manufacture, sale, repair, and use of pocket radios from the late '40s and '50s are still alive and can be interviewed. I was able to locate a few such individuals and secured a small sample of attitudes and recollections.

Contemporary evaluations of some consumer products are recorded in consumerist magazines, which many libraries conserve. *Consumer Reports* and *Consumers' Research Bulletin* were exhaustively searched, and treatments of a few radios with subminiature tubes were found. These magazines were useful for documenting radio performance and for sampling attitudes toward pocket radios.

Traces of the marketing of radios to the general public, particularly from major companies, survive in ads in newspapers and mass-circulation magazines. Fortunately, libraries commonly retain runs of these magazines from the post–World War II era. I intensively searched *Colliers, Holiday, Life,* and others, but ads for radios with subminiature tubes were as scarce as the proverbial hen's tooth. Limited samplings of newspapers turned up nothing.

By following the diverse pathways created by reuse processes, I was able to assemble a modest corpus of information that furnished relevant evidence on the technology, design, manufacture, and marketing of pocket radios with subminiature tubes. Research on these radios involved diverse activities not usually carried out by an individual investigator, including participant-observation in radio-collector clubs, oral history, library and archival research, and study of the radios themselves. The evidence I was able to unearth permitted me to piece together the story of a very obscure consumer product that, had the transistor not been quickly commercialized, would have been at the beginning of a significant technological trajectory (Schiffer 1991, 1992, 1993).

Creating a well-rounded account of the shirt-pocket radio with subminiature tubes depended on gleaning the traces of such sets from diverse and scattered sources. Table 7.1 shows the sources of evidence, grouped by type, in which each identified radio model was found. (It should be kept in mind that the list of models in the table is doubtless not exhaustive; I expect new models to turn up, especially those made by U.S. firms on the entrepreneurial fringe and by Japanese companies.) There are a number of intriguing patterns in these data, which underscore the need to assess biases in the evidence surviving through different pathways.

Mass-circulation magazines contain ads and blurbs about radios from established companies, especially the "name" brands. Even ads for the latter, however, are rare. Moreover, in this source there are no radio ads from firms on the entrepreneurial fringe or from Japanese companies that marketed clones in the United States. Consumerist magazines paid little attention to the Lilliputian radios; on the rare occasions reviews appeared, they usually concerned the products of established U.S. companies. Hobbyist magazines as well as trade and technical journals yield smatterings of information about radios from U.S. firms, especially those on the fringe. The Japanese clones, however, are not in evidence. *Sams PhotoFacts* is nearly exhaustive in its inclusion of radios from established U.S. companies, whereas sets from Japanese and U.S. firms on the fringe are absent. Oral history and information from surviving companies furnished evidence only about radios from established U.S. companies. I discovered that radios owned by collectors provided the most representative record, and it was the only source that included any Japanese clones. Other sources—the radios themselves—were rather impoverished.

Clearly, had I relied only on mass-circulation and consumerist magazines, my account of the pocket radio with subminiature tubes would have left out important parts of the story. For example, between 1946 and 1953, when no major U.S. company was making such radios, an entrepreneurial fringe was providing them to the marketplace. And, when a few established U.S. companies began to make pocket radios with subminiature tubes from 1953 to 1956, Japanese firms cloned them and marketed them in the United States. Inferring these developments required

TABLE 7.1. Pocket Radios with Subminiature Tubes in Various Sources of Evidence

Radio Models	Sources								
	A	B	C	D	E	F	G	H	I
Established U.S. companies									
Emerson 747	•	•			•	•	•	•	
Emerson 838[a]	•	•			•	•		•	
Emerson 856[a]			•			•		•	
Motorola 45 "Pixie"[b]	•	•		•		•		•	
Westinghouse H508P4 "Little Jewel"	•					•		•	
Westinghouse H493P4	•					•	•	•	•
Silvertone 4212[b]						•		•	
Crosley JM8[a]	•	•				•		•	
Automatic TT528						•		•	
Automatic TT600[a]					•	•		•	•
Firestone 4C28								•	
Firestone 4C29[a]						•		•	
Belmont Boulevard (5P113)	•		•		•	•		•	•
Hoffman BP-402 "Nugget"		•						•	
U.S. companies on the fringe									
Ekeradio AM					•			•	
Ekeradio FM					•				
Micro AM					•			•	
Micro AM kit					•			•	
Micro FM					•				
Privat-ear					•			•	
Trans-Mite Micro			•						
Hastings FM Jr.		•							
Pocket-Mite			•						
Florac				•			•		
Ear-radio								•	
German sets									
Grundig-Majestic "Mini-Boy"		•						•	
Japanese clones									
Excel KR-451								•	
Koyo Parrot								•	

NOTE: Column headings are as follows: A = mass-circulation magazines; B = consumerist magazines; C = hobbyist magazines; D = supplied by surviving radio companies; E = trade and technical journals; F = *Howard W. Sams PhotoFacts;* G = oral history; H = radios owned by collectors; I = radios from all other sources
[a]Tube-transistor hybrid
[b]Also contains miniature tubes

information from sources of evidence that scholars do not conventionally consult, including hobbyist magazines, trade journals, and radios in private collections.

Table 7.1 does not differentiate sources on the basis of the *kind* of information supplied, but there are marked differences. Magazines, journals, and *Sams PhotoFacts* furnished information for dating the radios. Evidence for inferring manufacturing technologies, on the other hand, was most abundant in the radios themselves. And mass-circulation magazines provided tidbits about marketing strategies. Judicious consideration of many lines of evidence was necessary for constructing higher-order inferences, for example, on the size of the market for pocket radios (it was small!).

These patterns—quantitative and qualitative—underscore the necessity of following diverse pathways to the widespread fragments of evidence that survive today. Because each line of evidence supplies biased and/or incomplete information, it is important to seek and assess as many lines of evidence as practicable. Relevant evidence does not respect boundaries between museums and private collections, between technical journals and popular magazines, between documents and commercial products, and between scholars and ordinary people. I cannot help but believe that this lesson is applicable to any research question concerning past human behavior.

NOTE

1. Ad for Raytheon in *Proceedings of the Institute of Radio Engineers* 34, no. 4, p. 24A. New York. Ad for Sylvania in *Proceedings of the Institute of Radio Engineers* 34, no. 1, p. 12A. New York.

REFERENCES

Braun, Ernest, and Stuart MacDonald. 1982. *Revolution in Miniature: The History and Impact of Semiconductor Electronics Re-explored in an Updated and Revised Second Edition.* Cambridge: Cambridge University Press.
Dixon, Bernard. 1984. "The Black Box Blues." *Discover,* June, 30–32.
Gilbert, Horace D., ed. 1961. *Miniaturization.* New York: Reinhold.
Goodyear, Frank H. 1971. *Archaeological Site Science.* New York: Elsevier.

Schiffer, Michael Brian. 1991. *The Portable Radio in American Life*. Tucson: University of Arizona Press.

———. 1992. *Technological Perspectives on Behavioral Change*. Tucson: University of Arizona Press.

———. 1993. "Cultural Imperatives and Product Development: The Case of the Shirt-Pocket Radio." *Technology and Culture* 34:98–113.

Stokes, John W. 1982. *70 Years of Tubes and Valves*. Vestal, N.Y.: Vestal Press.

8

The Destruction of the Archaeological Heritage and the Formation of Museum Collections
The Case of Denmark

KRISTIAN KRISTIANSEN

My title suggests, provocatively, that the formation of museum collections and the destruction of the archaeological heritage are interrelated phenomena, not as cause and effect but as alternative responses to social and economic developments in Europe and, probably, North America during the last 200 years. As a consequence of this growing recognition, it has become a major analytical and theoretical concern in archaeology to systematically trace and explain the formation of the archaeological record (Schiffer 1985). The aim of this new research paradigm is to asses how representative the archaeological record is in relation to questions asked about the past. A first step is to analyze systematically the known history of recovery, normally stretching back 150 to 200 years, including rates of destruction and recovery as far as they can be documented in museum collections. This is compared to statistics on land use, such as the intensity of plowing versus grass and forest coverage, drainage and the reclamation of wetlands, and so forth in order to uncover possible causes and effects between land exploitation and the recovery/destruction of the archaeological heritage (Kristiansen 1985). The objective is to interpret and explain the historical impact of these processes on the formation of the archaeological research environment and vice versa. This demands historical analyses of research objectives, conservation strategies, museum foundations, and policies of collecting and principles of museum display, just to mention a few. Such analyses transcend an internal description of the formation of the archaeological record leading toward a wider understanding of the social and political role of archaeology in society. In recent years such studies have come to play in increasingly important role as part of critical self-reflection and the formulation of new research and conservation strategies (Cleere 1989; Fowler 1987; Kristiansen 1993; Trigger 1984).

I propose that archaeology was shaped in the historical process that transformed much of the Western world from static mercantile-agrarian to dynamic industrialized societies. In that process history and natural science, including archaeology, replaced popular myth and religion as the dominant explanations of human origins (Grayson 1983; Schnapp 1994; Trigger 1989). It happened at a time when landscapes were transformed on a scale never seen before, bringing forth archaeological finds in the thousands. At the same time nationalism rose to dominance as a political and historical framework. In this ideological climate the first museum collections appeared as exhibitions of the origins of nations, reflected in the formation of numerous national museums throughout Europe during the first half of the nineteenth century. As one of the best documented cases, Denmark exemplifies these wider developments in the history of archaeology and formation of museum collections.

ECONOMIC DEVELOPMENT AND FORMATION OF THE ARCHAEOLOGICAL RECORD: 1800–1960

The rapid destruction of archaeological monuments in Denmark in the late eighteenth and early nineteenth centuries led to the uncovering of thousands of burial finds and hoards and a growing desire to preserve the archaeological heritage. Although attempts to protect monuments were largely unsuccessful, in 1807 a national museum was founded in Copenhagen. During the next one hundred years, the preservation of archaeological finds became a major objective of Danish museums. The growing number of finds and increasingly better information about find circumstances laid the foundation for the development of an archaeological science (Gräslund 1987; Kristiansen 1985a; Nielsen 1987). From about 1850 onward, provincial museums were founded, accelerating the growth of museum collections. During the same period a movement to protect archaeological monuments in situ started. The number of monuments had been declining as rapidly as museum collections had been filling up; now archaeological excavations would provide an inventory of all visible monuments and sites. These measures to save archaeological information in the landscape by recording it also provided a cultural context for the museum collections, which added a new scientific dimension to both museum archives and archaeological practice. In a race to rescue what could be rescued before destruction, archaeological excavations, mainly of barrows, and field surveying boomed in Denmark and throughout Europe at the turn of the century.

When agrarian expansion and intensification finally consolidated in the early twentieth century, the focus changed from excavation to protection in situ, and laws to safeguard what remained in the landscape were instituted in many countries. This happened at a time when museum foundations were declining in number and collections already established had been filled. The growing interest of the public in nature preservation, including monuments, also played a role. Restorations of medieval ruins and megaliths had raised interest in the archaeological monuments themselves, as an addition to the museum exhibitions. Later, university departments were established to consolidate the formation and reproduction of knowledge. This historical process is essential in understanding the context and representivity of two interrelated archaeological records: that preserved in museums and that preserved in the landscape.

First, I shall take up the relation between agrarian expansion and the destruction and preservation of monuments in Denmark. It can be demonstrated that barrows are mostly preserved in areas rich in pastures and heathlands, which were cultivated only in the later nineteenth and early twentieth centuries, when archaeological interest was established (Baudou 1985, Figs. 6–7 and 13). Inversely it can be demonstrated that the reclamation of grasslands and the intensification of agriculture during the nineteenth century on the Danish islands (Fig. 8.1) was directly linked to the frequency of finds handed to the museums from farmers who had leveled barrows. Figure 8.2 shows how the onset and expansion of professional excavations (in Zealand), in combination with increased popular interest in preserving the monuments, changed this picture, explaining the decrease of nonprofessional excavations after the change of the century.

Hoards from the Bronze Age represent a different picture. They cannot be looked up and looted; they are found accidently during plowing, drainage, and similar activities. Figure 8.3 shows a normal distribution,

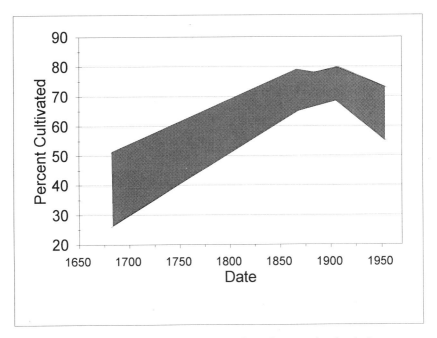

Fig. 8.1. Percentage of grasslands cultivated on the Danish Islands from 1700 to 1955. The expansion of cultivated land reached its maximum in the mid-nineteenth century. (After Baudou 1985, Fig. 8)

which can be linked to the intensification of agriculture, especially drainage and peat cutting. Because these activities, with the exception of peat cutting, have not ceased, the figure shows the discovery and exhaustion of an archaeological resource. Today, there are only few hoards left (Kristiansen 1985b).

If we total the number of museum foundations per decade (Fig. 8.4), the correlation with Figures 8.1, 8.2, and 8.3 is obvious, especially the correlation with professional excavations in Figure 8.2. At the same time that the number of museum foundations reached its height, the frequency of voluntary protection of monuments climaxed (Nielsen 1987). Only in 1937 were voluntary protections superseded by a general protection law. Figure 8.5 shows a characteristic situation from around the turn of the century: a group of farm laborers in the process of leveling a Bronze Age barrow with spades.

This brief scenario may be said to represent the first phase in the

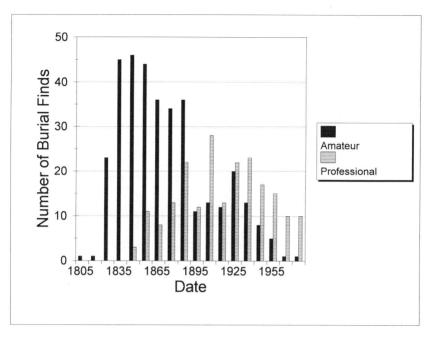

Fig. 8.2. Number of amateur and professional Early Bronze Age burial finds in Zealand. In most cases, barrows levelled for cultivation yielded the finds. Amateur finds reached their maximum number in the mid- to late nineteenth century, the same time the expansion of cultivated land reached its maximum. Note that the number of professional finds rises as the number of amateur finds falls. Due to the expansion of rescue archaeology after 1975, there has been an increase in the number of professional finds. (After Kristiansen 1985b, Fig. 4)

development and integration of archaeology in modern society, including museum collections. It was a period of mainly passive collecting and recording, when archaeology responded to the forces of economic development and developed measures to preserve what was possible, mostly material evidence in museums. Much was done voluntarily. The archaeological heritage was heavily exploited and sometimes exhausted in that process, providing the background to the formation of museum collections and a systematic and representative archaeological record for burial finds and hoards, which could probably not have been achieved in any other way within such a brief time span.

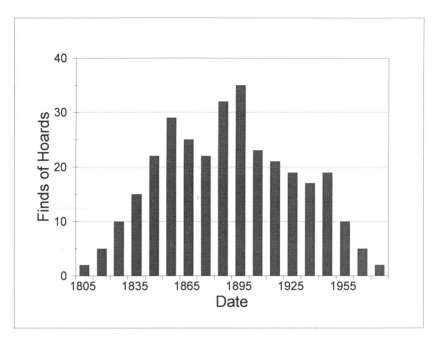

Fig. 8.3. Number of Early Bronze Age hoard finds in Zealand. (After Kristiansen 1985c, Fig. 1a)

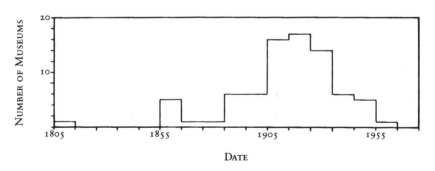

Fig. 8.4. The number of cultural-historical museums with an archaeological collection plotted against the date of their foundation. (After Kristiansen 1985a, Fig. 5)

Fig. 8.5. A Bronze Age barrow in northern Jutland, photographed during its excavation and removal by farm laborers in 1902. (After Kristiansen 1985a, Fig. 1; photograph courtesy of the National Museum, Copenhagen)

ECONOMIC DEVELOPMENT AND FORMATION OF THE ARCHAEOLOGICAL RECORD: 1960–?

I have demonstrated the interaction between economic development, the destruction/recovery of the archaeological heritage, and the formation of museum collections. These developments were reflected in research objectives and the cultural historical outlook of museum collections at the time: a preoccupation with isolated objects that were classified according to their dating and function—analogous to the grocery—with artifacts instead of commodities and identification labels instead of price tickets. Thus technological explanations of historical development predominated, and ritual and burial customs represented the dominant cultural context. This phase may be said to have lasted until the 1950s, although new developments were already underway from the 1930s onward within settlement archaeology.

However, a new phase began approximately thirty-five years ago, when industrializing, urbanization, and the development of infrastructure boomed at a scale not seen since the late nineteenth century. This time archaeology and museums were already in place and prepared, which meant that protective measures—new legislation that secured rescue excavations in addition to in situ conservation—could be taken instantly. It led to the largest boom in the development of archaeological resources and knowledge since the late nineteenth century, a development that has probably by now by now reached its peak, but whose consequences have not yet unfolded. The last twenty-five years changed the whole organizational structure of archaeology, from museums to state agencies to university departments. A whole new sector of conservation archaeology has been added to the existing structure of museums and university departments (Cleere 1989). Today most resources and jobs are created within the heritage sectors, which means that the power structure of archaeology has changed as well.

As a consequence of these developments, most archaeological work is based upon field surveying and settlement excavations in connection with rescue projects preceding construction works. But also, the intensification of agriculture and deeper plowing has forced archaeologists to focus upon the massive destruction of settlement sites. This new "settlement boom" can be parallelled with the "barrow boom" at the turn of the century, in terms of both destruction and uncovering of new archaeological material.

Figure 8.6 shows the increase in recorded Bronze Age settlements in Denmark. It coincides in a remarkable way with the increase in the number of tractors imported (leading to deeper plowing), which turned up new settlement material (Fig. 8.7). At the same time, following the curve of recorded settlement sites, new museum legislation and preservation laws were securing resources for the employment of professional archaeologists on a unprecedented scale. This reflects an archaeological response to the destruction of settlements sites, which is the main concern of today's fieldwork.

Thus settlements are now the most threatened part of the archaeological heritage, declining at the same rate as construction work and excavations fill the museum collections and archives. Plowing is causing gradual and irreversible destruction. Thus systematic field surveying has once again become a major tool in securing a representative sample of prehistoric settlement systems, as an interpretative platform for sites selected

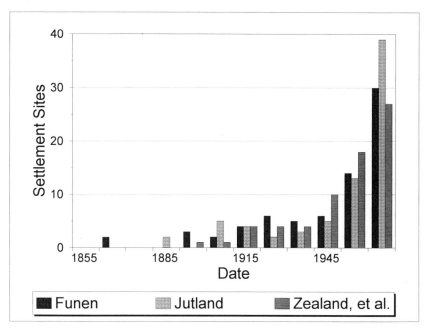

Fig. 8.6. Number of recorded Bronze Age settlement sites in Denmark, according to region. (After Thrane 1985, Fig. 2)

for excavation. In addition, conservation policies must be adjusted to take out of cultivation representative samples of prehistoric settlements. The damage caused by plowing is parallel to the massive destruction of the late nineteenth century, when so many barrows were destroyed, and has led to a recognition of the need to protect the archaeological record that remained. In much the same way we are only beginning to realize the degree of destruction of settlement sites and the need for more systematic protection in the future.

The changing configurations of archaeological conservation and research strategies during the last generation are also reflected in museum collections: the focus has changed from the life of the dead (burials) and artistic masterpieces to the living conditions of people in their houses, settlements, and environment. The so-called new archaeology can be seen as a response to these basic changes in the social and economic functions of archaeology in society.

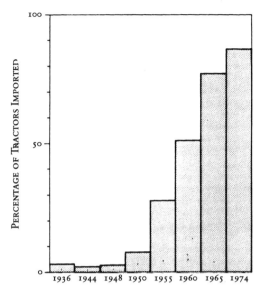

Fig. 8.7. The percentage of tractors imported into Denmark for selected years. Tractors allowed deeper plowing, thereby turning up new cultural layers from settlement sites. Today most sites have no or very little cultural debris, except in special circumstances. Plows have cut away the upper part of post holes and destroyed smaller post holes (from fences, etc). In many areas of eastern Denmark, only the deepest, roof-bearing post holes have been preserved.

CONCLUSION

Modern society consumes the past by destroying it and by preserving, in that process of destruction, select parts of it in museums (the movable heritage) and in the landscape (the nonmovable heritage). The composition of museum collections are thus a result of the historical forces that changed landscape and society during the last two hundred years, destroying a large part of the historical and archaeological heritage in the landscape in that process. Museums arose as a response to this development, in order to preserve some of the archaeological heritage—the movable part—from destruction. An interest in preserving the nonmovable archaeological heritage—monuments and sites—in the landscape, or at least preserving their full context through professional excavations, developed later.

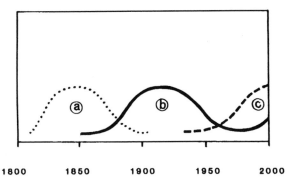

1800   1850   1900   1950   2000

*Fig. 8.8. The three main phases of archaeological conservation in Denmark,
1800–2000. a = destruction of monuments (metal hoards and burial finds);
b = excavation of barrows (field surveying, inventories, rise in number of museum foundations, restoration of monuments); c = settlement excavations/regis-
trations (rise in number of rescue excavations, rise in number of professional
archaeologists, monument maintenance, presentations and registrations).*

In Figure 8.8 I have presented graphically the three main phases of
archaeological recording and preservation in Denmark, demonstrating
their interaction in Figure 8.9. Following a decline of activities during
and after the Second World War, a new phase of archaeological rescue
work began after 1960, leading to a restructuring of both the institutional
and educational framework. All of these changes, including the "new
archaeology," are interrelated responses to the major social and economic
changes during the last thirty years. It is only during this period that
archaeology has achieved the status of a developed cultural and historical
science that is fully integrated into the administrative and political system.
Archaeologists and museum curators have become bureaucrats, serving
the needs of society.

REFERENCES

Baudou, E. 1985. "Archaeological Source Criticism and the History of Mod-
    ern Cultivation in Denmark." In Kristiansen, *Archaeological Formation
    Processes,* 63–80.
Cleere, H., ed. 1989. *Archaeological Heritage Management in the Modern
    World.* London: Unwin Hyman.

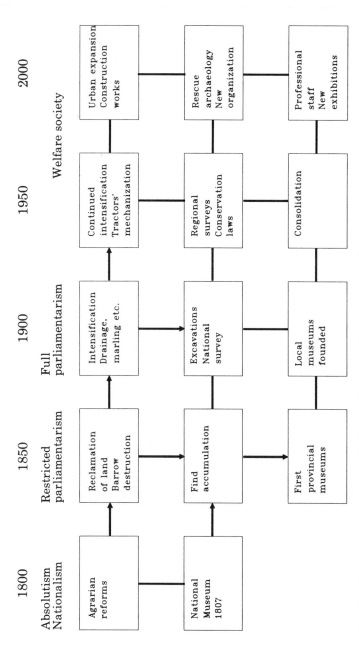

Fig. 8.9. Main interacting factors in the development of archaeology and society in Denmark, 1800–2000.

Fowler, D. 1987. "Uses of the Past: Archaeology in the Service of the State." *American Antiquity* 52:229–48.

Gräslund, B. 1987. *The Birth of Prehistoric Chronology: Dating Methods and Dating Systems in Nineteenth-Century Scandinavian Archaeology.* Cambridge: Cambridge University Press.

Grayson, D. K. 1983. *The Establishment of Human Antiquity.* New York: Academic Press.

Kristiansen, K. 1985a. "A Short History of Danish Archaeology: An Analytical Perspective." In Kristiansen, *Archaeological Formation Processes,* 12–34.

———. 1985b. "Bronze Age Burial Finds." In Kristiansen, *Archaeological Formation Processes,* 116–28.

———. 1985c. "Bronze Hoards from the Late Neolithic and Early Bronze Age." In Kristiansen, *Archaeological Formation Processes,* 129–41.

———. 1993. "'The Strength of the Past and Its Great Might': An Essay on the Use of the Past." *Journal of European Archaeology* 1:1.

———, ed. 1985. *Archaeological Formation Processes: The Representivity of Archaeological Remains from Danish Prehistory.* Copenhagen: National Museum Press.

Nielsen, I., ed. 1987. *Bevar din arv: Danmarks fortidsminder 1937–1987.* Copenhagen: Gad, Skov- og Naturstyrelsen.

Schiffer, M. B. 1987. *Formation Processes of the Archaeological Record.* Albuquerque: University of New Mexico Press.

Schnapp, A. 1993. *La conquête du passé: Aux origines de l'archéologie.* Paris: Éditions Carré.

Thrane, H. 1985. "Bronze Age Settlements." In Kristiansen, *Archaeological Formation Processes.*

Trigger, B. 1984. "Alternative Archaeologies: Nationalist, Colonialist, Imperialist." *Man,* n.s. 19:355–70.

———. 1989. *A History of Archaeological Thought.* Cambridge: Cambridge University Press.

9

Passionate Possession
The Formation of Private Collections

MARJORIE AKIN

The obsession with the possession of things has affected us for a long time, and apparently collectors in the past were every bit as devoted to their collections as their modern counterparts. In China during the eleventh century, Ouyang Xiu, a collector of carved jade and scrolls, wrote in the introduction to his catalogue of antiquities: "Someone mocked me saying: 'If a collection is large, then it will be hard to keep intact. After being assembled for a long time, it is bound to be scattered. Why are you bothering to be so painstaking?' I replied: 'It's enough that I am collecting what I love and that I will enjoy growing old among them'" (Zeitlan 1991, 5–6).

There is no way to gauge the percentage of humanly manufactured goods that have passed through collections at some point, but the volume must be staggering. Certainly no study of material culture, past or present, can be called complete without examining how and why private collectors have amassed the objects of their desire, how they have kept them, and how the collections were subsequently broken up, reformed, and circulated though societies. Examining collecting behavior by looking at the collecting process, the motivating forces, and the principles of organization of collected material will, in turn, reveal new sources of information that can enhance our understanding of the past and increase our awareness of our own behavior.

Michael Schiffer has pointed out that when things no longer serve the purpose for which they were created, they are sometimes transferred into the realm of collected material, a process he has described as "conserving," that is, a shifting of material from technofunction to socio- or ideofunction (1987, 32). Conservatory processes—collecting—are functional shifts that terminate in what is intended to be permanent (or longterm) preservation. Any given object may move back and forth between the realms of public and private collections, but this discussion will focus on the formation processes that affect privately collected materials. When does an assemblage of goods become a collection? It is not sufficient to note the functional shifts of individual items. Although it is generally true that a functional shift marks the conserved or collected item, sometimes the shift is only partial, and sometimes an item serves all three functions (technological, social, or ideological) at once. There is often no strict division between an item that is "in use" and an item that is collected. The way a person views and uses an object can, and does, change from time to time.

Two examples of commonly collected materials can serve as examples. Many people who read own books, but only a small percentage of them would identify themselves as book collectors. What differentiates someone who simply owns books from the collector? Using Schiffer's definition of conserved items, we would say that those books no longer being used for the purpose for which they were created (to be read) were the ones being conserved. Although many of the books a collector owns have been set aside to protect them from handling, which incidentally prevents them from being used for the purpose for which they were created, many are still read. The owner may acquire some books with the intention of reading them, but even if he never reads them, they are incorporated into the collection. There is no absolute book user/book collector dichotomy in this case—there is, rather, a range of behaviors.

The production, use, and conserving of tools can provide another example of the fact that there is no firm user/collector dichotomy. It is not uncommon for people who use a particular class of tools for work or recreation to collect a wide selection of those tools. An auto mechanic may possess any number of wrenches and gauges that are used on a regular basis, but that mechanic may also be seen at a swap meet, or a specialty shop, purchasing some obscure, rarely used tool. The mechanic may not have a specific use for that tool but will want to possess it anyway. The tool may be attractive because it is capable of performing an unusual operation, because of rarity, or simply because it is aesthetically pleasing. The tool can be used, but is unlikely to be used for the purpose for which it was made. A mechanic may obtain antique or obsolete tools, even though there is no chance of using them effectively. Is the mechanic a tool user or a tool collector? The answer is that there is no either/or but, rather, a range of behaviors.

Collecting behavior consists of a continuum of activities in which the collector obtains and maintains objects, and in which the primary functions of a substantial number of the pieces in the group are no longer those for which the items were originally created. Additionally, some items created especially to be collected may form a portion of a collection. A "serious" collector is someone with knowledge and expertise who spends a significant proportion of available resources on acquiring new material.

Formation processes of small-scale, private collections have not been investigated to the same degree as formation processes of museum, academic, and other formal institutional collections. There is extensive literature on collecting, especially on how and why it has been done for formal institutions, or by the sophisticated and presumably wealthy "connoisseur," but literature on private collecting, especially on a smaller scale, is primarily the province of collector's clubs and other non-academic organizations. Scholarly inquiry has underrated the value of private collections, especially those that do not contain "important" or particularly "valuable" material.

THE IMPORTANCE OF UNDERSTANDING COLLECTING

Examining collecting behavior helps us understand how material culture circulates through time and space. Knowledge of what motivates collectors, and what other forces may shape a collection of objects, helps us understand the meaning of the material to the collector. This can reveal a great deal about individual collectors' values and the cultural norms of their society.

Because of the idiosyncratic nature of personal collecting habits, the criteria for private collections are different, and in some respects more complex, than the more standardized criteria of formal institutions.[1] The criteria for determining what belongs in any given collection are different because individuals differ, and the motivations for personal collecting vary greatly from those of institutions. Items of material culture that have been privately collected may fall into the category of "commodities" (items intended for exchange), and thus become the subject of investigations of "value" that are economically based, but more often materials in personal collections have meanings for the owner that result in the material being pulled from circulation, removed from the world of markets and circulating commodities, at least for the lifetime of the owner.[2] For these items, the principles that govern economic exchange are often suspended, and replaced with other "values" drawn from subjective motivations. What we learn by studying privately collected material is that its movement through space and time depends on these motivations for developing any particular collection.[3] Once we realize that collected materials may be either examined as commodities or viewed as materials removed from intended exchange through "passionate possession," it becomes clear that this distinction has implications for the history of the objects.

Understanding the different motivations that lead to personal collections can provide us with new information. For example, understanding the desire for private collections and the various methods of their acquisition may enable us to gain access to previously excavated (or looted) material or to items that circulated, sometimes through black markets, in and out of the hands of collectors. It is true that studying such materials may pose ethical dilemmas, but we should recognize that if we ignore the information contained in objects held in private collections, our interpretations of past and present cultures may be incomplete.

My research on Asian coins recovered from archaeological sites in the New World depended on just such privately collected materials. More than half of the database represented holdings in small, private collections, including some coins that came from what many would understandably call looted sites, though most were "looted" legally. In this case the analysis of an entire class of material culture, Asian coins in the New World, depended on the ability to see patterns in assemblages of coins. Individually these coins were of little artistic or economic value, and therefore they did not attract the attention of institutions. Instead, they were left to circulate in the world of the small-scale private collector. Only by tracking down a number of the coins in private collections, and adding the information they contained to the database, was I able to put together a meaningful analysis of either the assemblages or the individual coins. Without an understanding of how the material moved among collectors, or without developing ways of communicating with and enlisting the help of the current owners of the material, the project probably could not have been accomplished.

INTERPRETATION OF COLLECTIONS

Understanding the biases and other forces that shape collections, and developing our skill in recognizing their effect on the material culture record, is essential to our ability to use collections to interpret the past. The different motivations that lead to the formation of a collection result in patterned assemblages. For example, the porcelain collection of a nineteenth-century missionary might be identified as such by certain patterns in the collection: dates of manufacture of the collected materials, location of manufacturing workshops, and the presence of items considered fashionable during that period.

Can we actually determine what type of collection we are looking at, or for that matter if we are looking at a collection at all? Yes, sometimes we can through contextual analysis or by searching for patterns of attributes in an assemblage. For example, a low rate of redundancy in an assemblage of artifacts may indicate a collection. In the case of archaeologically recovered coin hoards, intentional collections have been differentiated from simple accumulations of bullion coinage because coin collections have a greater variety of dates, mint marks, and other features that might be valued in the culture in which they were formed (Bradley 1985; Crawford 1986).

Cultural bias and the quality of the material may also provide evidence that a given assemblage is an intentional collection rather than material that was simply in use. Using such criteria I was able to distinguish Chinese coins collected for their talismanic value from those used as gambling paraphernalia at an abandoned "Chinatown" in Tucson, Arizona. Coins used for gambling tended to have an extremely high rate of reign date redundancy, to come from certain mints, and to have other distinguishing characteristics, such as uniformity of size. These coins were the functional equivalent of checkers or other gaming equipment. In contrast, talismanic coins, more highly valued and collected, were older, larger, and had much more reign date and mint mark variation. By becoming familiar with the expected characteristics of the coins the Chinese collected, I was able to differentiate the collected assemblage from the coins that were used in gaming at the Tucson site (Akin 1993, 236–39).

Understanding the way collectors conceptually and physically organized their collections often reveals underlying value systems as well as the social relations between the producers and the owners of the collected material. Sally Price has presented insightful observations of how the methods and justifications of the collecting and presenting of "primitive" art in various museum settings reveals underlying social beliefs. One such belief, often held but rarely stated, is that Western museums are needed to, and thus have the sole right to, understand and preserve primitive art for the rest of the world:

> First, like the ear in the forest, the Western observer's discriminating eye is often treated as if it were the only means by which an ethnographic object could be elevated to the status of a work of art; this alone is a definitional prerogative of tremendous power. Second, collectors and museums act largely according to their own priorities when they employ Western technology to rescue Primitive Art from physical extinction; they decide on the life or death of objects that have been fashioned from perishable materials by people whose own priorities represent, to Westerners, little more than a naive insouciance of the need to conserve their heritage for future generations. Third, Western connoisseurs assign themselves the job of interpreting the meaning and significance of artistic objects produced by people who, they argue, are less well equipped to perform this task. (Price 1989, 68–69)

The underlying beliefs of private collectors can be extracted through the same type of examination that Price has applied to wealthy connoisseurs and museum collections. Because collectors often believe they are preserving something of importance from destruction, we can discern collectors' cultural values by examining what classes of objects have attracted their attention. Similarly, an examination of items in a collection deemed "exotic" or "quaint" can reveal attitudes about social relations between groups of people.

Collections of "Mammy dolls" can serve as an example for both points. These dolls, which depict stereotypical nineteenth-century southern African American women, have been collected by people of different ethnic and economic backgrounds for different reasons. An African American scholar might maintain such a collection to help educate future generations about the nature of racism, preserving the dolls because the information they represent should be saved from oblivion. On the other hand, a southern European American woman told me, at a craft fair in 1992, that she cherishes her collection because the dolls are "quaint," "precious," and a reminder of her childhood. She assumed that the people for whom she produced similar dolls felt the same way about them.

WHY PEOPLE COLLECT

Collecting seems to be part of the very human urge to put the universe in order, to categorize and name things. Some of the great organizers of natural history, including Christian Thomsen, exponent of the Three Age System, and Charles Darwin, were avid coin collectors (Nelson and Jurmain 1991, 21). I would argue that there are five major reasons individuals collect things: to satisfy a sense of personal aesthetics, to gain a sense of control or completion, to connect themselves with history, for profit (real or imagined), and for, as one avid collector described it, the "thrill of the chase" (Barrett 1976, xviii).

Collecting to Satisfy a Sense of Personal Aesthetics

People often collect material culture to satisfy a sense of personal aesthetics, to reify their own sense of wonder and marvel. In a way, even the impulse to name things and put them in order satisfies that sense. The aesthetic aspect of any collection is a combination of personal taste and culturally derived values.[4] Although some collections are completely idiosyncratic, most collections are shaped, to some degree, by the cultural norms of "taste" and "importance" in the collector's culture. For example, in Euro-American culture there is a broad range of things people will collect. However, there are categories of collectibles that are considered more "normal" than others, such as stamps, dolls, and records. Guidebooks dedicated to these categories are published, and clubs are organized so that collectors can work together in pursuit of their passion. Conventions and shows, where markets are established and information exchanged, are not uncommon. The market value of collectibles in one of these categories is relatively easy to determine, and the guidebooks normally contain much information on producers, dates, and distinguishing characteristics (see Walker 1985; Potter 1989; Cummings 1991; Alpert and Elman 1992).

Types of collections that reflect more personal, idiosyncratic tastes, possibly raising an eyebrow or two, include, for example, assemblages of caps with trucking company logos on them or saltshakers shaped like pigs. Many collections consist of such materials, things that do not conform to popular tastes, but are especially prized for their uniqueness. Collectors' taste for the unique and nonconventional is a source of pride, self-identification, or psychological comfort. Nonconventional collections are popular among Americans, members of a society that puts a high value on individuality.

The most extreme examples of idiosyncratic collections, such as a collection of burned objects, would be considered abnormal by society. One person who collected such objects did so because he was fascinated by the transformational effects of fire on different types of material, melted metal, burned plastic, and the like. Such a collection would be considered weird by most people (but it is perhaps more understandable in this case when we learn that the collector's father was a chemist). Measuring the relative popularity of a type of collection within a society can indicate cultural norms, and the way people relate to the rest of society is often defined in terms of the social acceptability of their collecting passions. Collectors define themselves, and are defined by others, in part, by what they collect. Obituary notices, for example, often mention the deceased's collecting passions.

Although perfectly understandable within their own cultural context, some of the collecting criteria of other cultures may seem surprising to us. For example, when substantial trade between China and western Europe developed during the 1600s, Chinese porcelains brought fantastic prices from European collectors, whereas Chinese calligraphy was considered a mere curiosity. But van Gulik reports of the Chinese:

> They have always been much more jealous of their pictures than their porcelains. They consider . . . that painting and calligraphy represent the essence of their culture, hallowed by association with the great statesman and scholars who made national history. Ceramics they viewed as part of the furnishing of their house—often of exquisite beauty, but definitely belonging to the sphere of the artisan rather than the artist. (xii–xiv)

Other art historians and anthropologists have presented us with many examples of values that provide non-Western cultures with different ways of judging aesthetic merit. The quality of *jijora*, "the siting of art at a point somewhere between absolute abstraction and absolute likeness," is of great importance in the judgment of art among the Yoruba (Thompson 1971:376), but is rarely, if ever, a standard that European art would be measured against. Likewise, the "sleeping" mats prized by Samoans are valued for characteristics of manufacture and history of ownership that are difficult for the non-Samoan to distinguish (Martin Orans, pers. comm.).[5] Clearly, both aesthetic norms and the criteria of what has artistic, economic, or even functional value, and therefore the ideals of what should be collected, are largely influenced by the collector's cultural norms.

Collecting for Control or a Sense of Completion

In addition to collecting to satisfy personal aesthetic values, people collect to gain a sense of control or completion. In preparing an exhibit of children's collections, William Ackerman, executive director of the Children's Museum of Manhattan, observed:

> Developmentally, kids generally start collecting at around age five or six. They do it, for one reason, because a collection is a world that they can control. You know, a lot of kids nowadays have nothing that they can control, so in them the instinct becomes more intense than ever. A collection is theirs, they created it. They decide if it is good. It is an expression of who they are. (*New Yorker*, April 20, 1992, 32)

A dramatic example of collecting for completion was provided by a man I observed at a coin show in 1992 who was discussing his collection of cents. He had just purchased a rare U.S. cent and mentioned that this coin filled the last space in the collection he had recently inherited from his father. His father had been trying to find this particular cent for years, but had died before he was able to do so. By purchasing this coin, the gentleman had succeeded in "finishing" his father's task, and as he explained this fact he was overcome with emotion and his eyes filled with tears: "It really made me feel close to my father; it was finally finished."

Control may also be evoked in terms of domination. Curtis Hinsley has pointed out that collecting can be a method of displaying territorial control that is not always politically neutral. He describes a "typical phenomenon of America's unique history of regional expansionism," the collecting of Native American relics from a settled area, as "symbolic capital." The boosters of small-town, nineteenth-century America often demonstrated their claim to new territory by collecting its material remains and sorting them into boxes, shelves, and "mantelpiece museums" (Hinsley 1993, 111). The process of taking items of importance to Native Americans and transforming them into showcase trinkets placed on the mantelpiece was a graphic display of Euro-American political and economic domination

Field collecting of ethnographic material (sometimes referred to as "tribal arts") was often a demonstration of the "cleverness" of the collector, who was going to "rescue" materials from the oblivion they surely faced if they remained in the hands of their less-civilized creators. This attitude smacked of many of the ugliest aspects of colonial attitudes, and as a response, Price points out, many ethnographers developed policies that keep them from removing any materials from indigenous cultures except those freely offered as personal gifts (1989, 75). This recent shift in the policy governing collecting practices indicates that these Westerners recognize and reject their political role as representatives of colonial power.

Collecting to Make Connections with the Past

A desire to make connections with the past is another motive for assembling a private collection. People like to collect things that connect them to their past, and they also like to own a part of the historical record. Fred Coops, who worked as a stamp and coin dealer for more than half a century and took part in hundreds of thousands of transactions, reports that collectors seek out coins from the reigns of historically significant rulers, such as Henry VIII or Ghengis Khan, because they like the personal connection with the famous past that such ownership gives them (Fred Coops, pers. comm. 1991). An antiquities dealer states that customers enjoy stories about "empires rising and falling," and that tying an article to a king or a queen, even indirectly, will help to ensure a sale (Reis 1993). Such a connection may have been a motivating force for the dilettanti of the Renaissance period, who sought to connect themselves with the classical world or the ancient Maya who collected Olmec jade (Drucker 1955, 61).

Whatever the category of objects or the general theme of a collection, the owners will often try to tie the items to his or her past. Collecting material from one's "homeland" is common among people in the United States. For people whose ancestors have lived in the same place for centuries, just having something old that may have passed through family hands at some time may be important. Individual experience can also play a role in collecting behavior. Collections of baseball cards or seashells may evoke pleasant memories of childhood, and other assemblages may help the owner to remember visits to foreign places. Such is the case for Naomi Beckley, who said of her inscribed souvenir demitasse spoons, "If anybody looks at the spoons, they'll know where I've been" (*New Yorker,* February 19, 1992, 27). Personal history may play some role in the choice of the type of material to be collected or the particular items one seeks out (as in the case of the man who completed his father's collection of U.S. cents).

Collecting for Profit

Another motive for collecting—although it has, I think, been confused with investing—is the desire for profit. Collecting as a method of increasing personal wealth appears to be an almost incidental aspect of collecting among nonprofessionals. Although there is no doubt that many collectors hope to realize some profit from their collections, that this is incidental to their collecting is demonstrated by the fact that most people will continue to collect their favorite items in spite of market fluctuations, violating common investment strategies. Dealers are aware that catering to the special, individual desires of their customers can allow them to increase the price they can charge for an item, and those of questionable integrity may use this information to their advantage.

The desire to increase the market value of the collection can mold the general shape of a collection or be the deciding factor in whether to add a specific item. There are many reasons an individual may want to increase the market value of a collection; three important ones are: the goal of resale for profit, to increase the value as a form of savings or insurance, and to justify the collecting activity.

Most people who collect things maintain some sort of record of the estimated market value of the material. Such records occasionally take the form of written accounts, but more often consist of an informal, but highly detailed and accurate, mental tracking system. The reasons for such efforts include the possibility of resale of part or all of the collection. But people who accumulate goods that are secured and maintained with the primary goal of eventual resale are, by my definition, investors, not collectors. How do collectors differ from investors? A collector may occasionally sell an item to secure funds for another purchase that will improve the quality of the collection overall, or because of some personal financial difficulty, but the intention is to permanently preserve the material. Most collectors view their accumulations as a store of wealth, something to fall back on during hard economic times, as something to leave as an inheritance upon their death, or perhaps as something they can donate as an endowment. For this reason they give some attention to the market value of the collection and may buy and sell for the collection with the goal of increasing its value, but they consider the insurance function secondary.[6]

In contrast, investors may have an interest in the historic value or aesthetic virtue of a piece, but their overriding concern is with an item's market value. There is no absolute investor/collector dichotomy, however. As with other aspects of collecting behavior, these activities represent a range of behaviors. Occasionally, collectors who feel it necessary to justify collecting, to potentially hostile spouses or other significant persons, or even to themselves, will turn their attention to increasing the market value of their collection. This aspect of collecting behavior is accentuated in societies where wealth is measured in the possession of marketable commodities.

Collectors may try to increase their wealth in the form of demonstrated status, what Pierre Bourdieu calls "symbolic capital" (1993, 41). A fine collection of Pre-Columbian vessels may demonstrate that the owner has not only the wealth necessary to purchase such a collection but also the good taste, education, and black-market connections to get the material—as well as the political pull to keep it in the country. Certainly collectors desire to increase their status among their peers by demonstrating possession of the unusual, to gain prestige by having something different they can show people. Sometimes the status gained is self-proclaimed expertise. Jon Taleb, an educator, claims that her desire to own an original manuscript of a Byron work is motivated, at least in part, by her belief that "no one else in the world could appreciate it as much as I would."

Collecting for the Thrill of the Chase

The process of seeking out materials to collect and socializing with—sometimes competing with—fellow collectors motivates much collecting behavior. Finding the perfect item to fill a "hole" in a collection, finding the best, or even the unique, example of some class of objects, fills the collector with a deep sense of pride (Brook 1980, 17). Such finds demonstrate expert knowledge, tenacity, and good luck, which is not only satisfying to the owner but also may raise his status among other collectors. Occasionally such finds are financially rewarding, but objects added to a collection after a long search are rarely parted with. The long-sought-after piece that is finally added to a collection has a value to the collector that exceeds its market value: it satisfies the personal needs of the owner (Merkland 1993, 1–3).

The camaraderie of the collecting club, or the company of others with shared interests, is another motivating force for collecting behavior. These associations reenforce values and develop networks that overlap into other aspects of social life.

CHARACTERISTICS OF COLLECTIONS

Once a person has decided to maintain a collection, a number of personal, social, and economic forces come into play to help shape the collection. Like the different motivations for collecting, these forces can reveal much about collectors and the social context in which they are operating.

Forces that Shape Collections

In order to understand how and why a collection was put together at any particular time or place, we have to understand the collecting criteria of the associated culture. But there are other factors that influence the composition of a collection, including the financial means and collecting opportunities of the collector. Certainly the collections of the wealthy are going to differ significantly from the more opportunistic collections of those less well-to-do. Some people have opportunities to travel and are in a position to acquire materials that might be unavailable to others.

An interesting example of how traveling under special circumstances affected the formation of a collection comes from Britain, where late

Roman coins recovered in Scotland were presented as proof of a late Roman occupation of the area, an occupation unreported in any documentary evidence. However, examination of the coins showed that they were all minted in areas visited by crusaders. It was determined that these coins were, in fact, obtained by soldiers on military service who brought them back as souvenirs of the Holy Land. The coins were part of medieval coin collections, not evidence of early Roman occupation (Casey 1986, 109). Only the recognition of the coins as parts of private collections prevented a complete misinterpretation of the archaeological record.

The contents of some collections represent another kind of special access, work-related collections. Examples of this phenomenon would include the stamp collection of a postal worker, Bibles collected by a minister, or old sheet music collected by a musician. For collectors whose work involves travel, occupation-related collecting can explain the presence of a class of material in a totally unanticipated location.

Determining Completeness

What makes a collection "complete" is often defined by catalogues and price lists. It is well established that such catalogues and lists strongly influence what people will collect. Stephen Album, a noted numismatist and coin dealer who recently produced *A Checklist of Popular Islamic Coins,* wrote:

> Collectors of Islamic coins have long bemoaned the lack of general literature on the subject. In particular there has never been a general listing of Islamic coin types that could serve as a convenient guide to what exists, what is readily collectable, and what is rare. . . . Whatever the collector may choose, it is my hope that this checklist will facilitate his endeavors, making it easier for him to set up criteria for his own collecting. . . . Moreover, he can use the checklist to mark off dynasties, rulers, or types, as he acquires them for his collection. (Album 1993, 3)

By producing the *Checklist,* Album has, in effect, defined the parameters of a collectable field and provided collectors with a mechanism for determining their own completeness. Album has produced several important academic works on Islamic coinage. If past patterns hold true, however, it will be this somewhat informal booklet, which he produced in his role as a coin dealer, that will help shape collections of Islamic coins in the coming decades.

Guidebooks, checklists, and price guides are produced for a wide variety of the commonest, and therefore most socially sanctioned, types of collections. Although occasionally such books and pamphlets are released through a mainstream publishing house, the majority are either produced by specialty presses or privately printed. These publications are often unavailable in libraries, and the researcher who is investigating a special class of material culture may find it necessary to contact a collector or dealer to get a list of the applicable publications and directions for obtaining them. The quality of these publications vary widely, but many small, private publishers have good reason to pride themselves on the accuracy of their work.

TYPES OF COLLECTING BEHAVIOR

The different motivations for collecting are only one source of the variation in the types of acquisitions. The overall form of a collection is also determined by self-imposed criteria of formality and intensity in the collecting behavior. Some collectors take more care to conform to whatever collecting guidelines they have established for themselves or are simply more disciplined than others.

Formality

Collecting behavior can vary in rigidity, from "formal" to "idiosyncratic." At the formal end of the spectrum are collectors who have self-imposed, narrow and specific parameters for their collecting activities and who conscientiously attempt to make every addition to the collection fit their circumscribed collecting criteria. Such collections feature a highly structured internal arrangement. At the idiosyncratic end of the scale are collectors with haphazard and scattered collecting habits, whose collecting is not well directed or defined and who add to their collections on the basis of what is available rather than what fits a constructed definition of the collection.

Dealers will often develop an informal, working taxonomy that describes collectors' range of collecting behaviors. Joel Anderson, who deals in coins and related numismatic items, devised such a folk taxonomy to describe his customers. According to Anderson's scheme, collectors fall into two categories, "open" and "closed." Collectors who are developing open collections collect material purely on the basis of what they like. They are unconcerned with determining what comprises a complete collection and are not bothered by the standard conventions of "correct" collecting for their field. Such a collector is at the idiosyncratic end of the range of collecting behavior. At the other end are the closed collectors. They define precisely what they wish to collect and systematically try to collect one representative of every available type. Typical of this behavior are coin collectors who collect pennies by date and mint; once they have an example that fills the "hole," they are satisfied. Authors of guidebooks produced for particular "collectibles" will also often provide descriptions of similar taxonomies of collectors (see Unden 1982, 20; Potter 1989, 10–21; and Alpert and Elwin 1992, 3). Dealers will employ different procurement and sales techniques for the customer, depending on the collector's habits.

If the collector is using the amassed material as reference for a study, the collecting behavior will, of necessity, fall into the formal end of the range. Steve Mains, a geohydrologist for the Western Municipal Water District of Riverside County, California, collects examples of bottled mineral water. His interest is work-related but also driven by a curiosity about marketing strategies and an enjoyment of the humor often displayed on the labels. He adheres very tightly to the criteria he has established for the collection; he collects only samples that contain a full chemical analysis on the label and only one example of each type, which must be the smallest possible commercially available bottle. He buys every new type that comes to his attention and enlists the help of friends in his search. He has arranged the bottles on shelves according to shape and size and uses them as a reference resource when preparing reports or giving public presentations.

Philip Wilke, a professor of archaeology who studies the development of lithic technology, has collected samples of materials commonly used in the production of stone tools. He needs a comprehensive representation of the varieties of suitable flint, and other stone used in tool production, for research purposes, but he also appreciates the intrinsic beauty of the material. However, collecting rocks on a casual basis, obtaining only those materials that please, would not satisfy him. Like Mains, Wilke has developed certain rather stringent criteria for his collection. The stone must be well-provenienced, and he collects only one sample from each source (or one sample of each type from a source that contains some variation). The samples are worked into bifaces of uniform shape and size and stored in an orderly fashion with uniform labeling. He enlists the help of friends and colleagues in obtaining new samples and proudly displays his collection to anyone who shows any interest or appreciation. He might even chafe at the idea of being referred to as a "rock collector," because he does not like his activities confused with the informal end of the collecting scale.

Because the desire to connect oneself with the past through ownership of material culture is such a common phenomenon, many collections are used to illustrate historic or technological developments and are actively put to use as reference materials. Anyone who saw the two collections described above would recognize some of their functions. The strict ordering, the comprehensive labeling, the uniformity, and, most important, the completeness of the collected material would suggest that the collections serve some purpose other than simply pleasing their owners.

Intensity

Collecting can take place at various levels of intensity, ranging from "maximizing" to "opportunistic." Maximizing collectors have a sophisticated knowledge of their field and are concerned, if not obsessed, with improving the quality and range of the collection according to culturally determined criteria such as aesthetics and value as "symbolic capital." Such collectors maximize their collections by making the most of their time and resources. Many collectors, falling into a middle range, are not as concerned with how well informed their choices might be but are more casual in their selections. For them, the pleasurable activities associated with the thrill of the chase, such as shopping or attending meetings with other collectors, have a mediating effect on absolute maximization (Merkland 1993, 1–3). At the most opportunistic collecting level, a few interesting or attractive items are put away in a convenient spot, or perhaps displayed on a shelf. They may have no culturally recognized aesthetic or commercial value but nonetheless please their owner.

Maximizing collectors are often experts in their field, commanding a detailed knowledge of applicable history, technology, and market values. Avocational specialists have spent years studying and may have a greater mastery of facts about their specialty than academics, and they usually command a detailed knowledge of the pieces they own. They are often associated with the appropriate society for the study of their beloved class of material culture and are available as resources to researchers wise enough to seek them out.

There are many factors that lead to opportunistic collecting. These collectors may, as a matter of personal taste and habit, be less concerned with possessing a complete or perfect collection than their maximizing counterparts. They may have limited resources, financial or otherwise, or may take special pleasure in obtaining only bargains, that is, purchasing or trading for less than the market value. Opportunistic collectors are not necessarily less informed about their material and thus may also be important resources for the serious academic investigator.

SPATIAL ORGANIZATION AND ITS MEANING

Collectors often separate their materials into different groups, or sections, kept in physically separate locations. The portion of the collection that contains the most important items, or the materials being actively worked on, may be stored in a more secure area or placed on display, depending on the individual tastes and needs of the collector. Duplicates, or materials the collector intends to trade or sell, are usually found in locations physically separate from the "active" or "important" pieces. Items that have to be identified, repaired, or cleaned will usually occupy yet another physical space.[7] These physical locations may be different boxes or containers, different rooms, or even different buildings.

Vince (last name not given), who collects high-fashion magazines, has organized his prized possessions in a manner typical of a twentieth-century urban setting:

> Vince lives in a seven-room apartment on Second Avenue in the East Village . . . the apartment is a magazine cavern, constructed of glossy paper masonry. Stacked in the front hall are sixties Vogues. In special Conran's shelves in the dinning room are Vogues from the thirties to the sixties. Piled in Vince's bedroom are purchases he hasn't yet read and sorted. In the spare bedroom Vince keeps his dupes. (*New Yorker,* April 15, 1992, 32)

Observing the way collections are spatially arranged can reveal a great deal about what collectors think about their material, what they consider valuable and their criteria for determining values, and how they process the material once it is in their possession.

Items of special importance to the collector are almost always stored or displayed in a manner that separates them from the more mundane objects. Important items are at the center of the display case or shelf, in the most important room of the house, or are otherwise distinguished. This phenomenon is carried over into institutional displays, where the "major" pieces receive more room on the exhibit floor and receive special labeling or lighting, whereas lesser items may be relegated to storage in the basement. Culturally determined and idiosyncratic taxonomies can be revealed by examining the way the owner has sorted the collection (although it may be difficult to distinguish culturally determined from idiosyncratic unless there are several collections to compare).

The intentional decontextualization of objects, that is, moving them from one physical location to another and changing their function in the process, can reflect a change in the meaning (or the appreciation of a new meaning) of the material for the collector. Edward Carpenter described the discovery, and subsequent decontextualization, of Northwest Coast ethnographic artifacts found in a New York shop by Max Ernst and other surrealists in the 1940s. They were purchased by the surrealists, who appreciated the artifacts for their visual puns. An exhibit, consisting of a combination of the privately collected pieces and specimens from the American Museum of Natural History, was instituted in 1946 at a New York gallery. As Carpenter reported:

> The American Museum of Natural History offered a curious paradox. On public display was an incredible wealth of Northwest Coast art. Yet every piece was classified and labeled as a scientific specimen. Tribal carvings were housed with seashells and minerals as objects of natural history. Art was displayed in the Metropolitan Museum. Far more than Central Park separated these collections. Part of the gap derived from the anthropologists' insistence that ethnological specimens had meaning solely in terms of the social matrices from which they came.
>
> The very accessibility of this great collection reinforced that classification, preventing viewers from experiencing these objects artistically. By taking them off display in one part of New York and putting them on display in a gallery a mile away, the Surrealists declassified them as scientific specimens and reclassified them as art. (1976, 56–58; emphasis added)

Collecting is normally a process of decontextualizing material. By collecting something, the owner is changing its primary function from its original, intended function to another, socially or ideologically based function. Therefore, the same process described above for publicly owned and displayed material applies to private collections. The context of presentation of privately owned materials can provide the same kinds of clues about the social and ideological meaning of the collection as in public displays.

FROM PRIVATE TO PUBLIC, AND BACK AGAIN

It is a mistake to consider collections in private hands an intermediate stage of "conservatory practices," to be followed by absorption into formal museums and archives. Museums have always obtained materials from private sources, but the flow of the collections is not a simple progression from private collector to museum to bigger museum (if the piece is "important" enough), rather there is an ebb and flow of ownership, a shifting back and forth between public and private hands.

Michael Coe has recently produced a detailed study of such a flow.[8] He has examined the movement of Pre-Colombian art, as a system, from its source through a series of "distributors" and "consumers" for a period of about fifty years, beginning at the end of World War I (Coe 1993, 271–88). Coe views this specific flow of a particular class of goods as historically unique. However, the general pattern of the movement of material through a circle of collectors, curators and experts, museums, and dealers is rather common. In the circulating process outlined by Coe, materials were brought from the "producing" country to the "recipient" country by dealers, couriers, and agents who then introduced the material into the market. During the period investigated by Coe, artifacts moving in the loop of dealers, museums, and private collectors circulated freely "in any direction . . . [,] and desirable items were often swapped between dealers and between collectors" (276). Although increasing international enforcement of laws governing the sale of antiquities has affected the circulation of this particular type of artifact, the general system outlined by Coe can be observed by visits to specialty "shows" or through the examination of the catalogues of the major auction houses.

There has always been a flow of materials in and out of major public collections, depending on changing political and economic situations.

The world is undergoing rapid changes. As political boundaries shift and nations break apart, national museums are undergoing changes. Some changes are simply realignments with newly emerging political states, but other museums appear to be privatizing their collections and in the process returning the materials to the universe of the private collector. As demonstrated by the case of Pre-Columbian materials, this is not a new process. The current repatriation of Native American materials is resulting in the break-up of some centralized North American collections. James Clifford has documented several such cases in the Pacific Northwest. He has characterized these changes in ownership as turning to "unanticipated ends," when materials long held by public museums were returned to tribal councils; when "master narratives of cultural disappearance and salvage could be replaced by stories of revival, remembrance, and struggle" (1991, 214). The whole question of who "owns" the artifacts is continually up for reexamination in response to changing political and economic conditions.

Collecting criteria change as well. The definition of what is "desirable" in a collection changes over time in response to the cultural milieu of the collectors. The key piece in an assemblage today can become irrelevant, and even an embarrassment, in a very short time. The combination of the change in collecting criteria and the reorganization of major museum collections in response to changing political and economic conditions produces a constant ebb and flow of collections being formed and broken up. This process takes place on both an institutional and personal scale and is accompanied by a shifting of ownership between private and public sectors. Materials in private collections do not inevitably end up in public museums, and even when they do, there is certainly no guarantee that they will stay there.

ACCESS AND ETHICS

As discussed earlier, one of the most important motivations for collecting is the desire to connect oneself with the past. People like to collect old things, and this desire has had a strong impact on the fields of inquiry that rely on the material culture of the past for their investigations— primarily archaeology but also, to a lesser extent, history.

The conflict between private collectors and academics has produced serious problems and ethical dilemmas. The position of most scholars has been forcefully stated by Colin Renfrew and Ricardo Elia in a series of discussions, carried by the journal *Archaeology*, centering on the ethics of authenticating, displaying, and using looted materials for research (in this case Early Cycladic sculpture). The authors differ in their view of how scholars should interact with the various owners of the pieces, both private collectors and public museums. They agree, however, that "collectors are the real looters." Renfrew writes: "Most archaeologists would argue that to participate in the process of clandestine excavation/illegal export/private sale is not the role for the serious scholar. Those who agree to 'authenticate' pieces for sale catalogs of major sellers . . . have long been regarded with disapproval" (1993, 16).

Peer pressure is placed on serious scholars to avoid working with materials that have not been properly excavated and documented in the hope that their strong disapproval will help stem the tide of looting. Debates have arisen over the extent of cooperation that should be extended to the holders of such materials, and the effect that such sanctions will have on the black-market trade. The whole problem is aggravated by the fact that many improperly removed materials were obtained perfectly legally. This is especially true in the United States, where laws covering materials recovered from private lands, and certain classes of artifacts (such as arrowheads), are lax or ambiguous.

Collectors, of course, see their role differently, particularly the owners of relatively small, "unimportant" collections. Many view themselves as rescuers, saving their beloved possessions from oblivion. These collectors have often expressed a lack of confidence in museums and universities: they believe that donated objects are sold off, stolen by curators, or left to rot in forgotten basements and storerooms. Current museum practices of putting only a small sample of an institution's holdings on display at a time, and the lack of funds for changing permanent exhibits, feed into this common folk belief. The holders of small collections of material not deemed to be of "museum quality" are especially adamant in their belief that they are the guardians of the material, that they can protect the material better than formal institutions could.

Collectors are often afraid to cooperate with scholars for fear that their collections will be seized, or that they will be prosecuted, even when there is no legal basis for seizure or prosecution. As a result, many important pieces are never brought to the attention of researchers. The result of the conflict of values, and the lack of understanding of each other's position, is a high level of hostility between collectors and scholars that constantly interferes with research. Any working archaeologist can provide examples of such conflict. One of mine comes from the gold country of California.

In the course of my work I was informed of some Chinese coins unearthed by metal-detector enthusiasts. The coins had a low market value, less than ten dollars for the lot, but the information they could provide was crucial to my research. A schoolteacher and a shopkeeper had uncovered the coins near an abandoned temporary mining camp. They had offered the material to a local museum but had been turned away with a severe lecture about the destruction their looting might have done to a site. When I met them they had the coins, and excellent provenience information. But how was I to deal with them? The information they had was valuable to my research, but they had, in fact, recovered the coins by disturbing a site. The only way I could use the information was to work with the collectors, that is, to engage in what Elia, among others, would characterize as unprofessional behavior, activities that might contribute to the destruction of other archaeological sites (1993, 17).

I examined the coins and made a full record of their characteristics, gave a copy of the inventory to the coins' owners, and stressed to them, with perfect honesty, just how low the market value of the coins were. (A scholar's refusal to suggest a market value for an artifact, even an utterly valueless one, is often taken as confirmation that it is rare and valuable.) In this case, declining to examine or identify the coins would likely have led to more site destruction, as notions that the coins were valuable could have led to attempts to recover more. This approach clearly does not apply to Cycladic vases and other material with high market values. The situation does, however point out a basic paradox faced by anyone trying to reconstruct the past from material culture remains. We have to decide what strategies will result in the least overall loss of data. We have to balance the potential loss of data from looting that might be the result of cooperation with looters, dealers, or collectors against the loss of data that will result from refusing to examine materials that are currently in their hands.

The basic problem is this: removing an object from its original context without proper documentation destroys much of the evidence that gives the object meaning to us. The problem with unprovenienced material is that we lose information needed to interpret the past. We try to prevent this loss of information by refusing to cooperate with anyone involved with the material, in hopes that strong disapproval will stem the tide of looting. The paradox is that this lack of cooperation simultaneously prevents investigators from retrieving other information, information that is not dependent on provenience or contextual associations. In order to prevent loss of information, we must lose information.

The loss of information due to the looting of sites is a very visible problem. The loss of data because the material in private collections is not recorded or analyzed by people involved in academic research is not so visible, or even understood. It is important to recognize the scientific value, not to mention the sheer mass, of the materials in private collections and come to terms with the fact that if we are to get the data we must develop some methods of working with the people who "own" it.

I have had a great deal of success dealing with avocational collecting societies. They have led me to much of my data. I have also learned that agents, dealers, and brokers, although not subject to the rigorous standards of academic research, are often sources of considerable information, and the publications of collecting clubs contain information unavailable elsewhere. Avocational collecting societies maintain both formal and informal records on many types of material culture and are often able to direct researchers to sources. Material considered too "common" or redundant to merit space in the limited facilities of public institutions (a status that can change rapidly) can be traced through clubs. The full spectrum of an artifact type might not be apparent without looking at the not-so-precious, imperfect, or even incomplete specimens held by collectors of moderate means.

By understanding the formation processes of private collections we can gain physical access to materials that might otherwise be difficult to obtain, materials that have already been unearthed, legally or illegally, and are in circulation among collectors. We can improve our understanding of the significance of any piece of collected material culture if we understand the processes that brought it to a particular place at a particular time.

If scholars can develop ways of collecting the data that can be extracted through observation until issues of ownership are resolved, we might at least be able to salvage some of our heritage. How can we rescue information until questions of ownership, and the ethics of dealing with collectors, are resolved? Salvage archaeology has been accepted for several decades as a necessary evil. No one likes to excavate a site simply because the property owner has decided to install a strip mall. But salvage archaeology has proved somewhat effective in rescuing important data that might otherwise be lost. A similar type of salvage operation, perhaps one supported with legal sanctions, might help scholars rescue information from material in private collections.

The notion that an individual, institution, organization, or museum must have physical possession of an object in order to study, protect, and appreciate it is becoming an anachronism. Nonintrusive yet highly accurate methods of recording the physical characteristics of material culture are increasing rapidly. Although images and information can never substitute for the real object, many of the stated goals of museums, academic institutions, and private collectors—to preserve, protect, and present to the public their collections—can be accomplished without actual physical possession. Systematic salvage surveys that present no threat to ownership claims may prove acceptable to many private collectors. Being able to include recovered data as part of a unified, systematic collection of information might make working with owners of dubious ethics tolerable to those who, understandably, would normally refuse to do so. Like salvage archaeology, salvage data recovery should be considered a necessary evil. The potential usefulness of private collections is too great to relegate to oblivion because of unresolved questions about the nature and ethics of ownership.

NOTES

1. This is not to say that museum collections aren't also subject to the idiosyncratic whims of curators. For example Chester Dale, president of the National Gallery of Art from 1955 to 1962, was reported to have a "prejudice against small paintings . . . always implying that their small size made them unacceptable and not of museum quality" (Mellon 1992, 271).

2. Either a classic Marxist definition of a commodity as something that has a use value or exchange value (Marx 1906, 2) or Appadurai's more anthropological definition of commodity as "anything intended for exchange" (1986, 9) applies to this discussion.

3. This movement through space and time is what Kopytoff calls the "cultural biography of things" (1986, 65).

4. As Marshall Sahlins pointed out, "There is no such thing as immaculate perception" (1985, 147).

5. These mats are never slept on but are stored away from public view except during specific ceremonial occasions.

6. When the sale of his stamp collection was suggested to a financially

stressed, laid-off steelworker, his response was, "But what will I do with my time if I can't work with my stamps? They keep me from getting depressed and going crazy."

7. The "active" part of a collection is unlikely to be found in an archaeological context except in the case of fire, flood, earthquake, or similar catastrophe. In those situations the material would probably be found in context with other valuable items. Duplicate or damaged items are more prone to accidental discard.

8. His study has, in turn, followed the work of Dwight Heath (1973) and Joseph Alsop (1983).

REFERENCES

Akin, Marjorie. 1992. "Asian Coins in the North American West: A Behavioral Systems Approach to Numismatic Analysis." Ph.D. diss., Department of Anthropology, University of California, Riverside.

Album, Stephen. 1993. *A Checklist of Popular Islamic Coins.* Santa Rosa, Calif.: Stephen Album.

Appadurai, Arjun. 1986. *The Social Life of Things: Commodities in Cultural Perspective.* Cambridge: Cambridge University Press.

Barrett, Clifton Waller. 1976. Introduction to *Autographs and Manuscripts: A Collector's Manual,* edited by Edmund Berkeley. New York: Charles Scribner's Sons.

Boone, Elizabeth Hill, ed. 1993. Introduction to *Collecting the Pre-Columbian Past.* Washington, D.C.: Dumbarton Oaks Research Library and Collection.

Bourdieu, Pierre. 1993. *The Field of Cultural Production: Essays on Art and Literature.* Edited by Randal Johnson. United Kingdom: Columbia University Press.

Brook, G. L. 1980. *Books and Book-Collecting.* London: Andre Deutsch.

Casey, P. J. 1986. *Understanding Ancient Coins.* Norman: University of Oklahoma Press.

Clifford, James. 1991. "Four Northwest Coast Museums." In *Exhibiting Cultures: The Poetics and Politics of Museum Display,* edited by Ivan Karp and Steven Lavine. Washington, D.C.: Smithsonian Institution Press.

Coe, Michael D. 1993. "From Huaquero to Connoisseur: The Early Market in Pre-Columbian Art." In *Collecting the Pre-Columbian Past.* Washington, D.C.: Dumbarton Oaks Research Library and Collection.

Drucker, Philip. 1955. "The Cerro de las Mesas Offering of Jade and Other Materials." *Smithsonian Institution, Bureau of American Ethnography Anthropological Papers,* no. 44. *Bulletin* 159:25–68.

Elia, Ricardo. 1993. "Ricardo Elia Responds." *Archaeology* 46 (3): 17.

Hinsley, Curtis M. 1993. "In Search of the New World Classical." In *Collecting the Pre-Columbian Past*. Washington, D.C.: Dumbarton Oaks Research Library and Collection.

Marx, Karl. 1906. *Capital: A Critical Analysis of Capitalist Production*. London: Swan Sonnenschein.

Mellon, Paul, and John Baskett. 1992. *Reflections in a Silver Spoon*. New York: William Morrow.

Nelson, Hary, and Robert Jurmain. 1991. *Introduction to Physical Anthropology*. 5th ed. St. Paul: West Publishing.

Price, Sally. 1989. *Primitive Art in Civilized Places*. Chicago: University of Chicago Press.

Reis, Bob. 1993. "Danger Ever Lurking on the Edge of Hungary." *World Coin News* 20 (15): 14–20.

Renfrew, Colin. 1993. "Collectors Are the Real Looters." *Archaeology* 46 (3): 16–17.

Schiffer, Michael B. 1987. *Formation Processes of the Archaeological Record*. Albuquerque: University of New Mexico Press.

Thomas, David Hurst. 1990. "Who Owns the Past?" *Natural History* 8 (1990): 24–27.

Unden, Grant. 1982. *Understanding Book Collecting*. Woodbridge, England: Antique Collector's Club.

van Gulick, Robert. 1981. *Chinese Pictorial Arts as Viewed by the Connoisseur*. New York: Hacker Art Books.

Zeitlin, Judith. 1991. "The Petrified Heart: Obsession in Chinese Literature, Art, and Medicine." *Late Imperial China* 12 (1): 1–26.

10

Formation Processes of Ethnographic Collections

Examples from the Great Basin of Western North America

CATHERINE S. FOWLER AND DON D. FOWLER

The American Association of Museums (1992, 91, 94, and Tables D:27-A, 28-A) estimates there are about 78 million objects in U.S. museums; roughly 10 million of those are "ethnographic."[1] There are perhaps an equal number of ethnographic objects in museums elsewhere in the world. We can but marvel at so many millions of things formed into collections by various processes. As several commentators have noted, it is a wonder that "native peoples" have any of their own traditional objects left! Indeed, many have very few (Hardin 1983; Parezo 1986, 1987).

Our present concern is with collections in U.S. museums. By *ethnographic collections,* we mean collections made from living peoples defined by museum curators as "native," "tribal," or "folk." For illustrative purposes, we focus on Native American Great Basin collections. We consider not only collection formation processes but also "taphonomic" processes, which act on collections once they are assembled. Further, we are concerned with the formation processes of systematic collections, that is, collections made for museums within a framework of achieving a "complete" or "fully representative sample" of the material culture of an ethnographic group (Ford 1977). More randomly assembled collections of objects, seen as "curios," or objects of "primitive or tribal art" have their own formation processes. Objects formed by both processes wind up in museum collections. Once there, they are subject to the same processes discussed below. But their further uses are quite different.

The formation of many systematic ethnographic collections took place from about 1870 to 1940, during the so-called Age of Museums (Barber 1980; Holmes 1903; Holmes and Mason 1902). Twenty-three museums with anthropology components were established between 1875 and 1905 in western and central Europe, seventeen in the United States and Canada, and at least a dozen elsewhere. Nearly all of them set out to collect as much as they could (Feest 1992) from as many cultures as possible. The operative framework was inductive: to know (i.e., make generalizations about) humanity, we must know as much as possible about the range and variety of humans, physically, linguistically, and culturally. Objects were, literally, begged for, bartered for, bargained for, bought, and now and then stolen. Nineteenth-century collectors were sometimes in the employ of museums but more often were professional collectors who made their living by acquiring objects from native peoples and selling them, by the piece or the barrel, to museums (Cole 1985). Modes of acquisition changed over time. Between 1879 and 1883, the Smithsonian's James Stevenson bartered Euro-American trade goods to the Zuni, Hopi, and others in the American Southwest for railroad box-cars full of traditional ethnographic items (Hardin 1983; Parezo 1985, 1986; Hinsley 1992). In the twentieth century, Indian people had sufficient amounts of Euro-American goods, hence Isabel Kelly and Willard Park purchased items from their sources with dollars provided by museums.

The same period (1870–1940) was also the heyday of world's fairs (Rydell 1984, 1993). Museum curators played major roles in presenting exhibits at world's fairs (Fowler and Fowler 1991). Indeed, fairs often provided the funds for the formation of many major ethnographic, natural history, and art collections, as well as for the creation of several major museums to house them, including the United States National Museum, the Field Museum, the San Diego Museum of Man, and art museums in Cincinnati and St. Louis, among others.

Nineteenth-century collectors were guided by the concepts of the Vanishing Savage and the Ethnographic Present. From at least 1634 in Anglo America, it was expected that native peoples would "vanish," either physically or socially, an expectation that intensified after 1800 (D. Fowler 1990). From a museum perspective, the problem was to collect traditional culture items before it was too late. The concept of the ethnographic present held that collections should be made from a tribe, band, or village, preferably on a timeless "day before" they were subjected to acculturative forces. This day before was the ethnographic present (Feest 1992, 8), in the New World, myopically defined in terms of Anglo- or Franco-American contact. The influence of the Spanish, or of other native groups, somehow did not count. Conceptions of when the ethnographic present ended influenced *how* collectors defined "traditional" objects—and therefore *what* they collected. For example, in the American Southwest, objects made before 1821, or in a traditional style thought to be prevalent before 1821, became collectibles; those made later often did not. The same was true in other areas as well (Berlo 1992, Cole 1985).

FORMATION PROCESSES

Knowledge of formation processes is of vital importance for assessing the representativeness of any collection and therefore its value in answering questions of anthropological significance. But what constitutes a collection? For purposes of maintenance, exhibit, and research, museum professionals distinguish between "collections" per se and "systematic research collections." Here, we focus on the latter.

In defining formation processes of ethnographic collections, we agree with Parezo (1987) that there are two major stages at which processes need to be considered: (1) when a collection is assembled in the field, and (2) after a collection comes under the care of a museum. At each juncture, a series of questions needs to be asked about the activities taking place, and the answer to these questions (satisfactory or unsatisfactory) will ultimately determine the representativeness and value of a collection. The answers usually depend on the quality and quantity of the documentation that accompanies a collection. With good documentation, excellent and worthwhile statements can be made about the nature and full anthropological implications of a collection. Without documentation, ethnographic objects, like archaeological artifacts, become only things, useful perhaps for contemplation as "art objects," but of no value for scientific study (Fowler 1986, 26; Fowler and Givens 1992, 43–52). Wittgenstein's epistemological distinction between "seen" and "seen as" is central here (Aronson 1984). Some students of material culture attempt to "read" objects as "texts." An item from Euro-American culture is *seen to be* a metallic object. It also may be seen as a small silver spoon. It (perhaps) may be "read," that is, *further seen as* a social-status marker, as either a special gift to an infant (with implications about the social standing of the infant's parents) or a fancy piece of tableware suitable for stirring liquids in demitasse cups (again with status implications). Both readings are possible because the reader "knows" her or his own culture and hence can "document" the object from cultural knowledge. A metallic object from another culture may be seen as a "small silver spoon," but without documentation we cannot know anything of the ritual or social significance of the object, except to suspect that it probably is very different from its significance in Euro-American culture. It can only be read as a silver spoon: a cryptic, and not overly enlightening, "text." Because ethnographic objects derive, by definitions, from other cultures, reading them, sans documentation, is an exercise in imagination, not in analysis.

Formation Processes in the Field

The representativeness of any ethnographic collection is dependent on the perceived universe of what is manufactured by a group, by what is retained, and by factors that influence collectors' sampling procedures. Parezo (1987, 3) tells us that "a museum collection is never a random sample: it is always biased . . . the [final] problem is to determine what sort of explicit or unacknowledged sampling procedure was used in [forming the] . . . collection." She suggests, in agreement with Sturtevant (1967), that this is best approached by doing a thorough collection history, hopefully through the documentation provided. Matters to be determined and assessed are: (1) the purpose of a collecting trip, (2) the status of the trip, (3) the theoretical orientation of the collector, (4) the collector's view of the native culture and its future, (5) practical considerations, (6) historical considerations, (7) methods of collecting, (8) native views of collectors and their activities, (9) the field records on objects collected, and (10) the basic perspective on why the collection is made. As these factors have been scrutinized, the data on formation processes have become clearer, and the interpretations of the collections richer.

Formation Processes in Museums

There are processes that affect collections once they enter a museum. We refer to these processes as *taphonomic*, borrowing a useful term from paleontology. Taphonomy is the study of post mortem relationships between organic remains and their contextual environments (Efremov 1940; Gifford 1981). Here we expand the term to mean the postfield relationships between a collection and its museum environment. Various processes and procedures operate on collections in the museum setting, changing their value and representativeness: cataloguing procedures, records maintenance, storage, movement, exhibition history, conservation history, deaccessioning (including trading, condemnation, or outright loss), facilities, overall management (Ford 1977), breakage, theft, and insect damage. All these processes and procedures affect collection taphonomy, that is, whether a collection remains in a steady state, declines, or is enhanced.

The passage of the Native American Graves Protection and Repatriation Act (Public Law 101-601; 25 U.S. Code 3001) by Congress in 1990 has, and will continue to have, a major impact on formation processes of museum collections relating to Native Americans. The law mandates that human skeletal materials and related objects derived from archaeological contexts, as well as ethnographic objects deemed of major cultural significance, be returned to tribes that can demonstrate a claim to them (Morell 1994). By mid-1995 (when this chapter was put in final form), a required process of identifying relevant materials and notifying appropriate tribes was underway by all museums and other agencies holding relevant collections. There is little doubt that many museum collections will be depleted to some degree. However, the law, and the regulations being written to implement it, are very specific (Hutt and McKeown 1994) and do not require willy-nilly wholesale return of artifacts and collections, as some museum curators fear. Meeting the legal requirements will be difficult for both Native Americans and museums, and the full outcome will not be known for a number of years. There undoubtedly will be court cases to clarify a number of points in the law and the regulations—thus adding a new dimension to collections formation processes.

GREAT BASIN COLLECTIONS

We turn now to a review of formation processes of specific ethnographic collections. The collections of John Wesley Powell, made between 1867 and 1880, and Stephen Powers, made in 1875, represent the start of the era of collecting for big museums and world's fairs. Collections made by Robert H. Lowie and Samuel Barrett between 1906 and 1915 and collections made by Isabel T. Kelly and Willard Z. Park in the 1930s were each subject to somewhat different formation and taphonomic processes.

The Powell Collection

John Wesley Powell gathered an extensive ethnographic collection between 1867 and 1880 from Numic-speaking groups in the Great Basin culture area (Fowler and Fowler 1971). The collection was made for and deposited in the Smithsonian Institution. The bulk of the collection was formed in 1872 and 1873. During those years, Powell was accompanied by Jack Hillers, who worked for many years as Powell's photographer (Fowler 1989). Those portions of the collection that remain in the Smithsonian have been studied and described in some detail (Fowler and Matley 1979).

Several aspects of Powell's field collecting require comment. First, we know very little about the actual collecting procedures Powell used, or about his methods of field documentation. He seemingly traded for many of the items he received (Dellenbaugh 1962, 253), but with what is not known. Second, specific field documentation for the collections— if it ever existed—is no longer extant. Catalogues of the collection (Powell 1873, 1878), seemingly incomplete, appear to have been made well after the collection reached the Smithsonian, if not later, when the collection was transferred to the United States National Museum. These catalogues usually list the tribal or band provenience of an item and give a brief description; in some instances the native name for the object is also given, but little else. Some additional detail is provided in Powell's ethnographic fieldnotes (Fowler and Fowler 1971) and in Hillers's photographs, but even with those, a number of objects cannot be adequately interpreted. Third, there is considerable confusion in the catalogues (Powell 1873, 1878), owing to the taphonomic processes acting on the collection once it reached Washington.

Powell attempted to make a "complete" collection. However, the catalogue records indicate a total absence of items related to religion, medicinal curing, or women's events. Raw materials and items reflecting Euro-American contact are also missing. Hillers's numerous photographs document the use of Euro-American material culture objects and clothing by Native Americans, but these items were not collected, not being "traditional." A major problem with the collection is authentication and provenience for some items. Powell brought northwestern Colorado Ute clothing to southern Utah in 1872–73 to dress up the Southern Paiute to "look more like Indians" for Hillers's photographs (Fowler 1989, 45–54). One beaded dress, no longer in the collection, worn by a Kaibab Paiute woman in two 1873 Hillers photographs, has "Colorado 10800" written on the bodice (Fowler and Matley 1979, Figs. 17–18). The Kaibab Paiutes also made "traditional" clothing to order under the watchful eye of Powell's sister, Ellen Thompson, including Plains Indian style headdresses, not a part of their traditional clothing.

It is a truism of museum life that there are funds for collecting, but not for accessioning, storage, and care. The Powell Collection, probably numbering in excess of two thousand items, was transferred to the United States National Museum in about 1878. On July 1, 1884, his first day on the job, Otis T. Mason wrote in his diary, and later to James Pilling, Powell's chief clerk: "Took charge of the Department of Ethnology in the National Museum. . . . The specimens could hardly be in worse confusion. . . . I find Major Powell's specimens in the worst condition. . . . Between breakage and the moths, things are fallen on evil times" (Mason 1884a, 1).

Mason was unable to give the collection much care, inundated as he was by the tons of materials being collected from the Southwest by James Stevenson and others under Powell's direction (Hinsley 1992; Parezo 1985, 1986). The first catalogue of the Powell Collection lists some 1,560 items, a probable loss of one-quarter of the original (Judd 1915). By 1967, only 466 items remained in the Smithsonian. Some portion of the missing items fell to Mason's moths, breakage, and "evil times," some items studied and illustrated seem never to have made it back to storage (Fowler and Matley 1979, Tables 1–2). Other items seem to have disappeared through world's fairs and other exhibits; the remainder is presumed to have been traded to other museums as "duplicates." Indeed, Powell Collection items are in the University of Pennsylvania Museum, the Harvard Peabody Museum, several European museums, and as far away as the National Museum in Auckland, New Zealand.

Despite its taphonomic trials, the Powell Collection, made at a time of rapid cultural change, is still a valuable resource for the study of Great Basin peoples, especially when combined with Powell's ethnographic accounts and Hillers's photographs (Fowler and Fowler 1981).

The Powers Collection

Stephen Powers (1877; Fowler and Fowler 1970; Park 1975) was assigned by the Smithsonian Institution to collect ethnographic objects from California and western Nevada for the Philadelphia Centennial Exhibition of 1876. He collected 121 items from the Northern Paiute of Pyramid Lake. The documentation is minimal but has some native names and brief, but informative, descriptions. Powers also made some ethnographic notes, written more from the perspective of their precontact culture, but with many interesting observations on their postreservation condition. He apparently had a collecting guide, which O. T. Mason (1875) developed for the Philadelphia centennial, but it is difficult to determine whether he followed it. The Powers Collection is hardly of the "complete" type called for by Mason's instructions. He did obtain several of the "models" called for, including a tule house and a tule boat. Catalogue cards indicate that he was able to obtain some religious items, but these have disappeared.

The history of the Powers Collection once it arrived at the Smithsonian is as bleak as that of the Powell Collection. Of the items catalogued, by the early 1980s, only twenty-four had survived. Some items were traded, some condemned; there are no records as to the fate of the others. Unfortunately, most of what is gone includes extremely important fishing gear, a duck decoy, religious items, and all of a seed and medicinal plant collection—the first made in the region and thus of exceeding interest. Powers recorded native names for many ethnobotanical specimens. Using these names, reasoned guesses can be made as to the identification of the specimens, based on past (Colville 1895) and present day (C. Fowler 1990, 1993) ethnobotanical work.

The Lowie and Barrett Collections

Robert H. Lowie, of the American Museum of Natural History, and Samuel Barrett, of the Milwaukee Public Museum, gathered collections between 1906 and 1916. Both subsequently wrote ethnographic monographs on the Great Basin groups they visited, using collected specimens for illustrations (Lowie 1909, 1924; Barrett 1917). Lowie wrote that it was by 1909 impossible "[to obtain] much in the way of showy specimens. . . . [But] worth-while material could still be collected, especially good models where originals are no longer available" (Lowie 1924, 191). He obtained sixty-six specimens from the Northern Paiute and eighty-three specimens among the Southern Paiute people. The collections have survived reasonably well. The objects apparently have never been on exhibit, nor removed from storage for any other purpose. Some damage occurred through "benign neglect," but roughly 95 percent remains. The Lowie and Barrett Collections take on added significance for Great Basin studies because so much of Powell's and Powers's collections has been lost.

Barrett's collection is much larger than Lowie's, because he was collecting for a new museum and wanted to exhibit materials and build the general collection. He collected some 710 specimens among the Northern and Southern Paiute, and 84 among the Washoe. He seemingly went beyond the standard categories in collecting. For example, he collected weasel skins, used by midwives in the birthing process (to stroke the abdomen of the parturient), as well as slow matches and other unusual items. He also did not shy away from items reflecting contact and acculturation, for example, fishing spears and other objects with metal parts.

The Barrett Collection has fared well. A number of items are presently (1995) on exhibit, and seemingly have been on exhibit in the past. No items were traded. But because the catalogue makes no differentiation between Northern and Southern Paiute (which are distinct groups, not "branches" of the same group), it is of reduced primary research value. The collection is important, however, particularly to those with sufficient knowledge of Great Basin material culture to properly use it.

Isabel T. Kelly and Willard Z. Park

Isabel Kelly and Willard Park were commissioned by museums in the 1930s to make "representative collections" incidental to their ethnographic fieldwork. Both spent considerable time in the field, conducting extensive interviews on all aspects of "traditional" native cultures: work characterized by Kelly as "unabashedly of the how-was-it-in-your-grandfather's-day approach." By the time Kelly and Park were in the field, the museums for which they collected had partly changed their focus. Clark Wissler of the American Museum of Natural History told Kelly: "We are interested in . . . objects illustrating the present styles of decorative art, even though the objects may take on 'tourist characteristics'" (Wissler to Kelly, July 30, 1932, American Museum of Natural History, Anthropology Accession Records). Kelly actually collected much of ethnographic interest, including items used during childbirth and for menstrual isolation, but he collected almost no items related to religion. By contrast, Park's collection, although similar in general respects, contains items reflecting religion, as he became interested in shamanism, the ultimate topic of his doctoral dissertation (Park 1938; C. Fowler 1989). Both Kelly and Park relied heavily on models, because apart from some heirlooms and some basketry pieces that were still being made for use or sale, they found little traditional material left to collect. Interestingly, neither Kelly nor Park collected much in the way of beadwork, or beaded buckskin items, which certainly were available in the area in the 1930s, for the tourist trade as well as for personal use. Both still sought the ethnographic present, if not explicitly, at least by overall orientation (Kelly 1964; Kelly and Fowler 1986).

Kelly collected about 350 specimens, including for the first time in the Great Basin, items with the names of makers. The collection was divided between the American Museum of Natural History in New York City and the Laboratory of Anthropology in Santa Fe. Park collected about 190 specimens among the Northern Paiute and divided his collection between the American Museum and the Peabody Museum at Harvard, but specimens at both institutions have suffered the taphonomic degradation provided by insects. The Kelly and Park Collections were formed in a later era of collecting and influenced by changes in what was available to collect as well as some changes in collection orientation.

In sum, the six largest Great Basin ethnographic collections, made between 1871 and 1940, were formed through different collection processes. They subsequently suffered greater or lesser taphonomic indignities, but taken together tell us most of what we will ever know about "traditional" Great Basin material culture (Fowler and Fowler 1981).

New Museums: Tribal and Otherwise

Finally, we come to the present situation, and some suggestions as to future collection formation processes in the Great Basin. Although it is doubtful that many new publicly funded anthropology museums will be formed in the region in the near future, several Great Basin tribes are interested in developing museums and cultural centers. What are their prospects for collections? And what types of processes might be used?

Some tribal museums and cultural centers, such as the Paiute-Shoshone Museum in Bishop, California, have worked out arrangements with older and larger public museums for the loan of specimens, especially those representing older cultural traditions. Some have also acquired, through donation or loan, family heirlooms held by tribal members. Some hope to acquire objects from older museums through the provisions of the Native American Graves Protection and Repatriation Act of 1990. Some intend to commission new pieces, including models or copies of older specimens, but also other works representing more contemporary themes. Purchase of older, expensive items is as much out of reach for tribal as for other museums. Cultural preservation programs are also fostering a new awareness of cultural materials and new research interests on the part of tribes. This will undoubtedly have implications for collection formation processes—including some new views of what is important and what is representative. Thus, perhaps the processes of collection formation have changed, and will change less in the future, than orientation.

Great Basin tribes, as well as other tribes planning new museums, also have set out to collect and exhibit contemporary culture items. They will thereby define a new ethnographic present, one that emphasizes that native peoples are still here and still actively participating in various types of cultural activities. Perhaps this is born of necessity (the few older items available are expensive), but not wholly so. All of the extant or planned tribal museums also focus on performance—song, dance, hand games, and so forth—as these practices have been retained and are important markers of ethnic identity.

Thus, a turn toward a new orientation, one more in line with modern culture, is what is occurring now, and will carry forward into the future (McCormack 1992). Some older museums are following suit and formulating new collecting policies aimed at acquiring modern material culture reflecting contemporary times. In short, although it is regrettable that the Washoe tribe of Nevada and California may never have a Datsolalee basket (originals command tens of thousands of dollars on the art market), it may have some things that are more important to the cultural identity of its members: items overlooked by previous generations of museum collectors who focused too narrowly on antiquated and, at least in part, erroneous definitions of who Native Americans were and are and on how they should be represented. This can only be a healthy trend.

SUMMARY

There are several implications that can be drawn from the study of formation processes of ethnographic, or for that matter, any type of museum collection. The first has to do with documentation. As we have noted, ethnographic collections, sans documentation, have no knowledge value. They may be seen as "art" objects within the perceiver's own cultural tradition, and, indeed, untold numbers of unprovenienced ethnographic objects, seen as what used to be called "primitive art," have been collected. The second implication is that concepts of what is "traditional" and what is "representative" were conflated, which skewed the contents of collections. Collectors often defined traditional in terms of an ethnographic present, an imagined period and state of affairs in which European or Euro-American influence was not present. Hence, objects outside the ethnographic present were not collected, even though they were in use by the native peoples at the time the collections were made. This bias has been corrected, or should have been corrected, in most collections made since the 1950s (Sturtevant 1967). Finally, the wear and tear on collections once they are in museums, the taphonomic processes, as we call them, are major factors in the continued existence of ethnographic, and all other material culture, collections.

ACKNOWLEDGMENTS

Studies of Great Basin collections on which this paper is based have been supported over the years by grants to Catherine Fowler from the National Endowment for the Humanities, the National Science Foundation, and the University of Nevada–Reno Research Advisory Board, and by a Smithsonian Institution/National Research Council Post-doctoral Research Associateship to Don Fowler. We extend our thanks to the curators, archivists, and administrators of many institutions for aid and assistance, including the Harvard University Peabody Museum of American Archaeology and Ethnology; the American Museum of Natural History; the Museum of the American Indian and the Museum of Natural History, both of the Smithsonian Institution; the Chicago Field Museum of Natural History; the Milwaukee Public Museum; the Laboratory of Anthropology of the Museum of New Mexico; the School of American Research; the Heard Museum; the Idaho State Natural History Museum; the University of Utah Museum of Natural History; the Nevada State Museum; the Southwest Museum; the Los Angeles County Museum of Natural History; and the Phoebe Apperson Hearst Museum of Anthropology of the University of California at Berkeley.

NOTE

1. The AAM report lists about 7,600,000+ objects as "ethnological" or "ethnographic" and 2,400,000+ as "folk culture." For present purposes, we take both to be "ethnographic."

REFERENCES

American Association of Museums. 1992. *Data Report from the 1989 National Museum Survey*. Washington, D.C.: American Association of Museums.

Aronson, J. L. 1984. *A Realist Philosophy of Science*. New York: St. Martin's Press.

Barber, Lynn. 1980. *The Heyday of Natural History, 1820–1870*. Garden City, N.Y.: Doubleday.

Barrett, Samuel A. 1917. "The Washoe Indians." *Bulletin of the Public Museum of the City of Milwaukee* 2 (1): 1–52. Milwaukee.

Berlo, Janet C. 1992. *The Early Years of Native American Art History: The Politics of Scholarship and Collecting*. Seattle: University of Washington Press.

Cole, Douglas. 1985. *Captured Heritage: The Scramble for Northwest Coast Artifacts*. Seattle: University of Washington Press.

Coville, Frederick V. 1895. "Directions for Collecting Specimens and Information Illustrating the Aboriginal Uses of Plants." *Bulletin of the United States National Museum,* no. 39, pt. J. Washington, D.C.

Dellenbaugh, Frederick. 1962. *A Canyon Voyage: The Narrative of the Second Powell Expedition Down the Green–Colorado River from Wyoming, and the Explorations on Land in the Years 1871 and 1872*. 1908. Reprint, New Haven, Conn.: Yale University Press.

Efremov, J. A. 1940. "Taphonomy: New Branch of Paleontology." *Pan-American Geologist* 74:81–93.

Feest, Christian F. 1992. "American Indians and Ethnographic Collecting in Europe." *Museum Anthropology* 16:7–11. Washington, D.C.

Ford, R. I. 1977. *Systematic Research Collections in Anthropology: An Irreplaceable National Resource*. Peabody Museum, Harvard University for the Council for Museum Anthropology, Cambridge.

Fowler, Catherine S. 1990. "Tule Technology: Northern Paiute Uses of Marsh Resources in Western Nevada." *Smithsonian Folklife Studies,* no. 6. Washington, D.C.

———. 1993. *In the Shadow of Fox Peak: Ethnography of the Northern Paiute People of Stillwater Marsh*. Portland: U.S. Fish and Wildlife Service.

————, ed. 1989. "Willard Z. Park's Ethnographic Notes on the Northern Paiute of Western Nevada, 1933–1940." *University of Utah Anthropological Papers,* no. 114. Salt Lake City.

Fowler, D. D., and D. R. Givens. 1992. "Preserving the Archaeological Record." In *Preserving Anthropological Records,* edited by N. J. Parezo and S. Silverman, 14–28. New York: Wenner-Gren Foundation for Anthropological Research.

Fowler, Don D. 1986. "Conserving American Archaeological Resources." In *American Archaeology Past and Future,* edited by D. J. Meltzer, D. D. Fowler, and J. Sabloff, 25–44. Washington, D.C.: Smithsonian Institution Press.

————. 1989. *The Western Photographs of John K. Hillers: "Myself in the Water."* Washington, D.C.: Smithsonian Institution Press.

————. 1990. "Images of American Indians, 1492–1892." *Halcyon 1990. A Journal of the Humanities* 11:75–100. Reno.

Fowler, Don D., and Catherine S. Fowler. 1981. "Museum Collections and Ethnographic Reconstruction: Examples from the Great Basin." *Annals of the New York Academy of Sciences* 376:177–200.

————. 1991. "The Uses of Natural Man in Natural History." In *Columbian Consequences,* vol. 3, *The Spanish Borderlands in Pan-American Perspective,* edited by D. H. Thomas, 37–71. Washington, D.C.: Smithsonian Institution Press.

————, eds. 1970. "Stephen Powers' 'The Life and Culture of the Washo and Paiutes.'" *Ethnohistory* 17 (3–4): 117–49.

————. 1971. "Anthropology of the Numa: John Wesley Powell's Manuscripts on the Numic Peoples of Western North America, 1868–1880." *Smithsonian Contributions to Anthropology,* no. 14. Washington, D.C.

Fowler, Don D., and John F. Matley. 1979. "Material Culture of the Numa: The John Wesley Powell Collection, 1867–1880." *Smithsonian Contributions to Anthropology,* no. 26. Washington, D.C.

Gifford, Diane P. 1981. "Taphonomy and Paleoecology: A Critical Review of Archaeology's Sister Disciplines." In *Advances in Archaeological Theory and Method,* vol. 4, edited by M. B. Schiffer, 365–438. New York: Academic Press.

Hardin, Margaret. 1983. *Gifts of Mother Earth: Ceramics in the Zuni Tradition.* Phoenix: Heard Museum.

Hinsley, Curtis. 1992. "Collecting Cultures and the Cultures of Collecting: The Lure of the American Southwest, 1880–1915." *Museum Anthropology* 16 (1): 12–20.

Holmes, William H. 1903. "Classification and Arrangement of the Exhibits of an Anthropological Museum." *Journal of the Royal Anthropological Institute of Great Britain and Ireland* 32:353–72. Reprinted in *Annual Report of the U.S. National Museum, 1900–01,* 253–78. Washington, D.C.

Holmes, William H., and Otis T. Mason. 1902. "Instructions to Collectors of Historical and Anthropological Specimens." *Bulletin of the United States National Museum,* no. 39, pt. Q. Washington, D.C.

Hutt, S., and C. T. McKeown. 1994. *Native American Graves Protection and Repatriation Act: Implications and Practical Applications.* Reno: Cultural Resource Management Policy Institute, University of Nevada.

Judd, Neil. 1915. "Memorandum on the J. W. Powell Collection. 1 August, 1915." U.S. National Museum Accession Catalog. Washington, D.C.: National Museum of Natural History, Smithsonian Institution.

Kelly, Isabel T. 1964. "Southern Paiute Ethnography." *University of Utah Anthropological Papers,* no. 69. Salt Lake City.

Kelly, Isabel T., and Catherine S. Fowler. 1986. "Southern Paiute." *Handbook of North American Indians,* vol. 11, *Great Basin,* edited by Warren L. d'Azevedo, 386–97. Washington, D.C.: Smithsonian Institution.

Lowie, Robert H. 1909. "The Northern Shoshone." *American Museum of Natural History Anthropological Papers* 2:165–306. New York.

———. 1924. "Notes on Shoshonean Ethnography." *American Museum of Natural History Anthropological Papers* 20 (3): 185–314. New York.

Mason, Otis T. 1875. *Inquiries Relative to the Indian Tribes of the United States, Prepared under the Direction of the Indian Bureau.* Washington, D.C.: Government Printing Office.

———. 1884a. Unpublished diary. National Anthropological Archives, National Museum of Natural History, Smithsonian Institution, Washington, D.C.

———. 1884b. Letter to J. C. Pilling, August 27, 1884. Bureau of American Ethnology Collection. National Anthropological Archives, National Museum of Natural History, Smithsonian Institution, Washington, D.C.

McCormack, Patricia A., organizer. 1992. "Contemporary Collecting: The Production of New Collections for the Future." Symposium presented at ninety-first annual meeting, American Anthropological Association, San Francisco, December 4, 1992.

Morell, Virginia. 1994. "An Anthropological Culture Shift." *Science* 264:20–22.

Parezo, Nancy J. 1985. "Cushing as Part of the Team: The Collecting Activities of the Smithsonian Institution." *American Ethnologist* 12:763–74.

———. 1986. "Now Is the Time to Collect." *Masterkey* 59 (4): 11–18.

———. 1987. "The Formation of Ethnographic Collections: The Smithsonian Institution in the American Southwest." *Advances in Archaeological Method and Theory,* vol. 10, edited by M. B. Schiffer, 1–47. New York: Academic Press.

Park, Susan. 1975. "The Life of Stephen Powers." *Contributions of the University of California Archaeological Research Facility* 28:1–44.

Park, Willard Z. 1938. "Shamanism in Western North America: A Study in

Cultural Relationships." *Northwestern University, Studies in the Social Sciences,* no. 2. Evanston, Ill.

Powell, John W. 1873. "Catalogue of Indian Collections Deposited in the Smithsonian Institution." Manuscript in Smithsonian Institution Archives, Washington, D.C.

———. 1878. "Catalogue of Works of Indian Art Collected During the Survey of the Colorado River of the West." Manuscript in Smithsonian Institution Archives, Washington, D.C.

Powers, Stephen. 1877. "Centennial Mission to the Indians of Western Nevada and California." *Annual Report of the Board of Regents of the Smithsonian Institution for 1876,* pp. 449–60. Washington, D.C.

Rydell, Robert W., II. 1984. *All the World's a Fair: America's International Expositions, 1876–1916.* Chicago: University of Chicago Press.

———. 1993. *World of Fairs: The Century of Progress Expositions.* Chicago: University of Chicago Press.

Sturtevant, William C. 1967. "Guide to Field Collecting of Ethnographic Specimens." *Smithsonian Institution, Museum of Natural History Information Leaflet 503.* Washington, D.C.

II

The Formation of Anthropological Archival Records

NANCY J. PAREZO

In 1992 I worked in the Mennonite Archives at Bethel College gathering material for an analysis of Henry Voth's collecting activities among the Hopi at Oraibi, Arizona. The physical results of Voth's endeavors, that is, ethnographic and archaeological collections, I had already examined in many museums: the Smithsonian Institution, the Field Museum of Natural History, the Carnegie Institute, the American Museum of Natural History, and the Heard Museum. Although the "official" home for Voth's papers was the Mennonite Archives, letters, reports, publications, some fieldnotes and ethnographic observations reside at these institutions and others I have not yet visited.

While reviewing Voth's correspondence, I talked extensively with the archivist, who had started an important and timely project: to gain intellectual control of the magnificent and irreplaceable photographs Voth took of the Hopi, Arapaho, and Cheyenne. He lamented the unfortunate necessity for this undertaking; no one knew where the photographs were, how they had come to be housed in scattered institutions, how many had been donated to repositories, and even whether photographs taken by Voth were properly attributed to him. This experienced archivist found it incomprehensible that Voth's photographs were at institutions other than Bethel College because it is the "official" Voth repository. He wanted the world to be controlled and logical so that he could satisfactorily do his job.[1] And he was right; all researchers have experienced the frustration of looking for records and finding that they are in a repository one would never have associated with their creator. It would be ideal if the records one needed for an anthropological research project were in "the right place," especially if it was convenient and exceedingly well organized. It makes perfect sense; Voth's photographs *should be* at Bethel, but they are not.

When one thinks about this situation from the standpoint of what happens to documentary records from the time they are produced until they are either archived or destroyed, however, the scattered placement of Voth's photographs is understandable. No scholar's papers, that is, documents produced over the course of a career, are gathered together before they are permanently preserved. Think about the activities anthropologists currently engage in that disperse documents. They send letters to friends without making copies, write reviews of books and National Science Foundation (NSF) proposals, consult, advance from job to job. They change research projects and move to new research locales, creating and leaving documents along the way; they work by themselves and with others in an ever-evolving constellation of colleagues. They send raw and processed data to each other; sometimes they pass these data down to students without keeping copies. They discard information "no longer needed," including that never published. Papers get lost in the mail, computers crash, janitors "accidentally" throw away analyses sitting on the floor, camera bags and briefcases are stolen.

Documents succumb to life; sometimes this is acceptable, but more often it is unfortunate and subsequent knowledge suffers. The type of record most susceptible to attrition is correspondence. Scholars place a great deal of unique and irreplaceable primary data, as well as information useful for understanding the intellectual development of the discipline, the underlying rationale for projects, and research agendas, in letters. As Sydel Silverman (1992, 1) has noted:

> In anthropology perhaps more than in other disciplines, the "raw data" of research and the records of personal lives and social relationships are interlinked. Everything we have learned about the anthropological enterprise argues for seeing the professional and the personal as in mutual interaction (mutually "constructed," we would now say) and for understanding them as a piece.

Voth's correspondence is full of information on Hopi culture, political factionalism, and interactions between Hopis and government officials, his own collecting activities and life at Oraibi. And it contains data on his photographs and hence provides clues on where to find the "missing" originals. Voth used photographs in exchange for goods and services. Thus, his ethnographic observations and photographs never constituted a single corpus; like other researchers, he scattered them unintentionally.[2]

Preserved anthropological data does not just happen. In order to understand the nature of our current archived database we must comprehend how historic anthropological documents have been created and how they have come to be saved. This is, of course, a tremendous undertaking, requiring an anthropology of anthropology, chronological and synchronic analyses of individuals and institutions, of how one learns to be an anthropologist, of personality types (pack rats versus ditchers, well-organized vertical filers versus chaotic horizontal dumpers), of ethics, socialization, friendship patterns, and authority networks, and an analysis of what constitutes useful disciplinary data as opposed to noise. Unfortunately, these factors vary by subfield and fieldwork situation: ethnographic, linguistic, biological, historic, and archaeological records can be very different.

Even though this array of variables and factors appears daunting when first inventoried, there are some overriding production and retention characteristics, and it is the identification of some of these that is the focus of this chapter. Three dominating characteristics can be definitively posited at the outset: (1) materials produced during the course of anthropological work are always of future research value; (2) although irreplaceable, everything produced in the course of anthropological work is not retained by the producer; and (3) archiving under professional records-management principles influences organization and subsequent access and use. These characteristics influence what is available and can be retrieved for current and future research projects.

PRODUCTION OF THE
ANTHROPOLOGICAL RECORD

The anthropological record consists of sets of materials produced by professionals who follow accepted disciplinary methods and techniques. Useful potential information also may be generated by others who record their observations about cultures and societies.[3] Basic data-carrying records created by scholars and amateurs may not be very different; most

T A B L E   I I . I . Types of Records Saved by Archivists

PERSONAL

Correspondence: Outgoing and incoming letters of a professional nature, personal letters if they contain some professional information, personal letters, telegrams, directives and instructions received, invitations to social and professional events, letters or memos fixing appointments, letter press books.
Curriculum Vitae: Old and recent resumes, certificates and awards, diplomas.
Legal Documents: Work contracts, wills, publishing contracts, inventories of estates.
Memoirs: Published and unpublished, diaries, journals, reminiscences.
Miscellaneous Materials: Card files, bibliographies, indexes, and any other materials produced and used in the course of professional activities; photocopies of articles and newspapers clippings; reminders and shorthand notes; books with marginalia; ephemera; old ballots.
Professional Activities: Minutes and proceedings in work for professional or avocational organizations; administrative records from place of employment, committee work.

RESEARCH MATERIALS

Preparatory Materials: Grant proposals, successful and unsuccessful; reviewer's comments; notes developing projects.
Legal Materials: Ledgers, financial documents, notes, human subject forms, permission forms for use and publishing photographs, work permits, transportation permits, administrative records, financial records, transportation records.

anthropologists (primarily socioculturalists) still have little training in the production of their own records. Observational and statement data are made in a variety of media, primarily paper and photographs, but also includes any of the research materials listed in Table 11.1. Thus when conceptualizing anthropological records, one must think in terms of kinds of data rather than in terms of items based on a producer's training and disciplinary affiliation.

Anthropology is a very eclectic discipline, and its records are varied. In general, anthropological records contain systematic, internally cohesive

TABLE 11.1. *continued*

RESEARCH MATERIALS

Research Records and Data: Notes; records and field/laboratory notes, scrap notes; types notes; daily logs; scratch notes; raw data in any form; transcriptions; texts; interviews; surveys; informants' comments; topical notes; life histories; lists of names and other types of information; household data; census surveys; diagrams and drawings; questionnaires; observation logs; time trials; informant notebooks and journals; maps; charts; diagrams; graphs; lists; genealogies; video tapes; audio recordings (with explanatory materials and transcriptions); photographic materials, such as slides, prints, negatives, movies, and transparencies; ancillary or special field/lab forms and analyses (i.e., isotopic analyses, pollen data).

Objects Collected in the Field: Gifts from collaborators, informants, and others, as well as supporting documentation on provenience, provenance, price, makes name, and any information on individual, use, collection method, native name, materials, and dates purchased or received, if possible; catalogues.

Cumulative Data: Including research analyses, outlines.

Research Outputs: Unpublished manuscripts; published manuscripts; rough drafts; page proofs; fair copies; reports to funding agencies and others; speeches; professional and popular lectures, including thesis and dissertation.

Teaching Materials: Class lecture notes and other educational materials; old grading books; exams from school (own and students); circulars of lectures, classes, and the like.

information on anthropological topics; at their best, they are comprehensive and organized. Each set has a central theme, which can serve as an identifying title. These theme sets are based on discrete research projects that involve a search for evidence (in order to answer a question or disprove a hypothesis), analyses, conclusions, and interpretations. Anthropological data may be either qualitative or quantitative and tend to be observational and statement-based rather than experimental. Whether data can be effectively reused depends on their crypticness, the availability of codes, reliability of the original source, and even the quality of the handwriting and stability of the recording material. Information in the form of preserved observational accounts, journals, and letters can be- come data when it is used for an anthropological study.

Modeling Fowler and Givens's (1992) conceptualization of the ar- chaeological record, we can describe the anthropological record as an extensive and multifaceted database that includes artifacts, ideofacts, and ecofacts generated in cultural settings—field, laboratory, library, and archives—and the written and visual observational documentation of contextual relationships.[4] Fieldnotes—as statement, provenience, and ob- servational records—are basic as primary and contextual data, for "with- out proper written and visual documentation, artifacts and observations are *meaningless* for scientific and culture history purposes" (Fowler and Givens 1992, 44). The resulting record can be subdivided into a number of parts based on purpose and the research process stage in which it was produced (see Table 11.2).

Some cultural researchers distinguish fieldnotes from other forms of field data (Jackson 1991, 20–21), such as gossip and idle conversations, purposeful discussions, highly structured and formal interviews and ques- tionnaires,[5] life histories, genealogical charts, census maps, linguistic nota- tions, stories and texts, surveys, projective tests, and research instruments based on native's statements. Fieldnotes have a shifting, ambiguous status; in general, they are a body of description, acquired and recorded in chronological order, consisting of shorthand references supplying context as well as information (Sanjeck 1990a, 1990b). They tend to deal with observational data but can contain text fragments, interlinear transla- tions, drawings, and diagrams. They constitute a "more or less coherent representation of observed cultural reality" (Clifford 1990) that are then used for writing and interpretation.

Methodology and technique greatly influence the type of record produced. For example, observation consists of systematic or haphazard descriptions of events and activities in original sociocultural settings, based on the assumption that behavior is purposive and expressive of values and beliefs. Observations vary greatly, however; they can be ran- dom or systematic, focused or impressionistic, diffuse and ambiguous or highly structured and detailed, a single notation based on a limited, casual scan or long-term, produced over an extensive period (Webb et al. 1966). A special type of account is based on participant observation, a procedure that demands firsthand involvement in the cultural or social situation under study. Participant observation varies in the same ways as other observation forms and is just as dependent on theoretical orientation

TABLE 11.2. Anthropological Record Categorization (Based on Fowler and Givens 1992)

Provenience: Field, accession, and specimen catalog records that are produced during and chronicle actual field research and the contextual data needed to construct culture histories and test scientific hypotheses. For archaeology this includes radiometric assays; identifications of pollen, plant macrofossils, and animal bones; metallurgical and chemical assays; and primary metric data, such as artifact measurements, identification, classification, and qualitative description.

Accession: Information deposited with collections in a curation facility or repository. Catalog records include information on specific objects and lots of materials, created either in the laboratory or repository. Accession records vary widely; ideally they contain copies of field records (or a clear statement as to where such records are housed) and repository documents, such as legal records that reflect previous and current custodianship. More recently conservation reports that chronicle actions (i.e., stabilization, preservation, restoration) undertaken in the field, laboratory, or museum have become critical research records.

Administrative: Materials relating to the context of a specific field or laboratory project: preproject materials such as research designs, requests for proposals, grant proposals, scopes of work, contracts, and related correspondence; project and postproject work, personnel and financial records, equipment and property records, newspaper clippings and publicity releases, artifactual loans, samples of project forms.

Analytical: Records of laboratory analyses; preliminary charts and statistical manipulations; primary metric data, such as artifact measurements, identification, and classification; and secondary analytical records, such as computer printouts of statistical and qualitative manipulations of primary data.

Project Reports: Published and unpublished project findings, data, analyses, and conclusions in relation to the larger body of anthropological knowledge, including preliminary as well as final reports, appendixes, and texts.

and research purpose (Marshall and Rossman 1989; Patton 1980; Pelto 1970).

A distinction should be made between artifactual data, direct audio and photographic/video recordings, and fieldnotes. The information in fieldnotes is an artifact of the researcher; it is new and unique because it did not exist before the research act. There is no displacement, change in cultural context and use, or a loss and gain of information as naturally accompanies the collection of objects—data that existed before the research process. Film, photographs, and video tapes combine both observational and statement-generated data. Film provides visual records of ephemeral events and is especially potent for documenting nonverbal behavior and communication. Like artifactual data, it requires the documentation of time, place, and subject, as well as researcher's intent and interests.

Anthropological records are never random samples, and we rarely know what was not recorded, the specific types of observations not made, or the reasons for selection. All researchers have both explicit and implicit sampling procedures in their heads based on the goals of their research and what they consider data and necessary information. Rarely is this recorded in their notes. For example, for my study on the commercialization of Navajo sandpaintings, I was given a great deal of unsolicited information on witchcraft. This had nothing to do with my project and was potentially volatile knowledge, so I did not write any of it down. One day, a woman asked me to record what she said so that she and her clan relatives could send their children to me to talk about this subject. Witchcraft cannot be spoken of by Navajos at certain times of year, but as a non-Navajo I could safely discuss it anytime. Also, the presence of the information outside the Navaho's core homeland and bounded by the four sacred mountains meant that it could not be obtained by witches and used against the People. These fieldnotes are an unpublished record for a Navajo clan, rather than data, yet nowhere in my field journal did I record this information.

The conditions under which a researcher works and whether he/she proceeds covertly or overtly also affects the type and quality of field records. In addition, what constitutes historic anthropological documents as research data has changed over the years through expansion and standardization.[6] Contextual information has increased in detail and complexity, resulting in an increase in the potential usefulness of data-carrying materials for more than a single research project (Fowler 1986a; Fowler and Givens 1992).

The creation of anthropological data is always an active, intentional event. The issues mentioned above are important because the decisions of scholars affect what is available for potential research data today. Unfortunately, the preservation of data is not always an intentional process. It can be either active and intentional or passive and accidental, and the heritage of anthropology is often saved in a haphazard fashion by change and circumstance.

RETENTION AND ATTRITION PROCESSES

Once produced, anthropological records do not save themselves, although they seem capable of purposeful self-destruction. Individuals preserve documents, and the manner in which they do this affects those documents' ultimate disposition. Like artifacts, records are placed in permanent repositories because someone physically transferred them. This may be through the purposeful collecting activities of an archivist or the initiative of the creator. Unfortunately, most creators think about their records only when they (1) retire and have to relinquish their offices, (2) no longer have space or cannot find a paper, (3) reach the end of a research project, or (4) change jobs. Many do not think about their documents at all; they passively leave everything for their heirs to deal with because they do not want to be bothered. Few scholars have records-management strategies; with luck most know where materials are.

Anthropologists generally do not save every piece of paper they ever produced or received, but most tend to be pack rats and save items produced during the course of a research project. Franz Boas and Elsie Clews Parsons appear to have saved everything—thousands of letters, extensive fieldnotes and research materials. Ruth Bunzel, on the other hand, discarded all her Zuni fieldnotes after she published *The Pueblo Potter* (1929) because she felt they were redundant and future scholars could discover anything of value in her book. It also appears that she kept very little personal correspondence or other professional documents.

There is almost no information on this saving/discarding process, but ethnologists seem to be the most insecure scholars and destroy more of their field records than archaeologists or biological anthropologists.

As Jean Jackson (1990) noted in her essay "I Am a Fieldnote" (1990) ethnologists are possessive yet ambiguous about their fieldnotes. As her interviewees remarked, field records evoke strong memories and emotions, for they reveal what kind of person one is. People are defensive because notes might reveal that their fieldwork did not live up to an imagined standard. Data are private and esoteric yet must be shared to be validated and valuable, because to replace them is impossible. For some anthropologists they are sacrosanct, for others all but worthless. They increase one's obligations to the profession, to posterity, and to the natives, for they symbolize the anthropological endeavor.

There are obvious reasons for this ambivalent mystique and for Tuzin's (1992, 32) finding that the more data-rich and descriptive the notes, the more likely they are to be lost to the permanent record. Ethnology has no minimally accepted standard for what constitutes evidence, as has archaeology and biological anthropology. One's ability to record and understand observations is very idiosyncratic and subjective. In addition, fieldnotes are complicated records. More than raw data generated by specific methodological operations using a set of identifiable techniques, "they are the product of intricate relationships between the personal and the technical, the anthropologist and the people he/she interacts with, the context and the content" (Silverman 1992, 4). Fieldnotes contain sensitive information that can easily be misused. Interestingly, this fear of having clay feet is not evident among amateurs, tourists, or explorers. Only professionals whose reputations (and hence their honor and authority) rise or fall on the strength of field-research skills are concerned with the structure, depth, and quality of their notes.

Archaeologists and biological anthropologists face the same issues, but the nature of their work partly obviates these concerns. Whereas most linguistic and cultural research is conducted by a single individual, archaeology and biological anthropology are team efforts that rely on a range of professionals and specialists. The reputation of each rests on more specific, standardized, and hence controllable techniques. The reputation of the director of a project depends on his/her synthesizing and interpretative abilities, skills all professionals have tested through peer review.

Non-fieldwork materials, including those generated and used for analysis and write-up, seem to be saved equally by practitioners in all subdisciplines. Crucial for understanding the nature of field records, retention varies by individual personality. This means, ironically, that we may have summary and supplementary data but not raw data for cultural anthropology. And even that which is saved may not be in its original form: everyone inserts and erase parts of their corpus for personal and professional reasons. Marginal notations that clarify and recontextualize data are added. Musings too personal to leave, information that turns out to be unwarranted speculation, potentially harmful or too easily misinterpreted if taken out of context, is erased. People change their minds as they discover that something previously recorded was erroneous, incomplete, or misinterpreted situations or events.

Even with this attrition, there is a tremendous amount of data-carrying material housed in repositories. In fact, no one has any feel for how many records have already been saved and are waiting to be rediscovered, but the numbers will be large. For example, the Nordic Museum in Sweden, a central repository for collections and documents on Sweden's cultural history, has more than one and a half million drawings and photographs of objects, environments, and practices (Becker 1992, 4). A survey of museums conducted by the American Association of Museums (1992) estimated that U.S. museums hold 12,739,433 linear feet of archival material and 6,124,565 bound volumes (178,703 linear feet). Most of these holdings are in general natural history or specialized museums.[7] Archival materials in history museums and at historic sites is smaller but not insignificant (593,317 linear feet). Of this material, 66 percent is accessioned but only 55 percent inventoried and catalogued.[8] The situation for natural history and anthropology museums is much worse: only 39 percent of archival materials have been accessioned, 21 percent catalogued and inventoried. Few have archivists so there is little intellectual control, especially at the item level.

It is a given that even if a scholar's research materials are housed as a single corpus in one archive, career and personal records will always be found in multiple repositories. For example, outgoing letters become part of the receiver's records if that person deemed them of some importance. The extent of the dispersal depends on the letters' breadth and depth, the scholar's network, the use to which the letters were put, the value placed on correspondence by the receiver, and whether the executors of the receiver's estate have ever heard of the sender. There is a tendency for people to save letters: (1) from the famous, (2) from people within their citation and acknowledgment network, and (3) that contain rather than request information. Potential retention also varies by time period; correspondence was more highly valued in the nineteenth century than it is today. Other records are found in the administrative and departmental files where an individual worked, in different countries if work was multinational in nature, in corporation headquarters or government files for consultants.

Another variable that influences the ultimate destination of records is the nature of a research project, specifically whether it was (1) pure or applied in nature, (2) of a consultative nature, (3) a single or multiperson project, (4) a short- or long-term project that was taken over by another individual or institution after the retirement of the original director, and (5) if the record generator-holder was director, supervisor, or staff. Legal or proprietary aspects are also important in applied research; some Cultural Resource Management (CRM) projects conducted for businesses are considered confidential and the property of the company. Some documents may even be classified. The nature of the contract and conditions under which the research was done is therefore important for preservation.

The processes of gathering these materials, from an institutional standpoint, are basically analogous to active and passive collecting by museums (Parezo 1987). Theoretically all collections that come into collections are assessed. Although this is true at the larger institutions, public repositories such as the Library of Congress, the National Archives, and university and state archives, many local historical archives and smaller museums do not have professional information specialists. The presence of professionals, like the presence of curators, affects what is collected, how it is retained, used, and codified, and its accessibility for research. Most passive collecting—papers "dumped" on the institution without prearrangement—tends to be haphazard. But this does not mean that the records do not contain little gems invaluable for anthropology.

Ideally researchers would like to use systematically collected papers that were gathered and arranged under the care of an archivist.[9] For anthropology this may still present an access issue, because most archivists are trained historians or librarians with little knowledge of anthropological research needs. This is not necessarily a disadvantage, but it does mean that materials are not organized using anthropological categories and can be a problem if an archivist will not let a researcher browse. And unlike museum collections, the rationale for the cataloguing schemes and taxonomies used for data control rarely meet disciplinary needs; different rules apply to the world of records management.

Archivists find anthropological records both similar in form to materials generated by other disciplines and unique and mystifying. Most archivists accept anthropological records based on models for history or one of the natural sciences. They also tend to think in terms of saving the core materials of key professional practitioners. This means that the data produced by avocational anthropologists do not find their way to repositories as quickly as the data of professionals and are generally passively acquired. Also, the materials of "key" figures (individuals who have produced macro-level theories and been remembered, in part, because of their structural centrality) tend to be actively sought and saved more readily than the materials of individuals who were data gatherers, taught at colleges rather than research universities, or were regional experts—that is, most of the profession's practitioners. Unfortunately, this may not be the "best" anthropological material to save, although it may have priority from the standpoint of the history of Western thought. It is not necessarily the Great Men and Women who generate the most valuable and useful data. It is the historical situation described, the scarcity of similar accounts, the rarity, thoroughness, quality, and reliability of the information, more than the renown of the generator and holder of the data, that valuate anthropological documents.

Even from the Great Men and Women, archivists do not uncritically accept materials; they selectively preserve in order to avoid squandering limited resources on redundant or relatively unimportant items. No archivist will accept a manuscript collection without appraising its permanent value. Underlying all appraisals since the nineteenth century is the contention that what is being preserved is information that has enduring historical, cultural, or research value, that is, records in any physical form that have been produced by individuals or organizations in the course of typical and extraordinary activities over time. As noted in Table 11.3, value is based on an assessment of the material's intellectual, historical, or research potential as well as its quality, age, physical form, completeness, and depth.

This emphasis on importance, future use value, and completeness is well noted in the archival community. Because the goal of archives is to preserve the society's collective memory, the act of retention is a visible symbol that the papers of individuals and groups are worthy of preservation. This act extends the producer's temporal and spatial range of communication by lengthening his/her influence beyond a lifetime. In 1956,

TABLE 11.3. Typical Archival Selection Criteria for Records

Research Value: The most important archival criteria includes the quality of the material and its future use value. Materials are worthy of retention because they are unique, irreplaceable, and have proven to be useful beyond the life of the creator. Papers are potentially useful to scholars in the future. Important is the intelligibility and legibility of the documents.

Age and Size: The turn of the twentieth century formed a watershed for the appraisal of documents. The older a document, the more important, because of rarity. Unpublished materials are more valuable than published items. For contemporary documents, quantity and repetitiveness are problematic, especially for certain kinds of government records and large surveys. Groups of documents that show action or change over time are valued. A current debate, therefore, involves sampling and representativeness. This is a problem for sociology, law, medicine, and political science, but generally not for anthropology, where projects are more discrete, of shorter duration, and involve small data sets.

Form: Few archives can afford to store duplicates, especially repetitive files containing both cumulative and primary (raw) data. Archivists also feel that certain types of documents, such as correspondence, field notes, site cards, laboratory diaries, and notes, carry information more frequently used by researchers than do discarded statistical analyses, used airline tickets, announcements of meetings, or invoices for office equipment. Increasingly important are the availability of codes for computer tapes and software for the programs. Also assessed is the stability of the materials and the actual conservation problems.

Evidential and Informational Characteristics: Materials collected contain evidence of the functioning, ideas, and activities of the creator. Records assessed on the basis of the information they contain on other persons, places, events, and actions.

Administrative Value: Records must be kept for continuing financial, legal, or administrative value. This is especially common for organizations.

Repository Collecting Policy: Each archive or record repository has implicit or explicit guidelines that underpin acquisition policy: this includes the scope, subject matter, and geographical range of the repository. This is based on the concept of collecting fields; the premise is that scholars can best study like or related materials together and that it is more economical for an institution to specialize in certain areas. The ability of the archive to safely house certain kinds of materials is also a factor.

Social Value: Records have actual or potential educational, social, or cultural value to members from different ethnic, social, or scientific communities.

Theodore Schellenberg argued that when appraising the value of records, the archivist "must take into account the entire documentation of society on the matter to which the information relates" (277). Since 1970, however, social historians have demonstrated how archives can err in favor of preserving the records of dominant social groups at the expense of the less powerful (Foote 1990; Hinding 1982; Miller 1981). This means that the historical records anthropologists use will tend to be produced by individuals from Western societies, not the peoples we have traditionally studied. Conversely, given that we have worked with these less powerful groups, retention of our records has added significance for documenting the histories and voices of the peoples with whom we work.

THE ARCHIVED RECORD

An archive both detaches meaning from and produces meaning in records and photographs. Materials to be saved take on the connotation of "that which is valuable," however value is defined. Archivists shape the record itself through the articulation of institutional goals (Becker 1992; Sekula 1975; Trachtenberg 1988). Photographs are a prime example of this. A photograph in a history museum has "evidential force" (Barthes 1981, 89) because it is conceptualized as an observation of an event in a social science paradigm; the same photograph, if taken by Ansel Adams, is conceptualized as artistic creativity and evidence of insightful imagination in an art museum. In addition, the networks of power in which these institutions are embedded and the ideas archivists have about what constitutes research evidence influences definitions of value. An anthropological photograph or document is generally conceptualized as that which bears facts or information in the form of scientific data, shows evidence of cultural forms, recovers of the past (ideal or actual), or captures the exotic. These assessments during collection thus validate the material, but in different ways.

The type of repository in which historic anthropological records are stored varies greatly. Records repositories are as varied as object repositories, although for anthropology these are often the same institutions. State and university museums have traditionally served as repositories for archaeological objects and their associated records. Local historical societies tend to have materials produced by amateurs. Records repositories are also in research centers, private and public museums, special federal facilities, university departments, libraries, and federal, state, local, public, and private archives and manuscript repositories. These may be general or specialized. In short, anthropological records are found in almost every type of repository.

Manuscript repositories are built on hierarchical classification systems that reflect the goals, ideals, and research needs current when the institutions were founded. These basic classifications may be added to and subdivided but are rarely changed. This means that when materials that reflect new research agendas and questions are acquired, there are classification inconsistencies. The taxonomic system under which most anthropological documentary materials are housed is one that was devised at the end of the nineteenth century; it reflects the needs and conceptions of history and natural science rather than the current state of anthropology. This same problem exists with library classification systems (see Parezo 1991). This does not mean that repositories do not change as the nature of research and what constitutes evidence evolves. Archival classifications are transformed following paradigmatic shifts, but slowly; categorization schemes resist reconceptualization based on evolving disciplinary research needs, which eliminates alterations in response to fads.

Archivists think hierarchically when they appraise and organize records. This includes at its most inclusive the record group or collection, which is analogous to an accession in a museum. Within a collection are series that are distinguished by the documents' main attributes. For anthropology this is often discrete projects, such as the records pertaining to an excavation or survey, the fieldnotes from an ethnography project undertaken in a single year or multiple years, all correspondence, or teaching notes. The documents in a series are always maintained as a unit because they relate to a particular subject (for an organization, this is a function), result from the same type of activity, have a particular form, or have some intrinsic relationship rooted in their creation, use, or receipt.

Each record series is composed of file units, which can be conceptualized as folders or loose documents. For example, although all the documents I produce during the course of my career will comprise one record group, I separate my individual field projects from my correspondence. My fieldnotes can also be divided by project into field interviews, object surveys, archival information, and field journals. For my letters, I put almost everything in folders based on half-year time intervals.[10] An archivist would consider each of these correspondence folders a file unit. For archivists, the relationship of documents in a file unit is determined largely by the characteristics of the individual documents: their dates, subject, and the quantity that can be placed conveniently in a folder. In this case, my semiannual letter files would be placed in several folders—in some cases almost twenty—because the number of letters I write varies greatly but is rather extensive. How an archivist would organize the individual documents, that is, each letter, would be interesting because I simply stuff the incoming letters and a copy of my responses into the folder. There is no real rhyme or reason to my stuffing technique.[11] An archivist could leave it as it is or rearrange it alphabetically (by correspondent) or chronologically.

Completeness of documents in a collection is a crucial archival variable. Archivists accept individual documents if they have value but prefer entire collections. They would like to have all the records from a project, but most accept incomplete series, especially if they are rare and have research value. Although some documents may be copies, the collection as a whole is considered unique and comprehensive if duplicates are available. Some records of less value by themselves are retained because they are part of a package.

Archivists try to keep the record group intact once it is acquired, because individual documents take on additional meaning in relation to other items in a record group. This idea is codified in the basic archival concept of respect for the integrity of a collection, the principle of provenance, and sanctity of the original order.[12] Archivists attempt to retain a collection's internal order so that future researchers can understand the creator's mind and logic, the order of events, or a decision-making process. Arbitrary or principled document reorganization by the archivist is thought to obscure information. This idea is based on the belief that every manuscript collection is unique because no two individuals or organizations have identical interests, work in the same way, or maintain the same quantity and quality of records. Individuality is valued. Thus the manner and shape in which documents enter a repository is critical to an understanding of how they are organized. Thus, although archivists do not deal with verbalized and codified preconceived arrangement schemes, they do organize materials based on a number of principles (see Table 11.4). Ordering by chronology is almost always used at the document level, frequently at the folder level, rarely at the series level, and almost never as the framework for the collections group.

As with object collections, attrition and loss occur in a repository;

T A B L E   11.4. Typical Archival Organizational Schemes

Date: Chronologically. This is the simplest and most common method of arranging manuscripts. It shows the relationship between documents and the events to which they relate. It is used to create time sequences.
Type: By type of information (i.e., correspondence, research notes, diaries, minutes and proceedings, printed material, financial documents, photographs, literary productions, legal documents, scrapbooks, maps, etc.) or by function or use, regardless of subject or date produced. These tend to be arranged internally either alphabetically or chronologically.
Project: Materials from a discrete research endeavor.
Topic or Subject: Materials that relate to a particular research locale or information subject (i.e., kinship, settlement pattern). This is rarely used because it is common for a single document to refer to more than one topic.
Media Type: By the material on which the information is recorded (paper, video tape, audio tape, photographs, computer disc).
Professional vs. Private Information: The separation of a person's papers into public and private spheres.
Locale: Materials based on culture areas, societies, or some geographical scheme. Photographs that are not part of a named collection, by photographer, are often placed in these types of arrangements.
Institutional Base: Materials based on place of employment or affiliation of an individual.
Alphabetic: By surname, organized alphabetically. The least commonly used ordering technique except on the level of the individual document.

some documents are destroyed through natural disasters and human error; some papers walk through the doors via intentional theft or scholarly forgetfulness, and insect infestations, fire, leaky water pipes, misfiling, old age, and brittleness take their toll. Institutions sometimes trade, and the records of these old transactions may or may not be retained. For photographs, a special situation can occur: the identification is lost from the document resulting in a loss of research value. Recataloguing also occurs; sometimes it increases accessibility, sometimes it hinders it. This reclassification depends in part on the logic of the original cataloguing scheme. For example, recently I began reviewing the papers of the Indian Arts and Crafts Board (IACB), which are housed at the National Archives as part of the Department of Interior's records. Once I began to use them it was obvious someone had rearranged and reboxed them since I had last looked at them in 1988; this made the basic box inventory useless. I began to work on the record set pertaining to the exhibits produced for the 1939 World's Fair in San Francisco. I knew about the exhibit produced by Frederic Douglas and René d'Harnoncourt; I did not know that Samuel Barrett and Alfred Kroeber had been called in to produce a second exhibit in 1940. The records produced by Barrett and Kroeber would have been kept in separate files during the fair's life for practical reasons. In the archive, however, the two exhibits are interspersed and then arranged, "sort of," by institutional affiliation of correspondent and topic—"sort of" because there are duplicates from the file of the University of California–Berkeley in the University of Pennsylvania file and originals from the Heye Foundation in the American Museum of Natural History file. Some documents appear to be original materials that had been transferred to Bureau of Indian Affairs (BIA) files, and interspersed are newspaper clippings that deal with the IACB's silver project. Regrettably, there is no record as to when this was done and whether all the BIA materials dealing in this file were so transferred. This means I will have to check the BIA files even though I may not find anything. In addition, there seems to be absolutely no rationale as to why certain folders were placed in one of the thirty-five manuscript boxes that hold these documents; their internal ordering is also a mystery. A researcher must look through all the records in the entire record set in order to find specific information.

An archivist's subject-matter knowledge and understanding of how researchers conceptualize data categories when they label files is as important for researchers' ability to find material as it is for the identification of object types in museum catalogue records. Historical biases obscure data. To call again on the records of the IACB, gender bias is evident in how the materials were labeled. Several folders deal with Native American demonstrators at the exhibitions in 1939 and 1940. Sometimes these are labeled tribally and categorically—"Navajo sandpainters," "Papago basketmakers"—at other times, by name of an individual or group. When husband-and-wife teams are given an individual folder (even though all the records regarding these individuals are not in this separate file), they are all labeled under the husband's name. Thus the file on María Martínez is under the name of her husband, Julian, and that on Zonnie Lee, a famous Navajo weaver in the 1930s, is under the name of her husband, John. This procedure erases the women from the level of researcher articulation and speaks eloquently of the categories considered significant when the materials were presented to the National Archives.

Sometimes materials are misidentified over the years, a problem common to museum collections, and pieces will be housed in different files and even in different parts of an institution. This requires that researchers think broadly when reusing material. For example, when I analyzed the collecting activities of Smithsonian scientists in the American Southwest, I searched specifically for the field catalogues of James Stevenson from his 1880s expeditions to Zuni, Hopi, and the Rio Grande Pueblos. I quickly found two catalogues in the National Anthropological Archives (NAA) listed under Stevenson. Another expedition's papers were microfilmed in the accession papers in the museum's central registration area, and those of the 1884 expedition were with the papers accompanying the catalogue cards in the anthropology department's processing laboratory. About three days before I finished my fellowship, one of the NAA archivists suggested I look in the John P. Harrington Papers which they were currently reinventorying. There were the Stevenson catalogues I had been looking for, along with many of Matilda Coxe Stevenson's hand-written fieldnotes (cut up by Harrington and incorporated into his own notes without attribution or reference but recognizable through penmanship). Because the principle of maintaining the integrity of a record group as it is given to an institution was followed, the materials had been left with the Harrington Papers. Luckily, today there is a finding aide that tells researchers that a good deal of both James and Matilda Coxe Stevensons' field data are incorporated throughout the Harrington Papers. Thus, this past use behavior has been incorporated and institutionalized by the archival community, even though we as researchers might think that the Stevenson Papers should be separated out by their original creator.[13]

There is a general tendency in the archival world to separate photographic and paper records because of differing conservation needs. Slides, still photographs (black/white and color), and movies have different physical requirements. The same is true of audio and video collections, but these have not been differentiated to the degree that paper and photographic records have. In many ways visual records are conceptualized and used differently than paper records. Worth (1981), Chalfen (1975), and Worth and Adair (1972) have all noted that photographs are cultural artifacts that take their shape and meaning from patterns rooted in shared cultural and historical experience. Like other forms of paper records, they are a form of data that is shaped by the cultural perspectives and time period of the researcher (Scherer 1975). Thus photographs and paper documents are catalogued either together or separately based on how the archival curators conceptualize their use. In actuality, the size of the institution and the complexity of its holdings determine whether these materials are kept physically together or are separated into separate collections. Today, cartographic and architectural records are also beginning to be separated; no one has quite decided what to do with machine-readable records. This will become an increasingly important issue for repositories in the future. (See Kemper 1992 for a discussion of such issues.)

DOCUMENTS RELATING TO COLLECTIONS

Is there anything special about those historic and anthropological documents that pertain directly and indirectly to material culture? In order to answer this question we must briefly discuss the position of archives in museums and reflect on how documents relate to collections.

Great variety is found in museums with regard to the location and categorization scheme of archival—institutional and manuscript—materials. Copies of related correspondence and financial records related to objects may be deposited in a separate archive, even though ideally they should be kept as part of the accession record. This is not always easy, given the manner in which curation facilities are organized; they often separate records dealing directly with artifacts. It is often the case that fieldnotes and analysis materials are placed in the institution's archive or library, physically removed from the collection. Here they are catalogued under a scheme different from that used for objects. And unfortunately, paper documents have received low priority in terms of conservation and the construction of informational controls. In fact, most documents dealing with collections and the projects that collected and assembled them for the institution have been "lost" (actually or temporarily) because some curators in the past have not considered collection documentation part of the collection or even their responsibility (see Trimble and Myers 1991 for the consequences of such a view). Others "knew" where these materials were and thus never bothered to write crucial information down; as these individuals have retired, the intellectual control over the location of vital information has been lost.

Another dimension of this problem is that historically researchers considered the fieldnotes produced on a project their own, whereas the artifacts belonged to the institution. This has meant that fieldnotes and analyses may not be housed in the same institution with the artifacts.[14] Researchers reusing materials must know a great deal about the history of specific research projects, as well as the intellectual history of the field with regard to how information was categorized when it was produced and deposited, before they can use artifacts to their fullest potential. Because of these past practices, most museums will not have complete records documenting the recovery and analysis of their artifactual material.[15]

Photographs taken on research expeditions should be conceptualized as part of the artifact collections. Researchers have used the camera as a special means to document objects it was impractical or impossible to collect: houses, boats, shrines, religious objects that were destroyed during a ceremony, ephemera, body decorations. By the turn of the century most anthropologists were producing photographs to document their work. For example, I took more than three thousand photographs of the ten thousand–plus Navajo sandpaintings that were being sold. To purchase these paintings would have been impossible and would have influenced the market in ways that would have masked actual economic patterns; the paintings were all sold within six months of my documentary shots. Each of my photos has an accompanying data sheet that provides provenience data.

Recently, Enid Schildkrout has noted that "as objects move from their place of origin into museums, they cross boundaries of space, time, ethnicity and class, thereby assuming new, frozen meanings as symbols of other cultures" (1992, 5). So it is with the records that accompany collections. Yet these records are different because they were often made by individuals who were not the makers and users of the artifacts. In this sense they are more fluid and cross fewer boundaries than artifacts; simultaneously, they are that which allows the crossing of boundaries and that which freezes the artifacts in their new meanings. Records are thus related to, that is, part of objects, yet distinct from them.

I should note that my conclusion with regard to the distinctions of records and objects may be challenged in the future by certain individuals who are currently recovering sacred objects under the Native American Graves Protection and Repatriation Act (NAGPRA). Although NAGPRA does not specifically deal with documentation, some tribes are requesting that all documentation be returned with repatriated items. These individuals do not distinguish the object from an oral explanation about the object as collected in the field, the written version of these words, or notes based on subsequent artifactual analysis. Others are not making such a request, considering the object distinct from what outsiders have written about it. Still others see the records and objects as related but would like to control access to records that contain sensitive or esoteric information. (And the debate is being extended to other kinds of fieldnotes as well.) There will be many debates on these and other intellectual property issues in the future. The nature of records relating to collections and the potential of all researchers—native and nonnative, scholarly and popular, professional and amateur—to use them and obtain a complete cultural picture in the future will very much depend on the outcome of these debates.

THE PAST INTO THE FUTURE

In a speech remarking on the importance of studying history, Bernard Bailyn observed, "The way the world develops has a relation to the way it was in the past. A community without history is like a person without a memory—incoherent."[16] So it is with anthropology. In our records we hold documentation of the history and collective memories of numerous peoples from around the world, of the past and present. We also hold our own history, a legacy for our scholarly descendants, and our always-active data. We can help ensure disciplinary coherence by responsibly preserving our records, thereby insuring the continuity and transmission of our cultural heritage.

As with collections of material objects, the routines an institution employs in gathering, selecting, and preserving records reveals strategies of representation and conservation that create and perpetuate the world and our knowledge of the past and present. All institutions have their unique problems and strengths; some do a better job of curation and intellectual control than others. A central problem for producing this essay and a critical barrier to ensuring our disciplinary heritage is that neither anthropologists nor archivists have any idea of the extent, scope, and quality of anthropological materials. As a result, all the principles and patterns I have identified should be considered preliminary. In order to test these principles, we need to inventory repositories, just as we inventory our collections before we can make definitive and informed conclusions on how the anthropological record was formed and can be used.

Because no one knows how many anthropological records are housed in repositories, or even where most of the material is located, it is difficult to say how much is being preserved. Nor is it possible to assess its overall quality, except based on the anecdotal tales of fellow archival travelers. But we can obtain a hint based on the data use, especially by ethnohistorians, historians of science, and anthropologists interested in historical questions. A brief comparison of past and recent issues of major anthropological journals indicates that the use of archival materials is increasing. I predict that this use will expand in the future, and that anthropological documents will be used by both scholars and the native peoples with whom we have worked in the past.

What will be saved in the future is debatable. Archivists have space problems and ethical responsibilities not to accept that which they cannot care for or make accessible. They will not be able to house thousands of linear feet of computer printouts or mountains of telephone-message slips. On the other hand, they may want copies in order to keep the original and provide researchers with duplicates for research use. Items on strange forms (toilet paper, napkins, shelving paper) will be weighted against their informational value.

I can predict that archivists will never have access to some materials because of changes in the way records are produced. Faxed letters, that crucial correspondence that documents and explains much of our activities, begin to disintegrate the minute they are received. Drafts of papers and preliminary analyses are no longer retained because we work on computers. We will still have finished products, but we will have less information on the research process. And there may be a time when, because of the speed with which computers and software become outdated, we do not even have these finished products. In twenty years the nature of the anthropological database will be very different, but it will still be worth saving.

NOTES

1. This is not meant to in any way belittle this individual's abilities. The Mennonite Archives is one of the best run, easiest to use, and friendliest institutions in which I have worked.

2. As we have noted in *Preserving the Anthropological Record* (Silverman and Parezo 1991), this production principle possesses a tremendous problem for anthropology. These data constitute a corpus of tremendous value to

anthropology for they are used over and over again by researchers. To ensure the future health and viability of the discipline we need to gain more control over our collective data. In order to do this we must know how anthropologists have used, saved, and distributed their documentary information. This intellectual understanding will help archivists control the location of anthropological documentary information so that researchers can use it effectively and efficiently.

3. Governments and their appointed agents have produced and maintained a variety of records concerning social statistics; churches and other private organizations have inventories with vital statistics on population size, births and deaths, crimes, genealogies, social relationships, and marriages. Information in newspapers, magazines, books, religious tracts, and the like can also be used when subjected to anthropological methods and techniques.

4. Fowler and Givens (1992, 44) define artifacts as "all physical remains of human cultural activity, from lithic debitage through 'works of art' to structures large and small" and ecofacts as "unmodified plant and animal remains, together with soils and geomorphological features useful in the reconstruction of past environments."

5. Interviews tend to be saved, pretesting instruments and protocols tend not to be.

6. In cultural anthropology, records began with noting down the story an elder told; later they expanded to include questionnaires, photographs, sound records, objects, interviews, and notes on observations. For archaeology, data began with whole pots, then expanded to whole pots, parts of pots, *and* written information on provenience, in short, adding paper documents. Physical anthropology began more like cultural; it started with observations, added records on measurements of human physical forms, then added objects.

7. Unfortunately, *specialized* is not defined in the figures from this report.

8. History museums are in better shape in this regard, as would be expected. Seventy-four percent of archival materials have been accessioned, 61 percent catalogued, and 59 percent inventoried.

9. Photographs are slightly different from paper records in this regard. An individual photo can have a great deal of evidential value, especially if it is well provenienced. Because of this, isolated photographs, passively collected with little documentation, tend to be more useful than isolated papers and undocumented objects.

10. I am not consistent in this regard. I take out some of the letters received from people whom I am studying, senior anthropologists, and put them in my bibliography files. I don't, however, do this with the letters I write to them.

11. Actually, my filing system reflects my lack of a secretary, my inability to say no to interesting projects, and my subsequent overwork and haste in

filing, as well as my periodic mad rush to find things that have been lost in my office.

12. This does not mean, of course, that an archivist will not refile a piece of paper that has obviously been misfiled.

13. Because archivists do not work on this principle, accurate, detailed, and extensive finding aides and cross-indexes are absolutely crucial for future research endeavors.

14. This will be an increasingly important issue in the next few years as institutions debate what records belong to institutions and what the individual's professional and ethical responsibilities are in this regard.

15. This is also true of institutional records. Past director of the Arizona State Museum, Byron Cummings took all the museum's institutional records with him when he retired, partly because he was angry with the University of Arizona for requesting that he retire (in his eighties) and because he considered them his personal property. Today, ASM's records are housed in the archives of the Arizona Historical Society as part of Cumming's personal papers.

16. Quoted in Winkler (1980, 3).

REFERENCES

American Association of Museums. 1992. *Data Report from the 1989 National Museum Survey.* Washington, D.C.: American Association of Museums.

Barthes, Roland. 1981. *Camera Lucida.* Translated by Richard Howard. New York: Hill and Wang.

Becker, Karin. 1992. "Picturing Our Past: An Archive Constructs a National Culture." *Journal of American Folklore* 105 (415): 3–18.

Bunzel, Ruth. 1929. *The Pueblo Potter.* New York: Columbia University Press.

Chalfen, Richard. 1975. "Cinéma Naïveté: A Study of Home Moviemaking as Visual Communication." *Studies in the Anthropology of Visual Communication* 2 (2): 87–103.

Clifford, James. 1990. "Notes on (Field)notes." In Sanjeck, *Fieldnotes,* 47–70.

Deiss, William. 1984. *Museum Archives: An Introduction.* Chicago: Society of American Archivists.

Fletcher, John A. 1984. *Native American Archives: An Introduction.* Chicago: Society of American Archivists.

Foote, Kenneth E. 1990. "To Remember and Forget: Archives, Memory, and Culture." *American Archivist* 53 (2): 378–92.

Fowler, Don. 1986. "Conserving American Archaeological Resources." In *American Archaeology Past and Future,* edited by David J. Meltzer, Don

D. Fowler, and Jeremy A. Sabloff. Washington, D.C.: Smithsonian Institution Press.

Fowler, Don, and Douglas Givens. 1992. "Preserving the Archaeological Record." In *Preserving the Anthropological Record,* edited by Sydel Silverman and Nancy J. Parezo, 43–52. New York: Wenner-Gren Foundation for Anthropological Research.

Han, F. Gerald. 1992. *Selecting and Appraising Archives and Manuscripts.* Chicago: Society of American Archivists.

Hinding, Andrea. 1982. "Toward Documentation: New Collecting Strategies in the 1980s." In *Options for the Eighties: Proceedings of the Second Annual Conference on American College and Research Libraries,* edited by V. Massman and M. Kathman, 35–42. Greenwich, Conn.: KAI Press.

Jackson, Jean. 1990. "'I Am a Fieldnote': Fieldnotes as a Symbol of Professional Identity." In Sanjeck, *Fieldnotes,* 3–33.

Marshall, Catherine, and Gretchen B. Rossman. 1989. *Designing Qualitative Research.* Beverly Hills, Calif.: Sage.

Miller, Frederic M. 1981. "Social History and Archival Practice." *American Archivist* 42 (1): 113–24.

———. 1990. *Arranging and Describing Archives and Manuscripts.* Chicago: Society of American Archives.

O'Toole, James M. 1990. *Understanding Archives and Manuscripts.* Chicago: Society of American Archivists.

Parezo, Nancy J. 1987. "The Formation of Ethnographic Collections: The Collecting Activities of the Smithsonian Institution in the American Southwest." In *Advances in Archaeological Theory and Method,* vol. 10, edited by Michael Schiffer, 1–47. Orlando, Fla.: Academic Press.

———. 1990. "The Challenge of Native American Art and Material Culture." *Museum Anthropology* 14 (4): 12–29.

Parezo, Nancy J., Nathalie F. S. Woodbury, and Ruth J. Person. 1992. "Saving the Past for the Future: Guidelines for Anthropologists." In *Preserving the Anthropological Record,* edited by Sydel Silverman and Nancy J. Parezo, 73–96. New York: Wenner-Gren Foundation for Anthropological Research.

Patton, M. Q. 1980. *Qualitative Evaluation Methods.* Beverly Hills, Calif.: Sage.

Pelto, Pertti J. 1970. *Anthropological Research: The Structure of Inquiry.* New York: Harper and Row.

Sanjeck, Roger. 1990a. "Fire Loss and the Sorcerer's Apprentice." In Sanjeck, *Fieldnotes,* 34–46.

———. 1990b. "A Vocabulary for Fieldnotes." In Sanjeck, *Fieldnotes,* 92–138.

————, ed. 1990. *Fieldnotes: The Makings of Anthropology*. Ithaca, N.Y.: Cornell University Press.

Schellenberg, Theodore. 1956. "The Appraisal of Public Records." *National Archives Bulletin*, no. 8. Washington, D.C.

Scherer, Joanna. 1975. "You Can't Believe Your Eyes: Inaccuracies in Photographs of North American Indians." *Studies in the Anthropology of Visual Communication* 2 (2): 67–78.

Schildkrout, Enid. 1992. "Introduction: Thinking about Things." *Museum Anthropology* 16 (3): 5–6.

Sekula, Alan. 1975. "On the Invention of Photographic Meaning." *Artforum* 13 (5): 1–12.

Silverman, Sydel. 1992. Introduction to *Preserving the Anthropological Record*, edited by Sydel Silverman and Nancy J. Parezo, 1–10. New York: Wenner-Gren Foundation for Anthropological Research.

Trachtenberg, Alan. 1988. "From Image to Story: Reading the File." In *Documenting America, 1935–1943*, edited by Carl Fleischhauer and Beverly W. Brannan, 43–73. Berkeley and Los Angeles: University of California Press.

Trimble, Michael K., and Thomas B. Myers. 1991. *Saving the Past from the Future: Archaeological Curation in the St. Louis District*. St. Louis: U.S. Army Corps of Engineers, St. Louis District.

Tuzin, Donald. 1992. "The Melanesian Archive." In *Preserving the Anthropological Record*, edited by Sydel Silverman and Nancy J. Parezo, 31–42. New York: Wenner-Gren Foundation for Anthropological Research.

Webb, E., D. T. Campbell, R. D. Schwartz, and L. Schrest. 1966. *Unobtrusive Measures and Nonreactive Research in the Social Sciences*. Chicago: Rand McNally.

Wilson, Thomas H., and Nancy J. Parezo. 1992. "The Role of Museums in Preserving the Anthropological Record." In *Preserving the Anthropological Record*, edited by Sydel Silverman and Nancy J. Parezo, 61–72. New York: Wenner-Gren Foundation for Anthropological Research.

Winkler, Karen J. 1980. "Wanted—A History that Pulls Things Together." *Chronicle of Higher Education*, July 7, 3.

Worth, Sol. 1981. *Studying Visual Communication*. Philadelphia: University of Pennsylvania Press.

Worth, Sol, and John Adair. 1972. *Through Navajo Eyes*. Bloomington: Indiana University Press.

Part Four

Materials Science in
Material Culture Studies

12

A Role for Materials Science

W. DAVID KINGERY

A major development in material culture studies during the last half-century has been the rapid development of scientific aids. A seminal event was the announcement in 1949 by Willard Libby of his invention of radiocarbon dating (Libby 1952). Since then a flood of books focusing on the application of physical science to archaeology and art has appeared (e.g., Brothwell and Higgs 1963; Biek 1963; Caley 1964; Hodges 1964; Young 1966; Levey 1967; Brill 1968; Tite 1972; Beck 1974; Fleming 1976; Jould 1978; Kempe and Harvey 1983; Lambert 1984; McKeever 1985; England and van Zelst 1986; Leute 1987; Sayre et al. 1988; Allen 1989; Vandiver, Druzik, and Wheeler 1991; Taylor, Long, and Kra 1992; Vandiver et al. 1992; and many others). The 1992 volume of *Art and Archaeology Technical Abstracts* (Brown 1992) contained 3,042 abstracts, as compared with 1,399 for the 1943–52 *decade* (Gettens and Usilton 1955). It is probably fair to say that art historians, archaeologists, and other material culture social scientists regard this avalanche with mixed emotions. On the one hand, some small fraction are invaluable; on the other hand, scientists' data are often seen as irrelevant to meaningful art and archaeological problems. Materials science can play an invaluable role in bridging the gap between these disparate cultures.

Materials science is a broad undertaking concerned with the selection, processing, production, structure, properties, applications, and performance of materials such as glass, ceramics, stone, wood, bone, paper, textiles, polymers, semiconductors, plaster, concrete, metals, and composites of these. These materials are used for the manufacture of everyday articles and art objects as well as sophisticated high-technology devices essential for both ancient and modern technologies. The core paradigm of materials science and engineering is that material selection and processing leads to particular structures of artifacts, giving rise to properties that determine artifact performance (Fig. 12.1). This paradigm is analogous to the process used by craftsmen in selecting materials, designing an object, and then creating an artifact with a form and properties suitable for some desired application. It models the behavior of modern and ancient industries as they create devices and products. An artist follows this same pattern in the creation of an object having special aesthetic properties. This coincidence of role gives the materials scientist a mindset sympathetic to the interpretation of artifacts in relationship to the materials and material properties involved in their production and use.

The special role of the materials scientist is to make explicit the nature and characteristics of "structure" and to use that knowledge as a guide for realizing particular structures and properties. By structure we mean the component parts of an object or assemblage—how they are arranged and how their interactions result in particular properties. There are many levels of structure, ranging from the atomic to the structure of artifact distribution (Fig. 12.2). Materials scientists are primarily concerned with the rich diversity of internal structure that determines the properties of an object and affects its use and performance. There is an

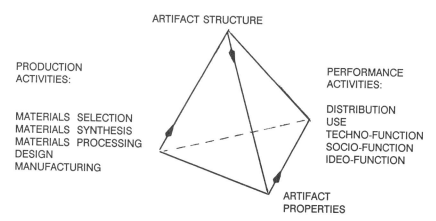

Fig. 12.1. *Materials selection, processing, design, and realization produce artifacts with a particular structure and with properties suitable for particular uses, functions, and performance.*

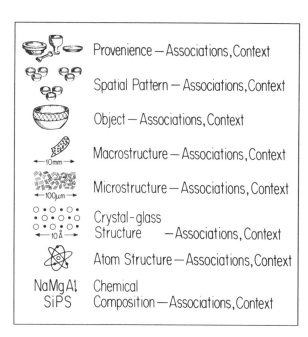

Fig. 12.2. The levels of structure associated with artifacts.

intimate relationship between structure and properties. One property of many silicate crystals is the emission of a dim luminescent glow when heated to a few hundred degrees centigrade. When minerals are bombarded by cosmic or other high-energy radiation, their internal electronic structure is modified. Some electrons are knocked out of their stable positions and become trapped at higher energy sites. It is the release of these electrons to their stable state during heating that results in thermoluminescence. This property resulting from the internal electronic structure is useful for inferring the time passed since the last heating of objects made from or containing appropriate minerals, as Michael S. Tite (Chap. 15 in this volume) discusses. The history of applying this property for dating purposes includes many misapplications resulting from an inadequate appreciation of the structure/property relationship. Understanding internal structure is a necessary prerequisite for understanding an interpretation of artifact properties.

All the levels of structure illustrated in Figure 12.2 are important for artifact interpretation. Our conclusions about human activities associated with artifact design, processing, and use are based on inference. Inferences justified by a single confirmation or a single refutation of a hypothesis are rarely convincing in studying the complexities of human behavior.

Conclusions become much more credible when several disparate lines of confirmation (or refutation) are in accord. Data ranging from the spatial pattern of artifact distribution to the artifact's microstructure, macrostructure, internal crystal and glass structure, atomic structure, and chemical composition provides a variety of evidence (Kingery 1981). Microstructure data combined with trace-element data combined with isotope measurements combined with stylistic analysis combined with spatial patterning leads to credible and convincing conclusions.

In addition to multiple evidences of different sorts, strong inferences are derived from confirmed quantitative deductions that would be wildly improbable standing by themselves, separated from their underlying hypothesis. Quantitative measurements of microstructure, phase structure, atomic structure, and chemical composition can often serve this purpose. Within a range of limits defined by tree-ring calibration, sample formation, and sample collection processes, such is the case for artifact dating based on carbon-14 determinations. This and other methods of sample dating from internal structure have revolutionized the practice of archaeological interpretation. Much structural and property characterization can be done on a quantitative basis and thus provides strong evidence. History has shown, however, that one piece of strong evidence should never be considered conclusive (Polanyi 1962).

The ability of materials science to provide a variety of strong evidences characterizing the internal structure and properties of artifacts made and used by humans is a powerful resource for material culture studies. The most widespread misapplication of materials science has been to rely on only one sort of evidence. This tendency arises quite naturally from the fact that many, perhaps most, materials scientists are specialists in one particular technique. The complexity of human behavior associated with artifacts requires that no one technique, whether stylistic analysis or chemical analysis, be relied on wholly by itself.

REFERENCES

Allen, Ralph O., ed. 1989. *Archaeological Chemistry,* vol. 4. Washington, D.C.: American Chemical Society.
Beck, Curt W. 1974. *Archaeological Chemistry.* Washington, D.C.: American Chemical Society.
Biek, L. 1963. *Archaeology and the Microscope.* London: Butterworth.

Brill, R. H. 1968. *Science in Archaeology*. Cambridge, Mass.: MIT Press.

Brothwell, Don, and Eric Higgs, eds. 1963. *Science in Archaeology*. London: Thames and Hudson.

Brown, Jessica S., ed. 1992. *Art and Archaeology Technical Abstracts*. Marina del Rey, Calif.: Getty Conservation Institute.

Caley, Earle R. 1964. *Analysis of Ancient Metals*. London: Pergamon Press.

England, P. A., and L. van Zelst. 1986. *Applications in Science in Examination of Works of Art*. Boston: Museum of Fine Arts.

Fleming, Stuart. 1976. *Dating in Archaeology*. New York: St. Martin's Press.

Gettens, R. J., and B. M. Usilton. 1955. "Abstracts of Technical Studies in Art and Archaeology." *Gallery of Art Occasional Papers*, vol. 2, no. 2. Washington, D.C.

Hodges, Henry. 1964. *Artifacts*. London: John Baker Publishers.

Jould, Robert F., ed. 1978. *Archaeological Chemistry*, vol. 2. Washington, D.C.: American Chemical Society.

Kempe, D. R. S., and Anthony P. Harvey. 1983. *The Petrology of Archaeological Artifacts*. Oxford: Clarendon Press.

Kingery, W. D. 1981. "Plausible Inferences from Ceramic Artifacts." *Journal of Field Archaeology* 8:457.

———. 1986. "The Development of European Porcelain." In *Ceramics and Civilization*, vol. 3, *High-Technology Ceramics—Past, Present and Future*, edited by W. D. Kingery, 153–80. Westerville, Ohio: American Ceramic Society.

———. 1990. "An Unseen Revolution: The Birth of High-Tech Ceramics." In *Ceramics and Civilization*, vol. 5, *The Changing Roles and Functions of Ceramics in Society*, edited by W. D. Kingery, 293–323. Westerville, Ohio: American Ceramic Society.

Lambert, Joseph B., ed. 1984. *Archaeological Chemistry*, vol. 3. Washington, D.C.: American Chemical Society.

Leute, Ulrich. 1987. *Archaeometry: An Introduction to the Physical Methods in Archaeology and the History of Art*. Weinheim, Germany: VCH.

Levey, Martin, ed. 1967. *Archaeological Chemistry*. Philadelphia: University of Pennsylvania Press.

Libby, Willard F. 1952. *Radiocarbon Dating*. Chicago: University of Chicago Press.

McKeever, S. W. S. 1985. *Thermo Luminescence of Solids*. Cambridge: Cambridge University Press.

Polanyi, M. 1962. *Personal Knowledge*. Chicago: University of Chicago Press.

Sayre, E. V., P. B. Vandiver, J. R. Druzik, and C. Sevenson, eds. 1988. *Materials Issues in Art and Archaeology 1*. Pittsburgh: Materials Research Society.

Taylor, R. E., A. Long, and R. S. Kra, eds. 1992. *Radiocarbon After Four Decades: An Interdisciplinary Perspective*. New York: Springer-Verlag and Radiocarbon.

Tite, Michael S. 1972. *Methods of Physical Examination in Archaeology*. London: Seminar Press.

Vandiver, P. B., J. R. Druzik, and G. S. Wheeler, eds. 1991. *Materials Issues in Art and Archaeology 2*. Pittsburgh: Materials Research Society.

Vandiver, P. B., J. R. Druzik, G. S. Wheeler, and I. C. Freestone, eds. 1992. *Materials Issues in Art and Archaeology 3*. Pittsburgh: Materials Research Society.

Young, W. J., ed. 1966. *An Application of Science in Examination of Works of Art*. Boston: Museum of Fine Arts.

13

Materials Science and Material Culture

W . D A V I D   K I N G E R Y

The focus of materials science is centered on artifact attributes that are but one part of a material culture system consisting of design and production activities creating and realizing a particular object, exchange activities relating to distribution, and use activities correlating function and performance behavior. Properties and performance are connected through feedback loops to materials selection, materials processing, artifact design, and artifact realization. Clearly, materials science is only one component of the intellectual tool kit required for the interpretation of this overall system of human activities, which must be considered in their physical, social, and cultural environment (see Fig. 13.1). Human perceptions, social organization, cultural concerns, and fiscal, educational, regulatory, and other aspects of the environment are important in understanding and interpreting system behavior. The environment changes continually, so that system responses may or may not be effective at any point in time. Artifact production and use are complex activities in which the feedback relationships are usually nonlinear. Often enough, perhaps most of the time, the system will not be in equilibrium.

In his book *The Evolution of Technology*, Basalla (1988) has argued that artifacts and artifactual evolution must be the central focus of any history of technology. This premise is congenial to many materials scientists, with their professional concentration on artifact attributes, but it also is dangerous. In order to be meaningful, material culture must, to warrant the signifier culture, be concerned with human activities,

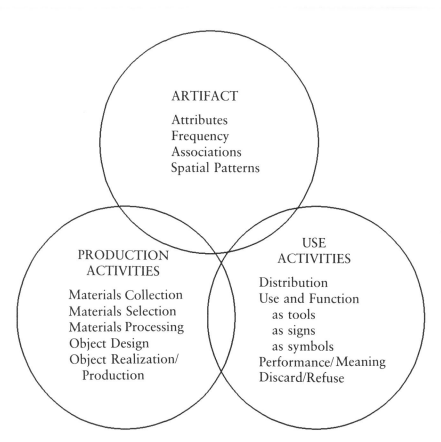

Fig. 13.1. Materials science, concerned with artifact structure and properties, is part of an interconnected system. Feedback from artifact use, performance, and meaning affects design and production to develop new properties.

organization, and behavior. From a behavioral point of view, the importance of artifacts relates to how they participate in, relate to, and inform us about human *activities* (e.g., Schiffer 1992). From an artifact change point of view, the importance of artifacts relates to the lifeways and interactions of the communities that make them, exchange them, and use them. Artifacts, artifact performance, and feedback loops to design and manufacture are social constructs, (e.g., Bijker, Hughes, and Pinch 1989). Finally, artifact use, design, performance, and manufacture are component parts of a larger system in which economics, aesthetics, and learned behavior are equally or more important than artifact structure and properties (e.g., Hughes 1989).

INTERNAL STRUCTURE

During the last few decades the capability and sophistication for characterizing materials, including nondestructive evaluation (Ruud, Bussiere, and Green 1991), has expanded almost beyond comprehension. A recent book on materials characterization lists some 150 acronyms for widely used instruments and methods (Wachtman 1993). These techniques can be characterized broadly as elemental analysis, microstructure analysis, and macrostructure analysis.

Elemental (Atomic) Analysis

In Chapter 12 I mentioned electron distribution in silicates and its use for thermoluminescent age determination. Capabilities for chemical-isotope analysis are increasingly sophisticated. Carbon-14 concentrations are widely used as a method of artifact dating. Carbon-isotope analysis is also applicable to studies of prehistoric diets. Lead-isotope concentrations have long been used for provenance studies. New developments in mass spectroscopy are allowing a wide range of other isotope ratios and trace-element concentrations in parts per billion to be readily determined. These concentration limits are a thousand times smaller than for neutron activation analysis, and a wider range of elements can be measured. A host of other analytical methods are available, many of which are noninvasive and nondestructive. Others require only microscopically small samples for analysis. Some widely available methods are:

Atomic absorption and emission spectroscopy
Electron-induced X-ray emission
Proton-induced X-ray emission
X-ray photoelectron spectroscopy
Auger electron spectroscopy
Electron energy-loss spectroscopy
Mass spectroscopy
Ion-scattering spectroscopy (high and low energy)
Nuclear activation analysis

Nuclear magnetic resonance
Various other chemical techniques

Microstructure Analysis

Solids consist of atoms, ions and molecules arranged in particular crystal-line or glass structures called "phases" in our scientific jargon. There are a variety of methods for identifying and characterizing these phases and their spatial arrangement which is called the microstructure. The arrangement of atoms within a phase and the arrangement of phases within the microstructure is of special interest to the materials scientist because these factors both *determine the properties* of a material and *carry the traces* of the processing and manipulations used during manufacture. From the Paleolithic period onward, humankind has been manipulating these material characteristics to suit many different purposes (Killick 1994). In the last few decades, increasingly powerful techniques and instruments have been developed, many of which are nonintrusive and nondestructive and most of which require only a tiny, often microscopic, sample. Some widely available methods are:

Optical microscope (petrography)
X-ray diffraction
Electron diffraction
Infrared absorption
Raman scattering
Light scattering
Scanning electron microscopy
Transmission electron microscopy
Scanning transmission electron microscopy
Ultrasonic scattering and imaging
Neutron scattering

Macrostructure Analysis

The resolution of the human eye viewing an object at fifteen or twenty centimeters is a bit less than a tenth of a millimeter. Surface structure at that level can be observed easily with a hand glass. Internal structure requires more specialized techniques, which are rapidly improving in capability, availability, and resolution:

X-ray film radiography
Xeroradiography
Fractography
Neutron activation imaging
Ultrasonic scattering and imaging
Magnetic resonance imaging
CAT scans
Infrared imaging
Ultraviolet imaging

PROPERTIES

Material properties are a major factor determining artifact performance. Just as the instruments and techniques for characterizing internal structure have multiplied and become more sophisticated in the past few decades, so with property measurements. Transparency, translucency, opalescence, reflectivity, infrared and ultraviolet absorption, color, hardness, brittleness, ductility, malleability, heat conduction, toughness, strength, elasticity, thermal-shock resistance, abrasion resistance, impact resistance, melting behavior, boiling point, viscosity, electrical and magnetic properties, solubility, vapor pressure, and corrosion behavior are some of the properties that can be quantitatively determined and may be behaviorally significant for material culture studies (e.g., Cotterell and Kamminga 1990).

MATERIALS SCIENCE AND HUMAN ACTIVITIES

Where to begin, where to end? The physical narrative of the life of an artifact begins with materials selection, design, and then realization; it is followed by distribution, use, performance, discard. This part of the story, particularly design and production, has been the focus of what most historians and archaeologists have thought of as "technology." Materials science has much to contribute to our understanding of these activities. The utilitarian, spiritual, emotional, creative, aesthetic narrative of the life of an object flows in the opposite direction. That story begins with use and performance, real or imagined, and only then turns to material selection, design, and realization. Materials science also has much to contribute to our understanding of use and performance. These fundamentally different approaches toward developing interpretations of material culture as a human endeavor have led to substantial differences in methods and theory. Reconciling these different points of view, these different starting points for study, is essential for the development of a holistic field of material culture studies.

ARTIFACT PRODUCTION

Outside of dating, provenance, and conservation studies, the most effective and well-developed application of materials science has been to elucidate the processes actually employed for individual, family, craft, or factory production. There are no written records for preliterate societies and for most historical artifact production. In any event, in written records both observers' and participants' descriptions are often suspect. One example from my own research is the 1897 patent application of Walther Nernst, a leading figure in the development of German chemistry, for his incandescent "Nernst glower" (Kingery 1990). During the latter part of the nineteenth century, Germany was pressing its national development as a modern state and its claim to recognition and a leading role among nations as an influential member of the international community. One aspect of this effort was governmental support of a new kind of research university with a potential for enhancing new industrial production. At the same time, Edison's patents for the carbon-filament electric light bulb were running out, and there was a ferment of investigation and invention of new alternatives. In Nernst's laboratory of physical chemistry, an exciting topic of investigation was ionic conductivity. In 1897 Nernst filed a basic patent application for a solid state incandescent conductor "of the second class," that is, a solid ionic conductor analogous to sulfuric acid, rather than an electronic conductor, such as carbon or metal. For the solid electrolyte, Nernst indicated "such substances as lime, magnesia, zirconia, and other rare earths," giving as his principle example "burnt magnesia," which were to be preheated as shown in Figure 13.2. In fact, as was discovered by those trying to imitate his art, none of these materials works in the arrangement shown. A very special, unique material, an alloy of zirconium oxide with 10–15 percent yttria, is required. This composition (Fig. 13.3) was subsequently disclosed in a patent filed on November 9, 1900, and was incorporated in the practical incandescent

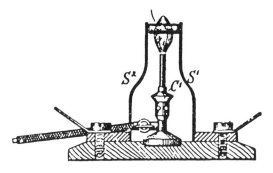

Fig. 13.2. Drawing from Nernst's first patent application showing how the "glower" cylinder was heated with a Bunsen burner. (U.S. Patent No. 653349)

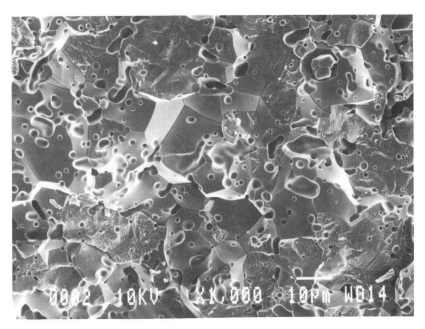

Fig. 13.3. Microstructure of the zirconia-yttria alloy Nernst electrolytic glower from a 1901 lamp. (After Kingery 1990)

lighting device shown in Figure 13.4. The written record obscures, probably intentionally, the essential element of Nernst's invention and has led
to a fair amount of confusion. On the other hand, recent studies of the
composition and structure of medieval glass have shown that "the most
remarkable aspect of the chapters of Theophilus (in his medieval work
on *Diverse Arts*) on glass is just how frequently and in what detail they
prove accurate" (Freestone 1992).

It is difficult for those unfamiliar with the craft to realize how much
a connoisseur of material structure can infer from the structure of objects
as seen under the microscope. Processes ranging from Han dynasty Chinese factory production of bronze objects to Neolithic production of
plasters and individual oil-painting techniques have been inferred from
microstructural and macrostructural analysis. (But beware; many, perhaps most, modern materials scientists are more qualified in chemistry
and physics than in structure and have little firsthand knowledge about
the realities of material manipulation.) With the experience and judgment
necessary to interpret the evidence, Cyril Stanley Smith has pointed out
that for metals,

> microstructures differ more from each other than do the external
> forms—and they instantly reveal to a knowing eye the technical history

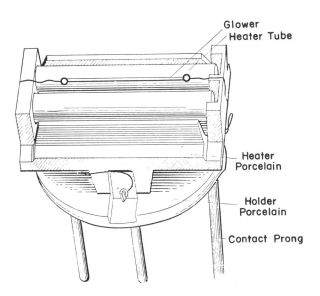

*Fig. 13.4. Heater
and glower configu-
ration of the 1901
Nernst lamp.*

Glower
Heater Tube

Heater
Porcelain

Holder
Porcelain

Contact Prong

of making the object. Such records are in a universal language, and they are free from the distortion that inevitably accompanies passage through a human mind. Through such records, I have communicated with dozens of craftsmen, including a Luristan smith of 800 B.C., a bronze founder of Shang, China, an ancient Greek goldsmith, and a 13th-century Japanese swordsmith; and I have understood them better than I understand some of my English-speaking colleagues of today! This newly found Rosetta Stone is making accessible records of a new world or, more correctly, an unnoticed aspect of culture in the old. As a metallurgist trying to understand the history of his profession, I had exhausted the literary sources without finding evidence of the beginnings of most of the techniques that interested me: only when I moved from libraries to art museums did I find the real origins of metallurgical (and other) techniques, and in doing so my whole view of man, matter and discovery changed. (Smith 1981a)

Curiosity and creativity are among the most basic characteristics of humanness; there is a deep human need to create and have things. Modeling clay, building sand castles, and whittling shapes from wood are part of everyone's experience. Examining the macrostructure and microstructure and feeling the shape and form of an object that has been created at another time and in another place allows one to participate vicariously in and understand the human experience of its creation. Knowledge and experience with materials properties and materials processing allows us to understand the need for a particular set of actions and to recognize the result of that behavior. Creativity and discovery seldom appear in a precise way in the archaeological or historical record. Nevertheless, Smith (1981) has shown in extensive studies of the development of metallurgical processes how the invention of new technologies has almost always been initiated by individual craftsmen playing about with new ways to make things and new things to make. Smith's contentions that "aesthetic curiosity is the very root of all discovery" and that "discovery is art, not logic, and new discoveries have to be cherished for reasons that are far more like love than purpose" (ibid., 351, 347) seem to apply from ancient antiquity to the present. Scientists and artists alike regard their creative activities as more play than work. Based on the traces left in the internal structure of artifacts, our understanding of the discovery and development process is enormously magnified by knowing not only what but also how and why particular methods were developed. One result of this is to enhance our respect for the innate creativity, intelligence, and capability of craftsmen developing complex sophisticated processes without the benefit of modern science. As Smith observed, essentially all of the fundamental techniques of modern metallurgy outside of iron and steel are illustrated in the decorative objects recovered from the third millennium B.C. royal cemetery at Ur. Metals have long been colored for use as jewelry and sculpture. Smith describes this as "an enormous field with a large literature, much of which is worthless. Here more than in most areas an examination of objects in a museum laboratory is more revealing than reading about them in a library" (1981, 339).

For ceramics, all clay-working techniques, including wheel throwing used for clay-based pottery shaping and decoration, were in place by about 3500 B.C. (Kingery and Vandiver 1986). Already in the Song dynasty, without the advantages of modern temperature measurement and analytical chemistry, potters in China were producing exquisite celadon and jun glazes. The latter depend on a process known as spinodal decomposition, the formation of a liquid-liquid emulsion such as oil and vinegar, at high temperatures. Success, which was regularly achieved, depends upon careful control of composition as well as the temperature cycle necessary to produce an internal structure (Fig. 13.5) that gives rise to the "white clouds, blue sky" opalescence much admired by connoisseurs. Even with the results of chemical analysis available, French scientists in the nineteenth century were unsuccessful in reproducing these results. The Song dynasty potters' persistence and ingenuity in achieving these glazes is one more evidence of the importance of aesthetic striving and accomplishment above and beyond utilitarian concerns.

The acceptance and growth of a material development that becomes a component of social behavior involves questions very different from those relating to the discovery process. Innovation has been widely studied and involves interactions between established users, new users, and producers (Schumpeter 1934; Freeman 1986; Scherer 1984; von Hippel 1987). The characteristics and requirements of the production process play an important role in the development and understanding of innovation. During the prepottery Neolithic period in Southwest Asia, one of the most important processed materials was lime plaster, which was used for a variety of applications, particularly for architectural purposes (Mellaart 1975). Lime plaster is formed from limestone, a widely available raw material, by heating it for a long time at a bright red heat. The decomposition of limestone strongly absorbs thermal energy, so that

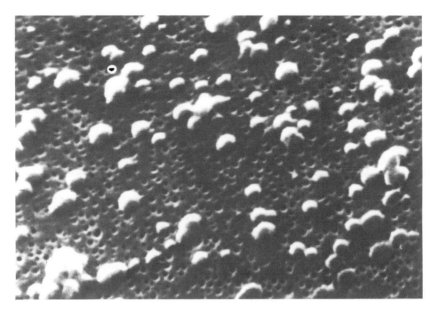

Fig. 13.5. The internal structure of the much-admired Song dynasty opalescent jun glazes consists of a fine-scale emulsion formation (the etched holes) combined with wollastonite precipitation (the white particles). Potters discovered and regularly produced this difficult result on a purely empirical basis.

sustained application of heat is necessary. For transfer of heat to substantial amounts of material, limestone must be calcined in the form of rocks, with sufficient open passages for flames and hot combustion products to pass through. This requires more than two tons of firewood for each ton of lime produced. Two to four days of continuous burning are necessary. Lime plaster is a resource-expensive and labor-expensive commodity. As a result, mortars with a lime plaster binder always include a substantial content of aggregate, which reduces cost and enhances properties. When it is used as a floor or wall material, the mortar is also often burnished with a small stone to apply high pressure at the surface and align the particles in a more dense array, achieving a greater resistance to mechanical damage and water degradation. The installation of lime plaster floors and walls requires skill and a significant labor commitment. These material requirements have had a direct influence on the use of lime plasters within and between sites. Poor village farming communities use little lime plaster; well-to-do towns use substantial amounts. In many large towns, lime plaster is restricted to buildings for ritual use.

For the construction of floors several centimeters thick, a significant amount of plaster is required for each room. We can calculate the amount of plaster used from the amount of aggregate added, the thickness of the floor, and the room area. One room in Neolithic Jericho required four tons of lime plaster with aggregate, necessitating the use of fuel equivalent to eight tons of wood. At another large residential site in Israel, seven tons of mortar (rather low in plaster binder) were incorporated in the floor of a large residential building (Garfinkel 1987). For cost effectiveness, a substantial amount of inert ingredients were mixed with the plaster. For construction purposes there are a variety of individual plaster formulations, which range from mostly limey clay with only 10 or 15 percent plaster to compositions in which the additive is finely ground white quartz or white limestone (for a more luxurious surface). In some special Neolithic buildings, there are floors that were abrasively polished to produce a smooth, often decorated surface with multicolored images. Thus, what at first appears to be a rather uninteresting, uninformative material in the archaeological record is found to have rich processing and compositional variability, satisfying a range of human needs (Gourdin and Kingery 1975; Kingery, Vandiver, and Prickett 1988).

In the Neolithic period the distribution of obsidian and sea shells at interior sites demonstrates a substantial trade interaction over wide areas. The distribution of plaster manufacture (Fig. 13.6) also illustrates a strong degree of interaction and widespread transfer of technology. Technology transfer is quite different from trade interactions. The passage of a skill from one place to another requires exchanges of workers familiar with the production and use of plaster. As with other skilled crafts, much of the necessary knowledge is tacit and can only be learned by seeing and doing rather than through written or verbal description. The existence of this wide range of technology over an area of hundreds of miles indicates that there was much more than trade interaction between inhabitants. Movement and exchange of individuals between different living groups is indicated. It is perhaps worth noting that the area in which lime plaster is predominant in the prepottery Neolithic later becomes the area in which a particular pottery (Amuq A) is found.

'Ain Ghazal is a prepottery Neolithic site in Jordan that was occupied for several centuries beginning about 7250 B.C. and then abandoned

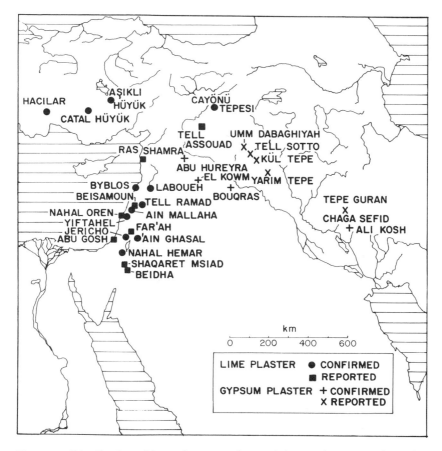

Fig. 13.6. Distribution of lime plasters in the Neolithic Mediterranean littoral.

about 5450 B.C. Why was 'Ain Ghazal abandoned? There is no evidence that abandonment was a result of warfare, and a climatic hypothesis seems untenable. It is known that the village is one in which goat herding was a major source of subsistence; also, there was extensive use of plaster. The site's earliest buildings had large post-and-beam construction and relatively large rooms. Over a period of time, the posts and beams and rooms all became smaller. Toward the latter stages of occupation, stone walls and even smaller rooms became common. Gary Rollefson (1991) has quantitatively measured the amount of mortar used and then estimated the amount of forest that would have had to be cleared to produce the required firewood. He calculates that over the time of occupation of the village, some 3,170 hectares, a circle of forest having a diameter of about 3.2 kilometers, may have been needed, an estimate that may be off by a factor of two. If one assumes that the goat population prevented reforestation, as has happened in many areas of the Near East over the last millennia, this deforestation would have created significant environmental pressure on daily life in 'Ain Ghazal. Rollefson suggests that the abandonment of 'Ain Ghazal may have been an early example of environmental degradation and ecological pressures resulting from compulsive use of a particular materials technology. We know that the deforestation of Attica for silver production in the Laurian mines was so severe that it required wood to be imported from Macedonia. Deforestation in England for iron and glass production in the sixteenth century required royal decrees forbidding such materials processing technologies. In our own time, we have seen the environmental effects of acid rain, holes in the ozone, and widespread smog as a result of our current materials processing technologies. Archaeology shows that humans have been destroying their resource base for millennia; environmental damage is not a new phenomenon (Diamond 1993). Behavioral aspects of historic and prehistoric patterns of ecological damage resulting from materials processing have not been as thoroughly investigated as one might hope.

Artifacts are created within families, communities, factories, or other social organizations. The methods and arrangements for production that can be inferred from internal structure and properties are an essential ingredient for studying this aspect of social organization (e.g., Costin 1991). The material culture record, properly interpreted, can lead to some understanding of manufacturing arrangements. Studies of craft specialization and the organization of factories and manufacturing systems must be built on a clear perception of the actual processes being employed. One exciting result of artifact study is the determination that there was factory organization for the manufacture of decorative bronze vessels during the Chou dynasty in fifth century B.C. China (Keyser 1979; Bagley 1993). Chinese bronze vessels are covered with repetitive decorations. The manufacturing process required great skill not only with metal casting but also with clay-mold making. The model for a vessel was the same size and shape of the finished vessel but was smooth, with no decoration. Clay was packed around this model and then opened vertically and removed from the model, forming an undecorated two-piece mold. The mold maker applied decoration, which was produced from "pattern blocks," to the interior of the mold. The clay pattern blocks had a positive design carved on their surface and were fired. A negative mold section was made from the pattern block with wet clay and then transferred to the interior of the blank mold. In this way, a complete pattern was built from repetitive impressions. The pattern blocks could be used for more than one part of the vessel pattern and also for more than one vessel.

The particular advantage of the pattern-block method of processing is that it allows what would otherwise be a long and exacting process—a single master craftsman carving a decorated model—to be divided among workers. The most skilled work, carving the pattern block, is done only once. One can infer from the process itself that a bronze casting was produced in a factory operation in which there was effective division of labor. Metal casting lends itself to this sort of division (Franklin 1983). There are inscriptions from the Han dynasty (200 B.C.–A.D. 200) describing the specialist workers who participated in the factory production of objects. The material culture evidence of the mold-manufacturing process five centuries earlier indicates that this factory manufacture with specialized labor has a long history of development.

As the examples illustrate, methods of materials processing and manufacture both reflect and affect human behavior and social organization. The macrostructural and microstructural attributes of artifacts provide what Cyril Stanley Smith referred to as a "Rosetta stone" for characterizing these processes and interpreting how they fit into the larger context of human development.

ARTIFACT USE AND PERFORMANCE

Artifacts are purposeful creations. The maker has some image, usually but not always correct, as to its function and how it will be used. His perceptions of its effectiveness, derived from customers and users, infect him with pride, satisfaction, happiness, and despair—and affect subsequent generations of production. The efficiency of the feedback process, the level of conservatism and complexity of the production process, and the ease or feasibility of modification will affect the rate of change, but not, I think, the fact of change. The relationships of consumer (peasant, trader, prince, housewife, wholesaler, art critic, government, corporation, pope) and producer (housewife, craftsman, artist, court retainer, government, small factory, large corporation) will clearly have an influence on both the speed and strength of the feedback process. Analysis of this process is not my aim; rather, I want to insist on the central role of customer perceptions about performance effectiveness in determining artifact design and manufacture.

But what about the internal dynamics of engineering design and production, the innate creativity of individual artists and craftspersons? What about Van Gogh, who never sold a painting in his entire life? Yes, often enough the artist, engineer, or craftsperson is his or her own most important customer, providing a critical evaluation of performance effectiveness in gauging the level of accomplishment. It seems to be a universal, or at least widespread, human characteristic to strive for success, to find satisfaction in accomplishment (Csikszentmihalyi 1990). Village potters in the Philippines recognize one another's work in a collection of cooking pots and have a keen sense of the quality of one another's product (Longacre 1993). The shortest feedback loop is when the producer and the consumer are the same person.

Effective performance of the potter, artist and engineer alike must be measured with regard to what Polanyi (1962) has termed the *operational principle* of an artifact, whether tool or sign. The most fundamental knowledge about an artifact is how its parts function together to achieve a particular purpose, something that is rarely obvious from the artifact standing by itself. There is almost always tacit knowledge embodied in artifacts, and it is not easy to interpret the function and use of a complex construction without culture-specific knowledge or specific instruction. Archaeologists well know how difficult it is to infer the use and function of a surprising and unknown shape or configuration. The excavators who unearthed the pattern blocks for the Chinese bronze vessels mentioned above were unable to explain their use or function (Bagley 1993). Vincenti has described this idea, essentially, "how it works," as the first notion of the engineer's Fundamental Design Concept, an idea that applies to both artists and artisans. A second fundamental notion of craftsperson, artist, and engineer is the idea of "normal" configuration, that which identifies an object as a painting, frying pan, airplane. How an object looks. Finally, there are the specifications, traditional tools, mental templates, intellectual kits, and standard methods of using these that permit and limit the process of design and manufacture (Vincenti 1990).

Recognizing the operational principal as a tool or sign or both, the user of an artifact judges the effectiveness of its performance. Here use is defined as the specific method and purpose of artifact employment. A person drives a Mercedes convertible back and forth to work, takes the top down, and drives to and parks at a tennis club to create a particular image with friends and acquaintances. The function of the car is both for utilitarian transportation and as a social signifier—both tool and sign. Some archaeologists have separated the social and ideological functions of the artifact as sign from its functions as a tool, that is, an object is described as having technofunction, sociofunction, ideofunction. In ceramics, Matson (1965) was a pioneer in advocating that we focus on how pottery was *made* and *used* rather than on reconstructing cultural and historical stories. Almost without exception, artifacts serve both utilitarian and social/ideological functions; they are both tools and signs. This is the underlying reason for the vision of some art historians that all objects, no matter how utilitarian and functional, must be considered art. All are signs!

The consumer is rarely familiar with the details of the internal structure, design process, or specific methods of manufacture. His or her perceptions arrive from performance characteristics as experienced in artifact use. Does the Mercedes convertible get its owner back and forth reliably, comfortably, economically? Does it evoke admiration, recognition, envy? Performance effectiveness depends on a wide variety of factors. Among many, the one that falls into the realm of materials science is the influence of material properties. Amongst the most obvious properties affecting a material performance through history are the shining luster, the ductility and easy workability, the corrosion resistance, and the rarity of gold, which have made it a material of choice for jewelry, adornment, and vessels that universally function as symbols of wealth, power, and prestige. Flint and obsidian are unusual, perfectly brittle, hard materials with conchoidal fracture that allows them to be formed into sharp points, sharp-edged scrapers, and knives that perform effectively. They have been used everywhere for these functions.

Everything has to be made of something, and a material's properties are basic to product performance, as materials scientists, engineers, and artists (who are well acquainted with the different techniques required and results obtained with fresco, tempera, oil, acrylic and other media) know well. We enshrine this idea in the story of *Goldilocks and the Three Bears,* as we teach small children to test soup, beds, and chairs for heat, hardness, and size as well as for their suitability to different kinds of people. As Friedel (1993) points out, the *value* attached to a particular material is one of cultural perception. In the case of cooking pots, functional concerns such as abrasion resistance, thermal-shock resistance, rate of heating, toughness and fracture resistance, and ease of cleaning are characteristics in which the feedback from performance effectiveness to materials selection has been effective (Schiffer 1992; Schiffer and Skibo 1987). But Kalinga villagers in the Philippines use metal cooking pots bought outside the village alongside traditional clay cooking pots made by village potters. One type is preferred for meat dishes, another for rice (Longacre 1981). We see a similar range of choices in materials available for modern American kitchen utensils.

The preeminence of gold and silver as materials signifying value, wealth and prestige has led to many efforts aimed at replication and imitation. There has been widespread use of super-thin gold foil and amalgam gilding to form superficial layers. In both western Europe and Peru, gold-copper and gold-silver alloys were acid-etched to remove the copper or silver from a thin surface layer that was then burnished or sintered to close the pores, a process called "depletion gilding" (Lechtman 1973). Silver has been enriched on the surface of silver-copper alloys by oxidizing the alloy, then removing, with an acid treatment, the copper scale that forms. As early as the third millennium B.C., copper and arsenic vapor were used to form a silvery coating of Cu_3As (Smith 1981). In the nineteenth century, one of the first commercial applications of electricity was for electroplating to make silver-surfaced objects available to a large consumer market (Smith 1981, 328).

For much of history, hard, sonorous, translucent white porcelain imported to western Asia and Europe from China, and then Japan, was the social equivalent of silver, perhaps even gold (Kingery and Vandiver 1986). Craftsmen and alchemists in various Persian and European royal courts made extensive efforts at reproducing this material. During the late fifteenth century, Italian narrative-painted maiolica combined the strong figurative pictorial art tradition of Italy with Moorish white-glazed ware to develop what came to be called faience or delftware. For more than two centuries maiolica was the premier European ceramic (Kingery 1993). The explosive growth of the maiolica industry came at a time of emerging capitalism and the beginnings of a consumer society in which "things" were becoming important to many (Goldthwaite 1987, 1989). The porcelainlike but indigenous European characteristics of maiolica made for its successful use as objects for both use and decorative display. The display and use of these objects gave a clear signal of participation in the new urban culture in which splendor was a virtue and luxury a respected achievement. Two hundred years later, the development of soft-paste porcelain in France and hard-paste porcelain in Saxony followed a similar course (Kingery 1986). Development of European ceramic decorative arts must be seen as the result of the confluence of material properties and the growth of capitalism, consumerism, and mercantilist national policies.

The role of effective utilitarian performance on the technological development of pottery cooking pots, flint/obsidian points and blades, and many other artifacts is very clear (Braun 1983; Skibo 1992). The role of effective symbolic performance of gold and porcelain as symbols leading to a range of new replications and imitative design and manufacturing technologies is equally clear. These paradigms illustrate the way in which material properties affect perceptions of artifact performance as tools and as signs. Recognition that all objects, even the most utilitarian, are also art objects in which aesthetic and symbolic elements enter into design and realization should sensitize us to the intermingled nature of art and technique. The Roman architectural revolution in which large covered areas became a characteristic feature of urban architecture is inseparable from the use of new Pozzolonic-cement building materials and associated building methods (Lechtman and Hobbs 1986). The extensive art history of *istoriato* maiolica ware encompassed a period of revolutionary change in the potter's craft. Cipriano Piccolpasso devoted almost half of his 1557 treatise *Three Books of the Potter's Art* to new pigment and glaze technology. As Cyril Smith has pointed out, armor production has everywhere focused on the development of tough strong materials. Armor's life-protecting function has always led its owners to recognize and signify its importance with decorative design and materials manipulation seemingly all out of proportion to its rough usage (Smith 1981). Although the roles of material properties and material manipulation working in combination to develop effective utilitarian performance in concert with aesthetic, symbolic, and ideological function is most obvious with the decorative arts, it is a characteristic universal to all material culture.

In materials choice and materials manipulation, aesthetics and technique are equally important. It is one positive aspect of the focus of materials science on both the internal structure and the properties of materials—which must be read in context with all the other levels of structure (which are outwardly more visible and equally or more important). The intertwining of art and technique in all levels of structure is an important constituent of material culture studies. Separation of aesthetics from technique, of tools from signs, of technofunction from sociofunction is an artificial construct of scholars searching for a reductionist mode of analysis.

In the study of material culture and the feedback loops from performance effectiveness to changes in artifact production, it is always important to know what the artifacts mean to the people who make them and use them (Maquet 1986, 1993). By contributing to our understanding of how artifacts are made and how artifacts are used, materials science contributes most strongly to the analysis of objects as tools, objects as instruments. The behavioral activities inferred are effective in locating an artifact in context but are limited in helping to comprehend an artifact's culture-specific meaning and semiotic functions. The same objects are viewed very differently by different audiences (e.g., Rawson 1993). By their similarity to other objects, as symbols and as signs for metonyms, artifacts have visual functions that cannot be fully understood without culture-specific information, which must be derived from the spoken or written record or from ethnographic analogy.

SUMMARY

Materials science contributes to material culture studies most directly through dating, provenance, and artifact conservation. The level of artifact structure that materials science is unique in exploiting for material culture studies is the internal structure. Inferences about human behavior and social organization that materials science has been most effective in helping to imagine and test are related to materials selection, artifact design, and artifact production. Material properties are critical factors for artifact use and performance and therefore determine materials selection, design, and realization. The way human behavior, culture, and social organization affect perceptions about material properties and the performance effectiveness of artifacts as tools and as signs is central to materials science studies of material culture and needs to be actively pursued as an aid to understanding the history and prehistory of culture, society, and technology.

REFERENCES

Bagley, Robert W. 1993. "Replication Techniques in Eastern Zhou Bronze Casting." In *History from Things: Essays on Material Culture,* edited by Steven Lubar and W. David Kingery, 231–41. Washington, D.C.: Smithsonian Institution Press.

Basalla, G. 1988. *The Evolution of Technology.* Cambridge: Cambridge University Press.

Bijker, Wiebe E., Thomas P. Hughes, and Trevor J. Pinch, eds. 1989. *The Social Construction of Technological Systems: New Directions in the Sociology and History of Technology.* Cambridge, Mass.: MIT Press.

Braun, David P. 1983. "Pots as Tools." In *Archaeological Hammers and Theories,* edited by James A. Move and Arthur S. Keene, 108. New York: Academic Press.

Costin, C. L. 1991. "Craft Specialization: Issues in Defining, Documenting and Explaining the Organization of Production." In *Archaeological Method and Theory,* vol. 3, edited by Michael B. Schiffer, 1–56. Tucson: University of Arizona Press.

Cotterell, Brian, and Johan Kamminga. 1990. *Mechanics of Pre-Industrial Technology.* Cambridge: Cambridge University Press.

Csikszentmihalyi, Mihaly. 1990. *Flow.* New York: Harper and Row.

Diamond, Jared M. 1993. "Sociological Collapses of Ancient Civilizations: The Golden Age that Never Was." Stated Meeting Report, American Academy of Arts and Sciences, San Diego, October 1, 1993.

Franklin, Ursala. 1983. "On Bronze and Other Metals in Early China." In *The Origins of Chinese Civilization,* edited by David Keightly, 279–96. Berkeley and Los Angeles: University of California Press.

Freeman, C. 1986. "Technical Innovation, Diffusion, and Long Cycles of Economic Development." *Bridge* 16 (3): 5–9.

Freestone, Ian C. 1992. "Theophilus and the Composition of Medieval Glass." In *Materials Issues in Art and Archaeology 3,* edited by Pamela B. Vandiver, James R. Druzik, George S. Wheeler, and Ian C. Freestone, 739–45. Pittsburgh: Materials Research Society.

Friedel, Robert. 1993. "Some Matters of Substance." In *History from Things: Essays on Material Culture,* edited by Steven Lubar and W. David Kingery, 41–50. Washington, D.C.: Smithsonian Institution Press.

Garfinkel, Y. 1987. "Burnt Lime Products and the Social Implications in the Pre-Pottery B Villages of the Near East." *Paleorient* 31 (1): 69–75.

Goldthwaite, Richard A. 1987. "The Empire of Things: Consumer Demand in Renaissance Italy." In *Patronage, Art, and Society in Renaissance Italy,* edited by F. W. Kent and Patricia Simons with J. C. Eade, 155–75. Oxford: Oxford University Press.

———. 1989. "The Economic and Social World of Italian Renaissance Maiolica." *Renaissance Quarterly* 42:1–32.

Gourdin, W. H., and W. D. Kingery. 1975. "The Beginning of Pyrotechnology: Neolithic and Egyptian Lime Plaster." *Journal of Field Archaeology* 2:133–50.

Hughes, Thomas P. 1989. *American Genesis.* New York: Viking Press.

Keyser, Barbara. 1979. "Decor Replication in Two Late Chou Bronze Chein." *Ars Orientalis* 11:127–62.

Kingery, W. D. 1986. "The Development of European Porcelain." In *Ceramics and Civilization,* vol. 3, *High-Technology Ceramics—Past, Present, and Future,* edited by W. D. Kingery, 153–80. Westerville, Ohio: American Ceramic Society.

———. 1990. "An Unseen Revolution: The Birth of High-Tech Ceramics." In *Ceramics and Civilization,* vol. 5, *The Changing Roles and Functions of Ceramics in Society,* edited by W. D. Kingery, 293–323. Westerville, Ohio: American Ceramic Society.

———. 1993. "Painterly Maiolica of the Italian Renaissance." *Technology and Culture* 34 (January): 28–47.

Kingery, W. D., and P. B. Vandiver. 1986. *Ceramic Masterpieces.* New York: Free Press.

Kingery, W. D., P. B. Vandiver, and M. Prickett. 1988. "The Beginnings of Pyrotechnology Part II: Production and Use of Lime and Gypsum Plaster in the Pre-Pottery Neolithic Near East." *Journal of Field Archaeology* 15:219–44.

Lechtman, Heather. 1973. "Gilding of Metals in Pre-Columbian Peru." In *Applications of Science in the Examination of Works of Art,* edited by W. J. Young, 38–52. Boston: Boston Museum of Art.

Lechtman, H. N., and L. W. Hobbs. 1986. "Roman Concrete and the Roman Architectural Revolution." In *Ceramics and Civilization,* vol. 3, *High-Technology Ceramics—Past, Present, and Future,* edited by W. D. Kingery, 81–128. Westerville, Ohio: American Ceramic Society.

Longacre, William A. 1981. "Kalinga Pottery: An Ethnoarchaeological Study." In *Patterns of the Past: Studies in Honor of David Clark,* edited by I. Hodder, G. Isaac, and N. Hammond, 49–66. London: Cambridge University Press.

———. 1993. Personal communication.

Maquet, Jacques. 1986. *The Aesthetic Experience: An Anthropologist Looks at the Visual Arts.* New Haven, Conn.: Yale University Press.

———. 1993. "Objects as Instruments, Objects as Signs." In *History from Things: Essays on Material Culture,* edited by Steven Lubar and W. David Kingery, 30–40. Washington, D.C.: Smithsonian Institution Press.

Matson, Frederick R. 1965. "Ceramic Ecology: An Approach to the Study of

Early Cultures of the Near East." In *Ceramics and Man,* edited by F. R. Matson. Chicago: Aldine.

Mellaart, James. 1975. *The Neolithic of the Near East.* London: Thames and Hudson.

Piccolpasso, Cipriano. [1557] 1980. *Three Books of the Potter's Art.* 2 vols. Translated and edited by Ronald Lightbown and Alan Craiger-Smith. London: Scolar Press.

Polanyi, M. 1962. *Personal Knowledge.* Chicago: University of Chicago Press.

Rapp, George, Jr., and John A. Gifford, eds. 1985. *Archaeological Geology.* New Haven, Conn.: Yale University Press.

Rawson, J. 1993. "The Ancestry of Chinese Bronze Vessels." In *History from Things: Essays on Material Culture,* edited by Steven Lubar and W. David Kingery, 51–73. Washington, D.C.: Smithsonian Institution Press.

Rollefson, Gary O. 1991. "The Critical Role of Technological Analysis for Prehistoric Anthropological Inference." In *Materials Issues in Art and Archaeology 2,* edited by Pamela B. Vandiver, James R. Druzik, George S. Wheeler, and Ian C. Freestone, 365–74. Pittsburgh: Materials Research Society.

Ruud, Clayton O., Jean F. Bussiere, and Robert E. Green Jr., eds. 1991. *Nondestructive Characterization of Materials,* vol. 4. New York: Plenum Press.

Scherer, F. M. 1984. *Innovation and Growth.* Cambridge, Mass.: MIT Press.

Schiffer, Michael B. 1992. *Technological Perspectives on Behavioral Change.* Tucson: University of Arizona Press.

Schiffer, Michael B., and James M. Skibo. 1987. "Theory and Experiment in the Study of Technological Change." *Current Anthropology* 28:595–622.

Schumpter, J. A. 1934. *The Theory of Economic Development.* Translated by Redvers Opie. Cambridge: Harvard University Press.

Skibo, James N. 1992. *Pottery Function.* New York: Plenum Press.

Smith, Cyril S. 1981. *A Search for Structure.* Cambridge, Mass.: MIT Press.

Vincenti, Walter G. 1990. *What Engineers Know and How They Know It.* Baltimore: Johns Hopkins University Press.

von Hipple, Eric. 1987. "The Sources of Innovation." In *Ceramics and Civilization,* vol. 3, *High-Technology Ceramics—Past, Present, and Future,* edited by W. D. Kingery, 125ff. Westerville, Ohio: American Ceramic Society.

Wachtman, John. 1993. *Characterization of Materials.* Stoneham, Mass.: Butterworth-Heinemann.

14

Optical and Electron Microscopy in Material Culture Studies

DAVID KILLICK

Contributors to this volume believe that the examination of manufactured objects can tell us much about the abilities and beliefs of their makers, and about the social context within which they were made. In other words, we hold that material objects are as much historical documents as anything written on paper. Historians may object that material objects are but a palimpsest of past social systems and that the material record can never compare to the richness of the written, and although we should be careful not to overstate our ability to extract meaning from things, we may counter that in some realms of the past much more can be read from the material than from the written record. This is obviously and trivially true for the vast span of prehistory, but it is equally true that even where written records are abundant, they may say little about some fundamentally important realms of human experience. Most of what we can ever know about these areas of the past is encoded in artifacts, and we must learn to read the message that they provide if we wish to understand these aspects of past lives.

The technological realm of human experience is particularly poorly recorded in writing. Compare, for example, the wealth of extant Greek and Roman writings in the fields of drama, philosophy, mathematics, science, and history with the lack of written records of technology. Most of our present knowledge of Greek and Roman technology derives not from documents but from the examination of material objects such as standing ruins, painting and sculpture, and finds recovered by archaeological excavation (White 1982). The inadequacy of the Greek written record on technology is perhaps most vividly illustrated by the recent discovery and reconstruction of the Antikythera mechanism (Price 1974), a complex analog computer of the first century B.C. that incorporates the earliest known differential gearing, which was used to model the relative motions of the major planets and stars. Its discovery came as a major surprise, for nothing in the written record suggests so advanced a knowledge of mechanical engineering in Greek times.

The Greek literate classes' apparent disdain for technology has been much discussed (e.g., Finley 1985; White 1982). The paucity of Greek writings in this area certainly stands in marked contrast to the wealth of documents on technology from the Han and subsequent dynasties in China, or to that for Islamic societies between the ninth and fourteenth centuries. Yet even where written records of technology exist, they are often difficult to interpret. This applies as much to the literature on technology in Europe before the late nineteenth century as to earlier Chinese and Islamic writings, and is particularly true of the chemical industry and the pyrotechnologies (pottery, glazes, glass making, metallurgy, etc.).

This problem reflects the facts that (1) the artisans themselves were almost invariably illiterate, and (2) those who produced written accounts had (with rare exceptions, such as Vitruvius and Biringuccio) no hands-on experience of the technology they were describing. A lack of direct experience was not much of a handicap in writing about water mills or mining technology, in which all aspects of the system were accessible to inspection with the unaided eye. But nonparticipant observation was of little use in understanding chemical processes and pyrotechnologies, in which the mechanisms were at a molecular scale and control of the processes depended upon the interpretation of colors, sounds, smells, and tactile clues. These are not sensations that could be described precisely in words, so artisans learned their analytical skills by working closely with an experienced master. We should not, therefore, be surprised by the inadequacy of written descriptions of these processes; only with the development of instruments for measuring temperature, viscosity, chemical composition, and the like could they be specified in writing.

How can we know what levels of technical knowledge and skill were current in preindustrial societies? Only by supplementing written records (where they exist) with the study of material remains of those technologies. There are three components to the study of material evidence: (1) the recovery of authentic, well-dated material remains in museums, private collections, or archaeological excavations; (2) the study of the remains with the tools and principles of modern science and engineering; and (3) experimental replication and testing of the object or process.

The balance between these three lines of inquiry will vary with the technology under investigation. If one wants to know how far a Roman catapult could hurl a projectile of a given weight, the appropriate strategy is clearly to build and test a full-scale replica, using documents and archaeological evidence for the design and for the selection of appropriate materials (e.g., Landels 1978, 107–32). A somewhat different emphasis is required to deduce how a object of metal, glass, or ceramic was made. In this case the first order of business is to study authentic remains by microscopy, chemical analysis, and the other tools of materials science and allied disciplines. The structure and composition revealed by these analyses may then be used to infer what raw materials were used and the conditions (of temperature, furnace atmosphere, etc.) under which they were processed (Kingery 1987). Such inferences are made by relating the observed properties of the object to those produced under known conditions in the laboratory. The relationships among process, structure, and composition may often be found in the scientific and industrial literature; if not, they must be obtained by experiment. The experimental conditions are adjusted until the microstructure and composition of the experimental products match those of the authentic object. With this information in hand, one may then return to the written descriptions or to the archaeological report and try to reconstruct the sequence of actions whose result was the artifact under study (e.g., McGovern 1989; Gordon and Killick 1991; Kingery and Vandiver 1986a).

Microscopy is of crucial importance in this type of study, and it is with the uses of microscopy in material culture studies that the remainder of this chapter is concerned. I shall concentrate upon what the examination of objects under the microscope can tell us about their makers, beginning with features that are barely beyond the resolution of the unaided eye and passing through increasingly greater levels of magnification to techniques that are capable of resolving individual atoms. My focus is not on the techniques themselves, but on what microscopy can tell us about the people who made the objects under study.

WHAT CAN MICROSCOPY REVEAL
ABOUT HUMAN BEHAVIOR?

At the level of the individual artifact, microscopy may reveal (1) of what materials it was made, (2) how it was made, and (3) how it was used. It may also reveal whether the artifact is authentic or a fake, and in some cases it may indicate where the artifact was made, or at least from which region the raw materials were obtained. Microscopy is the primary tool used to identify organic materials that have a cellular structure, such as fibers, wood, and basketry, and inorganic materials, such as the rocks and minerals used in sculpture, jewelry, and construction. Where inorganic materials have been substantially transformed by heat, as in the case of ceramics, glasses, and smelted metals, one must know both the microstructure and the chemical composition to reconstruct the technology. In these cases microscopy must be complemented by chemical analysis. In some cases physical techniques such as X-ray diffraction (XRD) and differential thermal analysis (DTA) also need to be enlisted. Microscopy is not very useful in the study of organic materials that lack a cellular structure (e.g., resins and plastics); here physical and chemical techniques of analysis are more informative.

Where objects have been shaped by grinding, cutting, or deforming them, close examination of the surface may reveal what tools were used in their manufacture and in which sequence they were applied. Wire that has been drawn through a die, for example, is easily distinguished from wire made by other means by the presence of continuous scratches parallel to the length of the wire (produced by contact with small burrs on the walls of the die). Where materials have been partially or wholly transformed by heat, inspection of the surface should be complemented by examination of a sample of the interior, removed by drilling or sawing, and also by chemical analysis. In combination, these three approaches can show what raw materials were used, how they were processed, the temperature to which they were heated, the approximate atmosphere (reducing or oxidizing) inside the kiln or furnace, and any subsequent treatment (cold forging, heat treatment, etc.). When considered together, these findings allow us to infer what the artisan knew about the properties of the material and how well he or she employed such knowledge to satisfy a particular task or need.

The use to which a tool was put may often be inferred from the use wear (surface damage) inflicted on the tool by contact with the material worked, or from residues of the worked material on or in it (e.g., charred food in cooking pots). (In Chapter 15 of this volume, Michael Tite gives some examples of use wear.) Microscopy is the primary technique for examination of use wear, and chemical or physical analysis is usually required for the identification of residues.

The evidence gleaned from examination under the microscope contributes to assessment of the knowledge and skill of the person or persons who made the artifact—in Marxist terminology, their labor power. Such assessments are relative rather than absolute. They are made by comparison to the work of other contemporary artists or artisans, to those of preceding and succeeding periods, and to the standards attainable today with the same materials.

Microscopy is therefore an essential tool in documenting the growth of human knowledge about the material world, and of the ingenuity of humans in manipulating natural resources to satisfy their desires for sustenance, shelter, security, and aesthetic satisfaction. Two examples of innovations that were detected by microscopy are the beginning of the use of wool for textiles in the fourth millennium B.C. (Barber 1990) and the development of new pigments, stable at high temperature, that made possible the delicately painted majolica ceramics of the Italian Renaissance (Kingery 1993). Microscopy was also central to Heather Lechtman's elegant demonstration that the thin gold surfaces on some Moche metal artifacts of the first millennium A.D. were produced by passive electroplating (Lechtman 1979)—but one of a number of discoveries, all stemming from the systematic application of microscopy to material objects, that have completely transformed our understanding of the technical abilities of early South American metallurgists (Lechtman 1989).

Microscopy also plays a role in tracing the diffusion of technical knowledge, or the lack of it. It is very striking, for example, that the practice of hardening steel by quenching and tempering, which is easily detected by microscopy, appears not to have been widely adopted in sub-Saharan Africa. This was certainly not for lack of hardenable steel, which Africans produced in abundance (Killick 1995). Quenching and tempering were employed in all other regions of the Old World where steel was produced, but the technology appears not to have been transferred to Africa.

On a larger scale, the evidence obtained by microscopy may be of value in addressing issues of social organization and political structure.

One current issue in archaeology is that of the emergence of specialization in production, and of the relationship of specialization to political stratification. Was the development of craft specialization a catalyst for political stratification, as Gordon Childe (1942) argued in *What Happened in History*? Or was craft specialization a consequence of the development of political and social hierarchy? Or is there no relationship between the two?

How, in any case, can one infer the former existence of craft specialists from the archaeological record? Examination of the structures, workshops, and tools revealed by excavation is obviously the first line of attack, but much can also be learned by studying the products and discards of the process. One potential indicator of craft specialization is standardization of the product (Costin 1991). In the case of prehistoric pottery, standardization has been sought in the dimensions of the vessels, and microscopy and chemical analysis have been employed to measure standardization in technological parameters such as the firing temperature and the amount and composition of added temper (e.g., Blackman, Stein, and Vandiver 1993).

THE HIERARCHY OF STRUCTURES

The interpretation of the microscopic internal structure (microstructure) of materials is a specialized skill. For this reason, microstructural studies of prehistoric or historic artifacts are usually conducted by materials scientists or geologists at the request of social scientists, conservators, or art historians. If neither side fully understands the aims and objectives of the other (i.e., where the study is multidisciplinary rather than interdisciplinary), the potential for major errors of interpretation exists.

In the case of microscopy, the most common mistake is for the scientist to examine too small a sample of the material: the report generated by the microscopist may be an accurate interpretation of the sample, but if the sample is not representative, the interpretation may be highly misleading. Perhaps the most blatant example of such an error is the much-publicized claim of Joseph Davidovits, a noted French cement chemist, that the pyramids of the Giza plateau were constructed by casting blocks of zeolitic concrete in situ (Davidovits and Morris 1988). This claim, based upon the microscopic examination of a few small samples, is easily refuted, as Folk and Campbell (1992) show, when the blocks of the pyramid are examined with the unaided eye. At this scale it is easy to see the bedding planes, joints, fractures, fossils, and other features that show that the blocks were cut from limestone, a sedimentary rock. The samples examined by Davidovits may indeed be zeolitic cement, as he claims, but are clearly not representative of the pyramids at large and thus do not help us to understand how they were constructed.

Although this is an extreme example, errors of this type are quite common. A more subtle case is the current debate over the environmental effects of lime plaster in the Neolithic of the Near East (c. 9000–7000 B.C.). Kingery, Vandiver, and Prickett (1988) were the first to call attention to the possible implications of the widespread use of lime plaster in architecture during the Neolithic. They noted that the burning of limestone to produce lime requires a large input of energy, which at that time could only have come from the burning of wood. This insight has been misapplied by some archaeologists. For example, Rollefson (1991) measured the volume of plaster at the Neolithic site of 'Ain Ghazal in Jordan, calculated the amount of timber required to make that volume of lime plaster, and concluded that lime burning would have resulted in deforestation of the surrounding region. This conclusion rests on the unproven assumption that all plaster floors at this site are composed entirely of burnt lime. Goren and Goldberg (1991) have subsequently studied large samples of Neolithic "lime plaster" from many sites in Israel by low-power microscopy and have found that these include a wide variety of materials, including dung, soil, stones, and crushed but unburned limestone. The proportion of burnt lime in many architectural plasters was small, and some had none. Claims that lime burning caused significant deforestation of the Near East in the Neolithic may therefore be greatly exaggerated. Future evaluations of this question must be based upon much more extensive sampling and identification of supposed lime plasters.

These examples serve to emphasize the need for careful, systematic research design. Any study of material objects that includes microscopy should begin with the consideration of whole objects in their archaeological or historical context. It should then proceed step by step from low to high levels of magnification, with the results obtained at any one level of magnification always being related to those obtained at lower magnification and to the context of their discovery. The best way to avoid errors is, of course, to make the project truly interdisciplinary. This means that all parties should fully understand the context of the material objects and the questions being asked, as well as the potential and limitations of microscopy to provide answers. Archaeologists, historians, and curators who treat scientific analysis as a black box will on occasion find that it contains nothing but a hornet's nest.

Low-Power Microscopy (5–50×) and the Examination of Surfaces

Microscopy above about 50× requires expensive equipment to obtain the images and specialized training to interpret them. Below 50×, the basic equipment is relatively cheap and the principles of interpretation are uncomplicated; so this realm of microscopy is accessible to almost any student of material culture. The most portable system for low-power microscopy consists of nothing more than one or two good-quality hand lenses and some compact means of illumination, such as a penlight. A great deal of useful information may be obtained with these very simple tools. A more versatile but less portable instrument is the zoom stereo microscope. The range of magnification varies with manufacturer and model, but it is typically between 5× and 50×. More sophisticated models may be coupled to a camera or video camera.

Some hand lenses and most stereo microscopes may be fitted with engraved graticules for the measurement of lengths, diameters, or angles. These are useful in measuring the precision attained by ancient artisans. Such measurements have proven useful, for example, in the debate over the first use of magnifying devices. Planoconvex lenses of rock crystal are known in the Mediterranean region from as early as 1400 B.C., but not until Roman times is there written evidence of the use of magnifiers. There has been considerable argument over the use of the crystal lenses. Were they used as magnifiers, or were they merely pieces of jewelry (Sines and Sakellarakis 1987)? The lenses themselves are mute; so attention has turned to the study of objects whose manufacture might have require the use of magnifiers. Sines (1992) has measured the circular borders around some Etruscan and Archaic Greek miniature carved gemstones and has shown that some are subdivided with quite remarkable regularity. We do not know yet know how the engravers laid out these minute divisions, but it seems probable that magnification (and therefore lenses) would have been required.

Low-power microscopy is most often employed in the study of surfaces. With rare or valuable objects, surface examination is usually the only form of microscopy permitted by the curators, but even such limited inquiry may reveal much about an object's manufacture and even help identify its maker. Low-power microscopy is routinely employed by art historians to compare fine details such as the brushwork and the signatures on paintings, as well as in detecting later repairs or overpainting. Low-power microscopy is also the most important tool in studies of textiles. The fibers of which the textile is made are identified by comparing their surface morphology to those of known fibers in reference collections; the weaving technology is reconstructed by studying the pattern of warp and weft. Kingery and Vandiver (1986a) discuss in great detail what may be learned from the study of ceramics at low magnification, and Scott (1991) provides a good example of the role of low-power microscopy in reconstructing the techniques of Renaissance silversmiths.

Where materials have been cut or ground to shape, it may be possible to deduce what tools were used by examining the damage left on the surface of the piece. These traces may then be compared to reference collections of damage produced by known tools on comparable surfaces. This method has been used for many years in prehistoric archaeology (Tite, Chap. 15 in this volume). Its value is not confined to the study of prehistoric technology, however, as is demonstrated by Robert Gordon's elegant studies of the role of machine tools in American armories during the nineteenth century (Gordon 1988a, 1988b).

The issue Gordon investigated is the displacement of skilled hand labor by machine tools in the nineteenth century. This is a landmark in the history of technology, and the question of where and when it originated is of some importance. The documentary record seems to indicate that this displacement was first achieved in the Springfield and Harper's Ferry Armories in the 1840s, a view that has become the standard interpretation among historians. Gordon chose to examine the material record. He first established that the microscopic wear patterns produced by hand filing are easily distinguished from those of machine tools (Fig. 14.1). He then disassembled firearms of known date from the Springfield and Harper's Ferry armories and examined the tooling marks on their internal mechanisms. This exercise revealed that even in the 1880s critical components of firearms were still brought to their final dimensions by hand filing. There is no question that machine tools were used in the armories from the 1840s (and indeed earlier) for the shaping of metal parts to approximate dimensions, but these early machines were not yet as precise as skilled hand labor and could not achieve the close tolerances required for truly interchangeable parts.

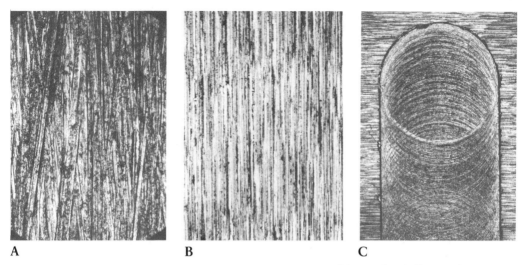

A   B   C

Fig. 14.1. Microscopic wear patterns produced on steel by (A) hand filing with double-action file (width of field 1.8 mm); (B) a machine tool (plane grinder; width of field 5.6 mm); and (C) a single pass of an end mill superimposed on marks made by a plane grinder (width of field 10.7 mm). (Photographs courtesy of Robert Gordon)

In publishing studies like these it is obviously desirable to submit photographic evidence. This presents no particular problem if the surface to be photographed is flat, but unfortunately, many surfaces of interest are not. The depth of field (i.e., the vertical zone of sharp focus) in conventional light microscopes is very shallow, even at low magnifications. A typical 10× objective lens on a light microscope (which when combined with a 10× eyepiece would give a final magnification of 100×) has a depth of field of 0.04 mm; a 45× objective (450× with a 10× eyepiece) has a depth of field of 0.01 mm (Bloss 1961, 32). If the topographic range exceeds these limits, some part of the field of view must be out of focus.

Much greater depths of field can be obtained, however, if the object is examined at the same magnification with a scanning electron microscope (SEM), in which a narrow beam of electrons is rapidly scanned in a rectangular pattern. Secondary electrons from the sample are detected and amplified to produce an image on a television monitor. A typical SEM can provide a depth of field of about 0.4 mm at 100×, or 0.1 mm at 450× (Goldstein et al. 1992, 165). This tenfold difference in depth of field between the light microscope and the SEM is evident in Figure 14.2.

Most modern SEMs can be focused at magnifications as low as 10× and thus are ideal for the study and documentation of objects with deep surface relief. Small objects may be inserted directly into the vacuum chamber of the SEM, though in a conventional instrument, nonmetals must first be coated with a very thin layer of carbon or gold to make them electrically conductive, so that the electrons can drain to ground. In the past this limited use of the SEM with rare or valuable objects, because curators often worried that in removing the coating or through exposure to high vacuum the specimen would be damaged. This is no longer an issue, for a new generation of scanning electron microscopes (the environmental SEM, or ESEM) requires neither high vacuum nor the coating of samples.

The research of John Gwinnett and Leonard Gorelick on the history of lapidary and stone-working technology is a good example of the application of the SEM at low magnifications to problems in material culture studies. By combining the unique imaging capabilities of the SEM with experiments in lapidary technique, they have produced evidence of technical advances that include diamond drilling (Gwinnett and Gorelick 1987) and the mass-production polishing of stone beads by tumbling (Gwinnett and Gorelick 1989) in Sri Lanka in the late first millennium A.D. Their

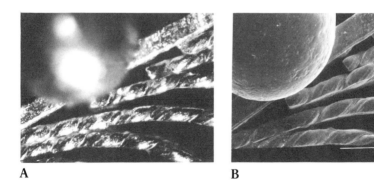

A   B

Fig. 14.2. Part of a Fulani silver earring from Cameroon, photographed at the same magnification with a light microscope (A) and a scanning electron microscope (B). The greater depth of field and absence of distracting reflections in the latter image show much more clearly how it was made. (Photographs by the author)

work also illustrates the use of flexible impressions to examine inaccessible detail, such as the striations produced by drilling in the bores of stone beads. To make an impression, a dental molding slurry is poured onto the surface to be copied. When set, the elastic impression may be peeled off, revealing a negative image of the surface. The impression may then be mounted on some rigid backing, coated with a very thin layer of sputtered gold, and examined directly in the SEM.

Impressions may also be used to study portions of the surface of objects that are too large to be inserted into the chamber of an SEM or cannot be removed from display. Such impressions have had a major impact in recent years in the study of the dawn of technology. Stone tools are often found in association with the bones of elephants, hippos, and other large mammals on archaeological sites in East Africa, dating between two and one million years ago. This does not necessarily mean, as earlier archaeologists tended to assume, that the hominids of that time were capable of hunting such large animals. These sites could represent scavenging by humans of the carcasses of animals killed by lions and other carnivores. The association of bones and stone tools could also be an accidental one, produced by flood or erosion (Binford 1981). Archaeologists have used the SEM to study replicas of the damage on the surfaces of animal bones from these sites and have developed criteria to distinguish the cut marks left by stone tools from damage produced by other means, such as the gnawing of rodents, trampling, or random abrasions from contact with rocks or soil (e.g., Potts 1988).

Intermediate Magnifications (50–1,500×)

The study of surfaces by low-power microscopy is important, but for many material objects of historical interest, it is not sufficient. Materials transformed by heat, such as glass, metal, and ceramics, preserve in their internal microstructure and in their composition some memory of the transformations they have undergone. An experienced microscopist can infer from this record the sequence of actions performed by the artisan in creating artifacts composed of these materials.

As an example, consider the four microstructures of steels in Figure 14.3. All have the same chemical composition, but each has been subjected to different physical treatments. The sample shown in Figure 14.3A has been held for several hours at 900°C and slowly cooled. It is tough (resistant to cracking on impact) and ductile (meaning that it can be

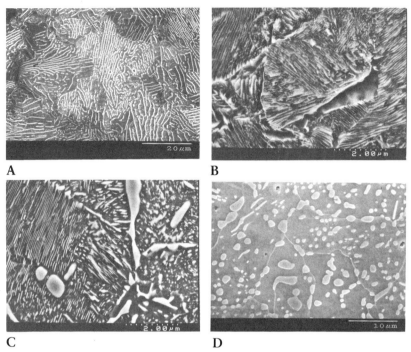

Fig. 14.3. Microstructures of four steel samples of identical chemical composition (0.97 percent carbon by weight) (A) cooled slowly from 900°C; (B) quenched into water from 900°C; (C) as B, but tempered for two hours at 540°C; and (D) as B, but reheated at 700°C for sixteen hours. All specimens etched with 4 percent nitric acid in ethanol. (SEM micrographs by Gary Chandler and the author)

substantially deformed without breaking), but it is not very hard (200 on the Vickers scale). It would serve well as an anvil but would not make a sharp cutting edge.

If, however, this same steel is immediately quenched from 900°C into water, the microstructure illustrated in Figure 14.3B is obtained. This steel is extremely hard (Vickers hardness 740) and thus would make an excellent cutting edge, but it is also brittle. A satisfactory compromise between hardness and ductility for many applications may be reached by reheating (tempering) this sample at 540°C for two hours to produce the microstructure shown in Figure 14.3C. This quenched and tempered steel is less hard (Vickers hardness 350) than the quenched sample, but is still hard enough to form a sharp cutting edge that is not easily blunted.

Unlike the quenched sample, it is tough enough to withstand sudden impact without cracking. It would therefore be suitable for applications such as the cutting edge of an axe.

A completely different microstructure (Fig. 14.3D) is obtained if the quenched and tempered sample is held for a very long time (sixteen hours) at 700°C. This spheroidized steel is soft (Vickers hardness 180) but can be repeatedly flexed without cracking; it is therefore a good material to use for springs.

This example shows that the microscopist can do more than simply reconstruct the techniques employed by the artisan. The macrostructure and microstructures of an artifact also reveal how well the artisan understood the differing properties of materials and employed his or her knowledge and ingenuity to satisfy human desires, whether for sharp cutting tools or for glazes that tease the eye with an illusion of depth. The engineering design and execution of many artifacts is extremely artful. Traditional Japanese swords are a much admired art form, yet the viewer who knows nothing of the technology of their manufacture (as revealed in their microstructures) is missing the greater part of the art. Japanese swords are composite structures, built of iron and steel, in which the inherent brittleness of the quenched but untempered steel cutting edge is countered by built-in compressive stresses that prevent any cracks in the cutting edge from spreading (Smith 1988, 40–62; Weins and Bleed 1991). This is a truly elegant engineering solution to the age-old problem of making edges that are very sharp but not brittle. An understanding of the engineering of the Japanese sword is essential to the proper appreciation of both the object and its maker, and the same can be said of many other pieces of material culture.

There are many specialized types of light microscopes in the intermediate range of magnification, and which type one uses depends to a large extent upon what material is being examined. Metals are prepared as flat, highly polished surfaces and are examined in reflected light, usually after a brief etching with some corrosive chemical to reveal features such as the boundaries between individual crystals, strain lines, and so on. Light microscopes are preferred to the SEM for microstructural studies of metals below 1,000× because they provide images in color, which is often important in revealing true microstructure. The SEM can only provide a monochrome image, but most modern SEMs have an additional capability that light microscopes lack: the ability to provide rapid chemical analysis, which is done by measurement of the characteristic X-rays emitted by each element as it is bombarded by electrons (energy dispersive analysis by X-rays, or EDAX). Because it is essential to know the chemical composition in order to fully interpret the microstructure, the light microscope and the SEM complement each other. Light microscopes are also limited by the wavelength of light to magnifications below about 1,500×; any features of interest that require greater magnification must be examined by electron microscopy.

Objects made of rocks or minerals are usually examined as very thin sections (conventionally 0.03 mm thick) cemented to a glass slide. Most of the rock-forming silicate minerals are transparent at this thickness, and the various mineral species present are identified by their shape, crystal form, and colorful interactions with polarized white light (Bloss 1961). Most rocks also contain oxide minerals that are opaque even at this thickness, so it is usual practice today to polish the upper surface of the thin section so that the opaque minerals may be identified in reflected light (Craig and Vaughan 1981). It is therefore advantageous when examining materials in polished thin section to use a microscope equipped with both transmitted and reflected polarized light sources—the so-called universal microscope. Other modes of illumination may be more appropriate with some materials. Many biological materials and some minerals are easily identified by fluorescence, meaning that they emit light of a particular wavelength when bombarded by other wavelengths of electromagnetic radiation. Bone, ivory, and many minerals (calcite, for example) fluoresce strongly when illuminated by ultraviolet light. The structure of some biological tissues may be rendered more clearly visible by staining with dyes that bond to specific tissues and that fluoresce strongly when illuminated with specific wavelengths of visible light. The whole area of fluorescence microscopy is one of very active development at present (Taylor et al. 1992), and many of the emerging techniques have obvious potential for the identification of historic and prehistoric materials.

Polished thin sections can also be examined in the SEM, where the chemical composition of areas of the surface or of individual crystals may be determined by EDAX. The combination of optical petrography and electron microscopy with EDAX is particularly useful in the examination of rocks, minerals, slags (metallurgical waste products), and coarse earthenware pottery. Discarded wastes such as slags, pottery wasters, and spilled glass may not be aesthetically appealing, but they are an invaluable source of information for anyone studying the history of work. Finished artifacts may have been be carried far from the place in which they were made, but in preindustrial times the waste products were usually discarded in or close to the workshop. One can therefore be fairly certain that the evidence they provide reflects the technical knowledge and prowess of the society with whose remains they were found.

The microscopic and chemical study of the slags, glasses, and ceramics can provide highly specific information, including the temperatures to which the sample was heated and an estimate of the composition of gases within the furnace. Both are indicative of the knowledge and skill of the artisan. Temperatures above 1200°C were particularly difficult to attain and maintain in ceramic and glass kilns before the nineteenth century, so evidence of the consistent attainment of such temperatures shows a high degree of skill. Such skills were not mastered in Europe until the eighteenth century, and then largely as the result of the long struggle to duplicate high-temperature technologies developed in the Orient, notably those of Chinese porcelain (Kingery and Vandiver 1986a) and Indian wootz steel (Smith 1988).

Before the SEM went into commercial production in 1965 (after some thirty years of development) microstructural studies of ceramics and glasses lagged behind those of metals. This is because critical portions of their microstructures consist of particles too small to be seen by light microscopy in a thin section of conventional thickness. The SEM revolutionized the study of ceramics, glazes, and glasses and made it possible to extract much more information from historic and prehistoric objects made of these materials (Kingery 1987; Freestone 1991; Tite 1992). One can even use the SEM to estimate the temperature to which a given historic or prehistoric ceramic has been fired. This is done by refiring the ceramic in increasing increments of temperature, inspecting the sample in the SEM after each increment. When a change of microstructure is noted, the refiring temperature must have exceeded that to which the piece was originally fired. Thus an upper limit for an estimate of the original firing temperature can be set (Tite 1992).

*High Magnification (1,500–100,000×) and Very
High Magnification (100,000–1,000,000×)*

The upper limit of light microscopy is about 1,500× in visible light and 2,000× in ultraviolet; the smallest particle that can be resolved by light microscopy is therefore about 0.1μ (0.0001 mm). The study of the microstructure of materials at higher magnifications is the province of electron microscopy. The SEM is most commonly used at magnifications below 10,000× in the examination of the products of prehistoric and historic technology but can provide much higher magnification if needed. The ultimate resolution of the SEM depends upon the type of electron source with which it is fitted, but most commercial instruments can be used effectively at magnification up to 50,000×.

For higher magnifications than those attainable with the SEM, one must turn to transmission electron microscope (TEM) or scanning transmission electron microscope (STEM). In these instruments the sample is placed between the focused electron beam and the detector. The sample must obviously be made thin enough (tens to hundreds of nanometers) that some fraction of the electron beam can pass through it to the detector. Variation in the chemical composition or microstructure within the field of view causes more electrons to pass some portions of the image than through others. This spatial variation in the number of electrons passing through the specimen forms an image on the detector, which may be a photographic negative or an electronic system that produces an image on a television monitor. The process of image formation is therefore analogous to that of a conventional medical X-ray image.

Other types of detectors may also be employed to identify the various phases seen in a particular specimen. The chemical composition of the phase of interest may also be inferred, as in the SEM, from the energies and intensities of the X-rays that are produced by the interaction of the electron beam with the individual atoms of the sample. The crystal structure of the phase of interest may be deduced by electron diffraction, in which electrons are diffracted by the atoms of crystalline phases in the sample and interfere with one another to produce a regular pattern of bright spots on a dark background at the detector (analogous to the brightly colored interference patterns produced by sunlight in an oil slick). The pattern of these dots reveals the spatial arrangement of atoms within the crystal (i.e., the structure of the crystal lattice and the spacing between the various crystal planes). This information, when considered in conjunction with the chemical composition, usually suffices to identify the particle being examined.

The field of view at such high magnifications is necessarily very small, so one must always ask whether the piece examined is representative of the artifact from which it was taken. Sampling problems are particularly acute in the examination of historic or prehistoric artifacts, which are usually much less homogeneous than modern materials. (Indeed, many of the triumphs of modern materials science and engineering stem from the ability to produce materials of remarkable purity and microstructural homogeneity). It is therefore rarely appropriate to employ the very high magnifications attainable by STEM or TEM on historic or prehistoric materials.

The major exception is in the study of ancient and historic glasses (including enamels and glazes), where chemical and microstructural variation is often on a sufficiently fine scale that the high resolution of the TEM is required. Strictly defined, glass is a substance without long-range crystalline order, but in fact many glasses contain dispersions of small particles that have crystallized from the melt or have precipitated from the glass after it solidified. (In materials science these are called glass-ceramics, to distinguish them from true glasses). These particles are often responsible for the color of the glass (Kingery and Vandiver 1986a, 261–77; Freestone 1991) but may be too small to be seen by light microscopy or even by the SEM. In such cases it is necessary to resort to the TEM to fully understand how past artisans achieved these effects.

The Attic Gloss pottery of classical Greece is among the most admired products of the potter's craft, and much effort has gone into discovering how it was made. It has been known for some time that the contrast between the glossy black and the matte red regions on Attic Gloss vessels is produced by firing the objects twice. The first firing was in a reducing atmosphere to produce a black vessel. In the second firing, under oxidizing conditions, the body of the vessel turns red while the painted decoration remains black. The interesting question here is why the black areas do not also oxidize to red in the second firing. Maniatis and Stalios (1993) have recently employed TEM to demonstrate that a very thin layer of glass, only a few microns thick, forms on the exterior surface of the black areas during the first firing. This layer is evidently impermeable to oxygen and thus prevents the black areas from reoxidizing during refiring. It is also responsible for imparting the characteristic gloss that gives the ware its name.

In the case of Attic Gloss the effect was fully reproducible, and it was controlled by careful selection and processing of the materials that made up the slip with which the glossy areas were painted (Kingery 1991). A more equivocal case is that of the Lycurgus Cup, an exceptional piece of Roman cut glass in the British Museum (Fig. 14.4). The most notable

feature of this piece, which is dated on stylistic grounds to the fourth
century A.D., is that the glass is dichroic—in reflected light the color is
pea green, but in transmitted light the vessel is wine red. Barber and
Freestone (1990) have examined some tiny fragments of this glass by
TEM and attribute this effect to a dispersion of tiny particles (c. 70 nm,
or 0.000007 mm in diameter) of a silver-gold alloy in the glass (Fig.
14.5). The silver content of this glass is only three hundred parts per
million and the gold content only forty parts per million. Experimental
work has shown that at higher contents of gold and silver, the glass is

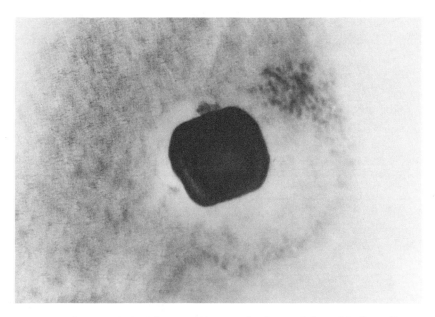

Fig. 14.5. A transmission electron micrograph of one of the gold-silver alloy particles responsible for the dichroism of the Lycurgus Cup. The width of the particle is seventy nanometers (a nanometer is one-millionth of a millimeter). (Photograph courtesy of Dr. David Barber and Dr. Ian Freestone; reprinted with permission of the British Museum [Natural History])

not dichroic. As it seems unlikely that such low concentrations could have been measured consistently in Roman times, Barber and Freestone (1990) suggest that the production of dichroic glass must have been a hit-or-miss affair and possibly the product of a single workshop. The fact that fewer than ten pieces of dichroic Roman glass are known appears to support this interpretation.

A similar study is that of Kingery and Vandiver (1986b), who used TEM to show that the transparent pink enamel on K'ang Hsi famille rose porcelain in the eighteenth century A.D. is attributable to a dispersion of tiny gold particles in the glass matrix. Unlike Roman dichroic glass, this enamel was fully reproducible, for many thousands of pieces of this ware were produced by an essentially industrial division of labor. The TEM was also employed in the investigation of shakudo, the beautiful purple-black patina produced on some Japanese copper alloys from the fourteenth century to the present (Notis 1988, 322–24). This effect is achieved by slight additions of gold to the copper, followed by extensive mechanical working and then by oxidation of the copper in a pickling solution. This is a marvelously sophisticated process, and its elucidation considerably increases our appreciation of the skills of the maker.

These examples in this section show the power of microscopy and chemical analysis to recover the technical prowess of preindustrial artisans. These and other discoveries should prompt us to probe the social circumstances that gave rise to these innovations. Out of what body of technical or philosophical knowledge did particular innovations arise? What were the social circumstances that favored experimentation in particular materials and technologies? What does the distribution of this technology through time and space tell us about its origins and mode of cultural transmission? None of these questions can be answered by microscopy or other scientific techniques. The role of these scientific methods is to bring the achievements of preindustrial artisans to light and to explain how their artifacts were produced.

QUANTITATIVE MICROSCOPY AND IMAGE PROCESSING

The discussion has focused on the qualitative observation of artifacts under the microscope, but quantitative measurements may also be of value in material culture studies. To give but one example, quantitative microscopy is being used to investigate a curious anomaly in the development of American industry. The documentary record shows that until the Civil War, American manufacturers were largely dependent upon European wrought iron and crucible steel for such critical manufactures as rifle barrels, files, saw blades, and the cutting edges of axes (Tweedale 1987). Both metals were manufactured in the United States, but the leading American manufacturers of these tools preferred to use imported materials. This situation left the United States extremely vulnerable to disruption of supply. Why were American manufacturers so loath to use American wrought iron and steel for these critical applications? Given that no reliable methods for testing the strength of materials had yet been developed, were there really significant differences between the performance of American and European iron and steel, or was this a myth perpetuated by ironworkers who had always used Sheffield steel or Swedish iron and refused to change?

This question is being answered by microscopy, chemical analysis, and mechanical testing of archival samples of American and imported metals from this period. The database so far (Gordon 1988c) is small, but it suggests that there were indeed significant differences between imported and locally produced iron. Some American samples were as good as imported Swedish iron, but the quality of American wrought iron was extremely inconsistent. Perhaps the most critical application for wrought iron was in gun barrels, and it was here that the preference for imported iron was most strongly expressed. At the outbreak of the Civil War, the Springfield Armory was entirely reliant on iron from a single English manufacturer (Marshall) and strongly resisted pressures to use American iron. Why was this?

Quantitative microscopic analysis of archival samples of Marshall iron (Gordon 1983) shows that this material was fully deserving of its high reputation. The quality of Marshall iron arose from repeated heating and rolling of the iron to produce a very homogeneous product in which the volume of residual slag was low and the remaining slag particles were small and well dispersed. (Because cracks spread rapidly along brittle slag particles, it is much less harmful to have the same volume of slag present as many small particles than as a few large ones.) One can also tell from the microstructure that Marshall used a low finishing temperature, giving rise to a small grain size in the iron matrix. This contributed to the quality of their product, because in most materials strength is inversely proportional to average grain size. The superior skills of the European iron makers at this time had, of course, been developed by empirical means—the microscopic examination of metals was in its infancy—as was the notion that metals were polycrystalline solids (Smith 1988).

Standard procedures for estimating parameters such as grain size and the dispersion of slag inclusions are defined and published by the American Society for the Testing of Materials (ASTM). These measurements may be made by simple but laborious techniques such as laying grids on photographs taken at a set magnification and recording what is present at each grid intersection. The advent of microcomputer-based image analysis software has taken much of the drudgery out of this work. In these systems the image is transferred by video camera from the microscope to a digitizer, which converts the analog signal (brightness) of the image at each spot (pixel) to a digital measure of brightness. Each pixel is assigned a number from o (black) to 256 (white). The image is then enhanced by various mathematical transformations, the purpose of which is to distinguish the features of interest (slag particles, grain boundaries, etc.) from everything else in the image. Once this is accomplished—and this is the most difficult part of the operation—software routines can be invoked to measure the percentage area, average particle size, shape and orientation, and other characteristics of the selected features.

Although a considerable investment of time may be needed to develop an effective image-processing routine for a particular application, great savings of time result when many similar samples are analyzed in this way. Computerized quantitative microscopy has not been much used in material culture studies to date, but it has obvious potential in archaeology, where it is usual to study large multiples of any class of object. It is probably of less interest to art historians, who tend to investigate singular objects or small multiples of them. Archaeologists have already shown considerable interest in using image processing to replace manual point-counting routines. These are used to measure the relative frequencies of the various rock and mineral grains that are present as natural inclusions or as added temper in earthenware pottery. The kinds and relative abundance of these inclusions may show whether the pottery was locally manufactured or imported, and the distribution of particle sizes provides evidence of the technology employed (it may show, for example, that the clay was screened or settled in water to remove larger particles). Unfortunately, this has proven to be too difficult a problem for computer image analysis. One needs to know more than just the relative brightness to distinguish the various minerals from each other, from the clay matrix and other features, such as holes in the section (Whitbread 1991). In this particular case the powers of discrimination of computer vision are as yet considerably inferior to those of the human eye.

Computerized image enhancement is also of great value in qualitative microscopy. In many cases the image obtained from the optical or electron microscope is unavoidably lacking in contrast or sharpness. These defects can sometimes be remedied by converting the image to digital form and applying one or more of the battery of mathematical transformations developed for this purpose (Goldstein et al. 1992, 231–46). The features of interest are then considerably easier to see. Image processing must, however, be used with care, as some mathematical transformations may produce features in the transformed image that were not present in the original!

CONCLUSION

I hope that the examples in this chapter demonstrate that microscopy is a powerful tool for appreciation of human accomplishments in both technology and the arts. But microscopy is of little use in and of itself; it must be fully integrated with the results of other scientific methods (chemistry in particular) and with all pertinent historical and archaeological evidence. Only then can material objects fulfill their potential as documents of human action and intent. The microscopist who is best able to draw such information out of objects is one who is as well versed in the methods of the humanities and the social sciences as in the methods of the sciences. Few among us can claim to have achieved this state of grace, but it is an end toward which we should continually strive. Conversely, those in the humanities who identify themselves as students of material culture have an obligation to set aside the idealist/materialist split in Western intellectual culture and take technology seriously. This applies in particular to art historians, who tend not to see the art in technology. An elegant solution to a difficult engineering problem is no less artful than the finest painting or statue.

REFERENCES

Barber, E. J. W. 1990. "Neolithic Textiles in Europe and the Near East." *Archeomaterials* 4:63–68.

Barber, David J., and Ian C. Freestone. 1990. "An Investigation of the Origin of the Colour of the Lycurgus Cup by Analytical Transmission Electron Microscopy." *Archaeometry* 32:33–45.

Binford, Lewis. 1981. *Bones: Ancient Men and Modern Myths.* New York: Academic Press.

Blackman, James, Gil A. Stein, and Pamela B. Vandiver. 1993. "The Standardization Hypothesis and Ceramic Mass Production: Technological, Compositional, and Metric Indices of Craft Specialization at Tell Leilan, Syria." *American Antiquity* 58:60–79.

Bloss, Fred D. 1961. *An Introduction to the Methods of Optical Crystallography.* New York: Holt, Rinehart and Winston.

Childe, V. Gordon. 1942. *What Happened in History.* Harmondsworth, England: Penguin.

Costin, Cathy L. 1991. "Craft Specialization: Issues in Defining, Documenting, and Explaining the Organization of Production." In *Archaeological Method and Theory,* vol. 3, edited by Michael B. Schiffer, 1–56. Tucson: University of Arizona Press.

Craig, James R., and David J. Vaughan. 1981. *Ore Microscopy and Ore Petrography.* New York: John Wiley.

Davidovits, Joseph, and Margie Morris. 1988. *The Pyramids: An Enigma Solved.* New York: Hippocrene.

Finley, Moses I. 1985. *The Ancient Economy.* 2d ed. London: Hogarth Press.

Folk, Robert L., and Donald H. Campbell. 1992. "Are the Pyramids of Egypt Built of Poured Concrete Blocks?" *Journal of Geological Education* 40:25–34.

Freestone, Ian C. 1991. "Looking into Glass." In *Science and the Past,* edited by Sheridan Bowman, 37–56. London: British Museum Press.

Goldstein, Joseph I., Dale E. Newbury, Patrick Echlin, David C. Joy, A. D. Romig Jr., Charles E. Lyman, Charles Fiori, and Eric Lifshin. 1992. *Scanning Electron Microscopy and X-Ray Microanalysis.* 2d ed. New York: Plenum Press.

Gordon, Robert B. 1983. "English Iron for American Arms: Laboratory Evidence on the Iron Used at the Springfield Armory in 1860." *Journal of the Historical Metallurgy Society* 17:91–98.

———. 1988a. "Who Turned the Mechanical Ideal into Mechanical Reality?" *Technology and Culture* 29:744–78.

———. 1988b. "Material Evidence of the Manufacturing Methods Used in Armory Practice." *IA: Journal of the Society for Industrial Archaeology* 14:23–35.

———. 1988c. "Strength and Structure of Wrought Iron." *Archeomaterials* 2:109–37.

Gordon, Robert B., and David Killick. 1992. "The Metallurgy of the American Bloomery Process." *Archeomaterials* 6:141–67.

Goren, Y., and P. Goldberg. 1991. "Petrographic Thin Sections and the Development of Neolithic Plaster Production in Northern Israel." *Journal of Field Archaeology* 18:131–38.

Gwinnett, A. John, and Leonard Gorelick. 1987. "Experimental Evidence for the Use of a Diamond Drill in Sri Lanka, ca. A.D. 700–1000." *Archeomaterials* 1:149–52.

———. 1989. "Evidence for Mass Production Polishing in Ancient Bead Manufacture." *Archeomaterials* 3:163–68.

Killick, David. 1995. "On Claims for 'Advanced' Iron Working Technology in Precolonial Africa." In *The Culture of African Iron Production,* edited by Peter R. Schmidt. Gainesville: University of Florida Press.

Kingery, W. David. 1987. "Microstructure Analysis as Part of a Holistic Interpretation of Ceramic Art and Archaeological Artifacts." *Archeomaterials* 1:91–99.

———. 1991. "Attic Pottery Gloss Technology." *Archeomaterials* 5:47–54.

———. 1993. "Painterly Majolica of the Italian Renaissance." *Technology and Culture* 34:28–48.

Kingery, W. David, and Pamela B. Vandiver. 1986a. *Ceramic Masterpieces: Art, Structure and Technology.* London: Free Press.

———. 1986b. "The Eighteenth-Century Change in Technology and Style from the Famille-Verte Palette to the Famille-Rose Palette." In *Ceramics and Civilization,* vol. 2, *Technology and Style,* edited by W. D. Kingery, 363–81. Westerville, Ohio: American Ceramic Society.

Kingery, W. David., Pamela B. Vandiver, and Martha Prickett. 1988. "The Beginnings of Pyrotechnology, Part II: Production and Use of Lime and Gypsum Plaster in the Pre-Pottery Neolithic Near East." *Journal of Field Archaeology* 15:219–44.

Landels, J. G. 1978. *Engineering in the Ancient World.* Berkeley and Los Angeles: University of California Press.

Lechtman, Heather. 1979. "A Pre-Columbian Technique for Electrochemical Replacement Plating of Gold and Silver on Objects of Copper." *Journal of Metals* 31:154–60.

———. 1989. "Traditions and Styles in Andean Metalworking." In *The Beginning of the Use of Metals and Alloys,* edited by Robert Maddin, 344–78. Cambridge, Mass.: MIT Press.

Maniatis, Y., E. Aloupi, and A. D. Stalios. 1993. "New Evidence for the Nature of the Attic Black Gloss." *Archaeometry* 35:23–34.

McGovern, Patrick E. 1989. "Ancient Ceramic Technology and Stylistic Change: Contrasting Studies from Southwest and Southeast Asia." In *Scientific Analysis in Archaeology,* edited by Julian Henderson, 63–81. Oxford University Committee for Archaeology Monograph, no. 19. Oxford.

Notis, Michael. 1988. "The Japanese Alloy *Shakudo:* Its History and Its Patination." In *The Beginning of the Use of Metals and Alloys,* edited by Robert Maddin, 315–27. Cambridge, Mass.: MIT Press.

Potts, Richard. 1988. *Early Hominid Activities at Olduvai.* New York: de Gruyter.

Price, Derek de Solla. 1974. "Gears from the Greeks: The Antikythera Mechanism—A Calendar Computer from ca. 80 B.C." *Transactions of the American Philosophical Society,* n.s., 64 (7): 1–70.

Rollefson, Gary O. 1991. "The Critical Role of Technological Analysis for Pre-historic Anthropological Inference." In *Materials Issues in Art and Archaeology 2*, edited by Pamela B. Vandiver, James R. Druzik, and George S. Wheeler, 365–74. Pittsburgh: Materials Research Society.

Scott, David. 1991. "Technological, Analytical, and Microstructural Studies of a Renaissance Silver Basin." *Archeomaterials* 5:21–45.

Sines, George. 1992. "Precision in Engraving of Etruscan and Archaic Greek Gems." *Archeomaterials* 6:53–68.

Sines, George, and Yannis A. Sakellarakis. 1987. "Lenses in Antiquity." *American Journal of Archaeology* 91:192–96.

Smith, Cyril S. 1988. *A History of Metallography.* 2d ed. Cambridge, Mass.: MIT Press.

Taylor, D. Lansing, Michael Nederlof, Frederick Lanni, and Alan S. Waggoner. 1992. "The New Vision of Light Microscopy." *American Scientist* 80:322–25.

Tite, Michael. 1992. "The Impact of Electron Microscopy on Ceramic Studies." *Proceedings of the British Academy* 77:111–31.

Tweedale, Geoffrey. 1987. *Sheffield Steel and America.* Cambridge: Cambridge University Press.

Weins, William N., and Peter Bleed. 1991. "Why Is the Japanese Sword Curved?" In *Materials Issues in Art and Archaeology 2,* edited by Pamela B. Vandiver, James R. Druzik, and George S. Wheeler, 691–701. Pittsburgh: Materials Research Society.

Whitbread, Ian. 1991. "Image and Data Processing in Ceramic Petrology." In *Recent Developments in Ceramic Petrology,* edited by Andrew Middleton and Ian Freestone, 369–88. London: British Museum, Occasional Paper 81.

White, K. D. 1982. *Greek and Roman Technology.* Ithaca, N.Y.: Cornell University Press.

15

Dating, Provenance, and Usage in Material Culture Studies

In considering past material culture, my viewpoint is that of an archaeo-logical scientist (Tite 1991). I am, therefore, mainly concerned with the artifacts (tools, weapons, vessels, ornaments, etc.) that have survived burial on and been recovered from archaeological excavations. Scientific examination is playing an increasingly important role in the study of this material. The contribution of materials science in answering technological questions such as how an artifact was made or how its raw materials were processed has been discussed in previous chapters. In this chapter, I am concerned with the application of a wide range of scientific techniques to investigating when artifacts were made (i.e., dating), where the source of the raw materials used to make the artifacts was located and over what region the artifacts were traded or exchanged (i.e., provenance studies), and for what the artifacts were used (usage studies).

The feasibility of answering the above questions and the appropriate techniques to use depend critically on the nature of the materials from which the artifacts were made. It is convenient to distinguish between organic materials derived from plants and animals (i.e., wood, bone, ivory, as well as extracts such as wax, resin, oil) and inorganic materials derived from rocks and minerals (i.e., stone, ceramic, metal, glass). The survival of organic materials depends on their burial environment. There-fore, in an archaeological context, the study of inorganic materials tends to predominate. However, radiocarbon dating of organic materials is of crucial importance to archaeology, and the analysis of surviving organic traces on stone artifacts and pottery is beginning to provide valuable information on both usage and diet.

DATING

In considering dating methods in material culture studies (Aitken 1990), a distinction should first be made between those methods that date the artifact itself and those that date the archaeological context in which the artifact was found. In the former case, a further distinction should be made between dating to a high accuracy and simple authentication to establish whether an artifact is genuinely ancient or a modern copy. When attempting to select the most appropriate dating method, other factors that need to be considered are whether the method provides essentially absolute dates or only relative dates, what materials can be dated by the method, and over what time range is it applicable (Fig. 15.1).

Radiocarbon dating of organic materials is the technique that has had most universal application and thus the greatest impact on archaeology (Bowman 1990). It can be used to date both the archaeological context and, particularly with the development of the accelerator mass spectrometry method, the artifact itself. Luminescence dating, which includes both thermoluminescence and optical dating, is probably the second most generally applicable method (Aitken 1985). Thermoluminescence dating can be used to date not only pottery but also burnt stones from Paleolithic sites that lie beyond the forty-thousand-year practical upper limit for radiocarbon dating. A recent extension to luminescence dating has been the optical dating of unburnt sediments, which again can provide dates beyond the range of radiocarbon dating.

The age limit for luminescence dating varies between 100,000 and 500,000 years, depending on the material being dated. The age limit of uranium-series dating, which has been used extensively for dating calcium carbonate deposits associated with human remains in caves, is in the range 300,000 to 500,000 years (Schwarcz 1980). For dating beyond about 500,000 years, one has to turn to potassium-argon dating of volcanic deposits. In particular, this technique has been successfully applied to early hominid sites in East Africa, obtaining dates of almost two million years for volcanic tuffs in stratigraphic proximity to hominid remains (McDougall 1981).

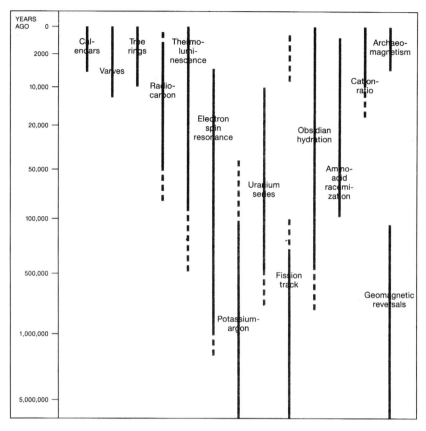

Fig. 15.1. Chart showing time spans for which different absolute and relative dating methods are applicable. (Reproduced with permission from Colin Renfrew and Paul Bahn, Archaeology: Theories, Methods and Practice, *Thames and Hudson, 1991)*

Other dating techniques applicable to specific materials include dendrochronology, or tree-ring dating, which can be used to date timbers from buildings and panel paintings (Baillie 1982). Ideally, the timber sample should contain at least a hundred rings, although a minimum of twenty rings has been used, depending on species and actual climatic variation of the time period under investigation. For the date to give the year of felling, the bark should be present. If the bark is missing, an estimate must be made of the number of rings lost during the preparation of the timber. Finally, to determine the date of actual usage of the timber, allowance must be made for the time spent in seasoning it.

For stone, there are a number of relative dating techniques that depend on measuring changes that have occurred at the new surfaces exposed during working in antiquity. These include hydration dating of obsidian artifacts (Stevenson, Carpenter, and Scheetz 1989) and cation-ratio dating of rock carvings (Lanteigne 1991). In addition, the possibility of dating stone on the basis of the measurement of the diffusion of atmospheric nitrogen into the surface is currently being investigated. With these relative methods, the rate of change inherent in the process must be independently calibrated using an absolute dating method. The calibration often has to be done afresh for each site or area because of environmental factors that influence the rate of change involved in these processes.

For metals and glass, no generally applicable absolute or relative method of dating exists. However, if a clay or sand casting core survives within a metal artifact, this will have been heated during the production of the artifact and therefore can be dated by thermoluminescence. Glass, in contrast, cannot be dated by this method because, being normally transparent, its thermoluminescence will have been modified *throughout* the body of the glass by exposure to light. The suggestion made by Brill and Hood (1961) that glass could be dated by counting the number of layers present in the surface crust has since been shown to be invalid, except possibly in very rare circumstances (Newton 1971). Some indication of the age and provenance of metal and glass artifacts that are otherwise without an archaeological context is possible on the basis of the raw materials and methods of fabrication used in their production. For example, the alloy composition and methods of surface decoration (gilding, silvering, tinning) of metal artifacts or the types of flux (soda or potash) and opacifier (tin- or antimony-based) used in glass are indicative of age and provenance. Such data, taken together with the nature of any surface corrosion or weathering, also provide the basis for authenticating metal and glass artifacts.

Radiocarbon Dating

Radiocarbon dating is based on the assumption that the ratio of carbon 14, which is formed through the interaction of cosmic rays with nitrogen in the earth's upper atmosphere, to the stable isotope carbon 12 is, and has been in the past, more or less constant in all living material. Once a plant or animal dies, however, its radioactive carbon 14 decays away with a half-life of 5,730 years period. Therefore, by comparing its carbon-14 content with that in living material, the time that has elapsed since death can be determined.

Unfortunately, the assumption that the ratio of carbon 14 to carbon 12 has remained constant in the biosphere is not strictly correct and therefore radiocarbon dates have to be calibrated. A calibration curve has now been established for the past nine thousand years or so, using long-lived trees such as bristlecone pine from California and bog oak from Ireland, the rings of which have been sequentially dated by dendro-chronology. The calibration curve reflects both the long-term and short-term variations in carbon-14 concentration, which are respectively associated with long-term changes in the earth's magnetic field intensity and short-term changes in solar activity. As a result of the long-term variations, the correction to the radiocarbon date tends to increase with increasing age, radiocarbon dates of 8,000 B.P. being too recent by as much as one thousand years. As a result of the short-term variations, the calibrated age range can be significantly smaller or larger than the radiocarbon age range. The problem is particularly severe in the postmedieval period, in part due to the injection of "dead carbon" into the atmosphere through the increasing use of fossil fuels (coal and oil). As a result, a radiocarbon date of 150 + 50 B.P. converts to a calibrated date of A.D. 1665–1950 (Fig. 15.2) and, therefore, the radiocarbon method can rarely be applied to material produced during the last three hundred years. Also, because of short-term variations, a single radiocarbon age range can convert to two, or even three, calibrated age ranges that are slightly separate from each other.

The conventional method of radiocarbon dating involves counting the beta particles emitted when carbon-14 atoms in a sample decay and as a result requires gram-sized samples. However, the accelerator mass spectrometry (AMS) method is now routinely available (Hedges 1987, 1990; Stulik and Donahue 1992). With this technique, the total number of carbon-14 atoms in a sample are counted, and as a result, only milli-gram-sized samples are required. The ability to obtain dates from such extremely small samples extends the application of radiocarbon dating to archaeological material and art objects to which unacceptable damage would have been done if sampled for the conventional method. The AMS method is also important for dating both inherently small samples, such

Fig. 15.2. Radiocarbon calibration curve for the period A.D. 1400–1954, showing calibrated age range (shaded) for a radiocarbon date of 150±50 B.P. (Reprinted by permission of Radiocarbon *and the authors from Fig. 1A, p. 8 in M. Stuiver and G. W. Pearson, "High Precision Bidecadel Calibration of the Radiocarbon Time Scale, A.D. 1950–500 B.C., 2500–6000 B.C.,"* Radiocarbon *35, no. 1 [1993])*

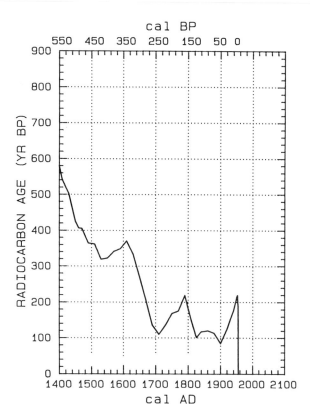

as individual seeds and organic residues, and samples reduced in size as a result of extracting those specific chemical fractions from materials such as bone that are least susceptible to environmental contamination.

The dating of human skeletal remains represents an important application of AMS radiocarbon dating. Unfortunately, the transition from Neanderthal to modern man in western Europe appears to have occurred about forty thousand years ago, which is just at the limit of practical applicability of radiocarbon dating. Similarly, the appearance of the first humans in Australia lie at or beyond the limits of the method. However, AMS dates for material with undoubted human association have taken the arrival of man in the Americas back to about 13,000 B.P. The AMS method has also been used to date some of the more spectacular recent finds of prehistoric man. For example, the body of the "Iceman," a mummified corpse of a man complete with clothes and equipment found on the edge of a glacier in the Alps, was unambiguously dated to about

3300 B.C. (Bonani et al. 1992). But the dating of Lindow Man, a well-preserved corpse of a naked man who had been struck on the head, strangled, and had his throat slit before being thrown into a peat bog, was less clear-cut (Gowlett, Hedges, and Law 1989). An AMS date of first century A.D. was obtained for the body, but the date obtained for the surrounding peat was fifth to third centuries B.C. The archaeologists involved favor a date of about 300 B.C., which would allow the man to be a sacrificial victim of the Celtic druids and thus perhaps explain the macabre way in which he died.

AMS dating is well placed to contribute to the investigation of the development of agriculture in that seeds of cultivated plants and bones of domesticated animals can be directly dated. Attempts are also being made to date prehistoric rock paintings by extracting from pigment samples the organic materials such as blood, oils, and resins added as binders (Watchman 1993). An obvious problem when handling such initially small samples is to ensure that the carbon being dated is not contaminated by more modern carbon, either from the environment (e.g., bird droppings, lichen, and fungi) or in the laboratory. Other archaeological applications of the AMS method include the dating of carbon extracted from both pottery and iron artifacts (Creswell 1991). In the case of the former, it is necessary to separate carbon added as temper in the form of rice husks or straw, which should be contemporary with the production of the pottery, from carbon already present in the clay, which could be several hundred years older. The carbon in iron presents less of a problem because it is likely to have come from the contemporaneous charcoal used to smelt the ore until the use of coal.

In attempting to date art objects, it must be remembered that, because of the peculiarities of the calibration curve, radiocarbon dating can only rarely be applied to material produced during the last three hundred years. However, the AMS method has been successfully applied to textiles, ivory, wooden sculpture, panel paintings, and manuscripts of earlier date (Stulik and Donahue 1992). A much-publicized application was the convincing medieval date (A.D. 1260–1390, with 95 percent confidence) obtained by three AMS laboratories for the Turin Shroud (Damon et al. 1989).

Luminescence Dating

Luminescence dating involves measuring the cumulative increase in the number of electrons trapped at defects in the crystalline lattice of minerals such as quartz and feldspar as a result of ionization produced by high-energy radiation from associated radioactive impurities.

In the case of thermoluminescence (TL) dating of pottery and burnt stone, the luminescence "clock" is set to zero and the cumulative increase in the number of trapped electrons is started by the firing process or chance heating, respectively. The current number of trapped electrons is measured in terms of the light emitted when the sample is heated in the laboratory, which in turn provides a measure of the radiation dose received, and hence the time that has elapsed, since the clock was set to zero. In the case of optical dating of sediments, the luminescence clock is set to zero by exposure to sunlight at their deposition, and the current number of trapped electrons is then measured in terms of the light emitted when the sample is exposed to a standard light source in the laboratory.

In TL dating of pottery (Fleming 1970; Zimmerman 1971), the annual radiation dose received since firing comes from radioactive impurities present in both the pottery itself and its surrounding burial soil. The alpha and beta particle contribution to the dose comes from the pottery, and, as a result of its greater penetration or range, the gamma ray contribution comes from the soil. Thus in order to obtain even a reasonably accurate date by the TL method, it is essential to know, and have soil from, the precise context in which the pottery was buried. Consequently, accurate dating of pottery from museum collections is not normally possible. A further complication is that some of the energy associated with the radiation dose is absorbed by water in the pores of the pottery and in the burial soil, rather than producing ionization in the pottery itself. Some estimate must therefore be made of the variations in the water content during the period of burial. For these and other reasons, the accuracy of TL dating of pottery tends to be poorer than that normally achieved by radiocarbon dating of organic material. Also, TL dating measurements tend to be more time consuming than those for radiocarbon dating. Therefore, although TL dating can provide a direct date for the pottery itself, radiocarbon dating of organic material from the associated archaeological context is generally preferred whenever possible.

TL has proved, however, to be extremely valuable for the authentication of art ceramics for which the demands of accuracy are less severe. The method can also be used to authenticate metal artifacts when a clay or sand casting core survives. An early and important application of the technique was to test a group of painted anthropomorphic vessels and figurines supposedly from the Neolithic site of Hacilar in southwest Turkey (Aitken, Moorey, and Ucko 1971). Following excavations at Hacilar from 1958 to 1960, painted pottery similar to that found during excavation began to appear on the antiquities markets of Europe and America. The quality of much of this pottery was such that experts were not certain whether it came from clandestine excavations or had been recently made by local potters. In due course a representative group of pottery in the Hacilar style from museums and private collections from around the world was tested for authenticity using the TL method, and out of a total of sixty-six pieces tested, forty-eight were found to be modern forgeries.

TL dating has been archaeologically important for burnt stone from Paleolithic sites whose ages lie beyond the practical limit of radiocarbon dating, even though the problems associated with determining the annual radiation dose still apply. A significant recent application was the dating of sequences of burnt flint from Paleolithic cave sites in Israel (Valladas et al. 1987 and 1988). TL results showed that strata at Qafzeh associated with modern man date to about ninety thousand years ago and therefore predate those at Kebara, which are associated with Neanderthal man and date to sixty thousand years ago (Fig. 15.3). Confirmation of these TL dates has been provided by electron spin resonance dating of mammal teeth from the two sites (Grun and Stringer 1991). Hence, in this part of the world, modern man appears to have been established at least as

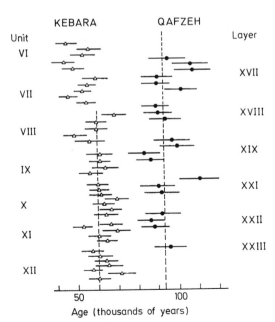

Fig. 15.3. TL dates for burnt flints from Paleolithic cave sites at Kebara and Qafzeh in Israel. (Reprinted with permission from Nature. M. J. Aiken, Fig. 6.13 in "Thermoluminescence Dates for Neanderthal Burial Sites at Kebara in Israel; Thermoluminescence Dating for Mousterian 'Proto-Cro-Magnon' Remains from Israel and the Origin of Modern Man," Nature 330:159–60; Nature 331:614–16)

long as Neanderthal man. These results, together with other data, make it unlikely that modern man evolved from Neanderthal man; instead, it is now suggested that Neanderthal man represents a separate branch of human evolution that died out some forty thousand years ago (Mellars, Aitken, and Stringer 1993).

Optical dating of airborne and waterborne sediments such as sand dunes, loess, alluvium, and ditch fills, although not providing a direct date for artifacts, has considerable potential for dating archaeological contexts in which human remains are found (Huntley, Godfrey-Smith, and Thewalt 1985; Smith et al. 1990). In particular, luminescence dating is beginning to make an important contribution to dating the arrival of man in Australia (Roberts, Jones, and Smith 1990). The earliest secure radiocarbon dates for human occupation in Australia are about 35,000–40,000 B.P. However, at some sites, artifacts associated with human occupation are found in levels well below those containing organic material suitable for radiocarbon dating. Thus, at sites located on sand aprons developed at the foot of the escarpment of the Arnhem Land plateau in northern Australia, both optical and TL dates for sediments associated with stone artifacts suggest that humans arrived in Australia some 45,000–60,000 years ago. Confirmation of the reliability of these early luminescence dates was provided by the good agreement found between luminescence and radiocarbon dates for younger strata from which samples for both methods were available.

PROVENANCE STUDIES

Provenance studies involve, first, the characterization of the raw materials used in the production of artifacts along with the identification of the sources of these materials and, second, the investigation of the extent of the trade or exchange of the finished artifacts (Scarre and Healy 1993; Baugh and Ericson 1994).

In the study of organic materials, some general indication of the possible regions of origin is provided by the identification of the plant or animal species from which the material derived, but precise location of the source of organic materials is only rarely possible. An exception is the fossil resin, amber (Beck 1986). On the basis of its distinctive chemical composition as characterized by infrared spectrometry or gas chromatography, it seems that amber from the Baltic can be distinguished from amber from sources in Italy, Romania, and France. Some support for the hypothesis that Baltic amber was traded through Europe as far as the eastern Mediterranean during the Bronze Age has thus been obtained.

Further, the source areas for organic materials can sometimes be narrowed down by measurements of stable isotopes (Ericson 1985 and 1989). The strontium-87 to strontium-86 ratio in soil varies according to the geological formation from which the soil was derived. The ratios observed in plants and animals will, in turn, reflect those of the soils within their habitat. Using strontium-isotope ratios, in combination with stable-carbon and nitrogen-isotope ratios, which reflect climate and vegetation, it has been possible to distinguish between modern elephant ivory coming from different habitats in southern Africa (van der Merwe et al. 1990).

Overall, the effort devoted to organic materials has been fairly limited, the great majority of provenance studies being concerned with the investigation of inorganic materials such as stone, pottery, metals, and glass. The analytical methods (Tite 1972; Kempe and Harvey 1983; Henderson 1989) employed in the study of inorganic materials fall into three main groups: optical petrology, minor- and trace-element analysis and stable-isotope analysis.

Optical petrology, which is applicable to both stone and pottery, involves the examination of a thin section in transmitted light. The mineral phases present are thus identified and their proportions, size, shape, and arrangement are determined. On the basis of these data, the general source area of the stone or the clay can sometimes be predicted from available geological knowledge. For confirmation, comparison with reference samples from possible sources is necessary.

Minor- and trace-element analysis involves determining the concentrations of elements at the 2 to 0.01 percent and 0.01 percent to 0.1 ppm, respectively. Artifacts made from raw materials from the same source can then be grouped together on the basis of a characteristic pattern of minor- and trace-element concentrations, which thus provides a "fingerprint" for that particular source. However, it is only rarely possible to predict even the general source area directly from these analytical data. Instead, it is necessary to compare the characteristic concentration pattern observed for a group of artifacts with those for all known sources of the raw materials.

A technique that has been extensively used in such provenance studies is neutron activation analysis (NAA) (Hughes, Cowell, and Hook 1991).

First, the specimen to be analyzed is irradiated with slow neutrons in a nuclear reactor. The neutrons react with the nuclei of the constituent atoms, transforming them into unstable radioactive isotopes. These unstable isotopes subsequently decay to form stable isotopes with the emission of gamma rays, which are detected using a semiconductor detector that determines both their energy and intensity. The gamma ray energies are effectively characteristic of the constituent elements, and the intensities provide a measure of their concentrations. NAA requires only a small sample (50–100 mg) and can provide data for a wide range of elements, typically down to concentrations of 1 ppm with an accuracy of better than 5 percent. There are now large NAA databases, principally for pottery and stone, in laboratories across the world that can be tapped for comparative analyses for source identification.

Stable-isotope analysis involves the determination of the relative abundance of the different stable isotopes of selected elements using mass spectrometry. For the great majority of chemical elements, the stable-isotope ratios are the same regardless of where, within the earth's crust, the elements originate. For certain elements, however, their isotopic ratios vary significantly, depending on the origin of the material in which they are found. In an archaeological context, the main elements of interest are lead (Pb204, Pb206, Pb207, Pb208), carbon (C12, C13), and oxygen (O16, O18). Again, the stable-isotope ratios can provide a "fingerprint" for artifacts made from raw materials from the same source. The isotopic ratios for lead depend on the age of the geological deposits from which the metal ore originated and, therefore, the general source area can sometimes be predicted from the lead-isotope data for a group of artifacts. Otherwise, as for minor- and trace-element analysis, the characteristic isotopic ratios observed for a group of artifacts must be compared with those for known sources of the raw materials.

Linking an artifact or group of artifacts to the source of its raw materials on the basis of petrology, minor- and trace-element concentrations, or stable-isotope ratios is not easy. First, there can be considerable variation in composition within a particular source as well as overlap or similarity in composition between sources that are widely separated geographically. Second, artifacts can be made from two or more raw material components, each of which contribute to its final composition. Third, the composition of the raw material can change during production of the artifact as a result of refining, volatilization, partitioning between different components, and reaction with subsequent burial environment.

Finally, locating and analyzing all the possible natural raw material sources can be extremely time consuming and is often impossible.

Stone

Stone is perhaps the ideal material for provenance studies, with the volcanic glass, obsidian, being particularly suitable. A single raw material is involved and there is no change in composition during its mechanical modification to produce the artifact. Furthermore, the number of possible sources is often limited and the resulting quarries are readily located. Thus, major and informative provenance studies have been undertaken, for example, on Neolithic stone axes from Britain (Clough and Cummings 1988), using optical petrology; on flint from northern Europe (Craddock et al. 1983) and on obsidian from the Mediterranean and the Near East (Renfrew, Dixon, and Cann 1966) and America (Glascock, Elam, and Aoyama 1991), using minor- and trace-element analysis; and on Classical marble from the Mediterranean world (Fant 1988), using carbon and oxygen stable-isotope ratios.

With stone, the researcher sometimes encounters the problem of trying to establish whether the stone was transported, from its primary natural source to the place where it was used, by man or by glacial action. For example, there seems little doubt that the bluestones used at Stonehenge come from the region of the Presceli Mountains in South Wales. However, whether they were transported all the way from the Presceli Mountains to Stonehenge by man or whether they were transported most, or part, of the way by glacial action is still in some doubt. Although recent analytical studies tend to favor glacial action (Thorpe et al. 1991), the results are not entirely convincing in that direct evidence for glaciation on Salisbury Plain remains ambiguous. Also, if the bluestones were brought to the region by glacial action, it is surprising that the occurrence of bluestone is minimal other than at Stonehenge itself.

Pottery

Provenance studies of pottery are in some ways less straightforward than those for stone because there are potential changes in composition both during and after production. The clay from which the pottery is made is often first processed either by refining to remove nonplastic inclusions or by the addition of further nonplastic inclusions referred to as temper.

Although there is normally no significant change in composition during firing to produce the pottery, some changes can occur during burial. Furthermore, very large numbers of possible clay sources exist in most parts of the world, and unlike stone quarries, they usually can not be located on the ground. However, where production centers can be identified by the presence of kilns or of overfired "waster" sherds, these can provide the control material for comparison with the pottery groups defined on the basis of their compositional fingerprint.

In spite of these difficulties, optical petrology (Middleton and Freestone 1991) has been successfully used to characterize, and sometimes identify, the clay source for coarse-textured pottery, particularly in regions of igneous or metamorphic geology, which generate distinctive rock fragments and mineral inclusions. For fine-textured pottery, minor- and trace-element analysis provides the most appropriate technique, and this approach, using principally NAA, has been extensively used for pottery provenance studies across the world.

The analysis of Spanish lusterware represents a typical application (Hughes and Vince 1986). Lusterware was produced at a number of sites in Spain from the thirteenth century onward and was exported to several other countries in Europe. The two major production centers were Malaga, which was in operation from the mid-thirteenth century until the early fifteenth century, and Valencia, which did not start producing lusterware until the late fourteenth century but then eclipsed Malaga as the major center during the fifteenth century. Early Malaga and late Valencia lusterwares are readily distinguished on the basis of style, but during the late fourteenth and early fifteenth centuries, the products of the two centers are difficult to distinguish. Samples of lusterware known to have been produced at these two major centers as well as samples from two minor production centers at Barcelona and Seville were analyzed using NAA. Applying discriminant analysis to the minor- and trace-element data, it was readily possible to distinguish between the products of all four centers (Fig. 15.4) and thus establish from which production center lusterware exported to other parts of Europe originated.

Metals

In the case of metals, a major problem is that the minor- and trace-element composition of a finished artifact can be very different from that of the ore from which it was produced. In the first place, this difference

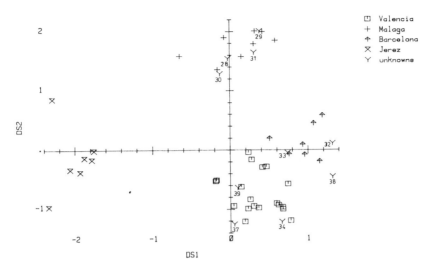

Fig. 15.4. Discriminant analysis plot for NAA data for Spanish lusterware from production centers at Valencia, Malaga, Barcelona, and Jerez (Seville) and for lusterware of doubtful provenance. (Reprinted from Proceedings of the 24th International Archaeometry Symposium, *Hughes, M. J., and Vince, A. G. [Washington D.C.: Smithsonian Institution Press], 363, by permission of the publisher. Copyright 1986. Illustration by courtesy of the Trustees of the British Museum, London)*

arises both through the loss of volatile impurities during roasting and smelting and through the subsequent partitioning of surviving impurities between the metal and the slag. Also, in addition to the ore itself, the charcoal used as fuel in smelting and the flux added to facilitate the formation of a molten slag contribute to the minor- and trace-element composition of the resulting metal. Finally, there are the problems associated, first, with the use of alloys of more than one metal, each of which contributes to the final minor- and trace-element composition, and, second, with the reuse of metal and thus the possible mixing of metals originating from more than one ore source. On the positive side as compared to pottery, there is the fact that the number of metal ore sources, at least for nonferrous metals, is finite and usually associated with mines and smelting sites, which are readily located.

Because of these difficulties, minor- and trace-element analysis has had only limited success in identifying the ore sources used in the production of metal artifacts. However, bulk chemical analysis, including major elements, has been of considerable importance in following the developments in the use of different metal alloys and in identifying different technological traditions (Craddock 1985; Northover 1989).

For example, from bulk chemical analyses, the sequences of copper-based alloys used in different parts of the world has been investigated and their chronology established. Typically, the sequence, which tends to reflect the different ore strata within a copper deposit, starts with the use of native copper, first hammered and annealed and later melted. Next copper was produced by smelting the relatively pure oxidized ores from the weathered upper part of the deposit. When the secondary enrichment zone within which the products of weathering are concentrated was reached, the ores would have been enriched in arsenic, resulting in the production of arsenical copper, a harder metal. Subsequently, when the unweathered primary ore below the enrichment zone were used, the metal produced would have contained much lower concentrations of arsenic and, therefore, in order the maintain its hardness, it was alloyed with tin, thus producing bronze. At a later stage, lead was added to the bronze, first in small quantities but eventually, when large quantities of lead became available as a by-product of silver production, in concentrations up to about 30 percent. The final copper-based alloy to appear in antiquity was brass, which was first extensively used in Roman times. In brass, tin has been replaced by zinc, the ore of which is generally more abundant and readily available than that of tin.

Instead of minor- and trace-element analysis, the prime technique for metal provenance studies is undoubtedly lead-isotope analysis because the lead-isotope ratios remain unchanged during the roasting and smelting of the ore to produce the metal (Stos-Gale 1989). It is possible that the charcoal fuel and any flux added could contribute to the overall lead content of the metal, but if these are local to the ore, they could well have a similar lead-isotope ratio. The possible reuse and mixing of metals from more than one source remains a problem. In addition to lead metal itself, the technique can be applied to silver produced from galena and to copper, which will contain small amounts of lead carried through from the ore. Of course, if lead has been deliberately added to the copper, the observed lead-isotope ratio will match that of the source of this added lead rather than that of the copper source.

The analysis of Late Bronze Age copper oxhide ingots from the Mediterranean region provides a typical application of the method that illustrates both its strengths and weaknesses (Gale 1991). A total of some

130 copper oxhide ingots weighing between ten and forty kilograms have been found on sites throughout the Mediterranean, from Sardinia in the west, through Sicily and Greece, to Cyprus and the Levant in the east (Fig. 15.5). In addition, a further 240 ingots have been found associated with two shipwrecks off the south coast of Anatolia. The oxhide ingots thus represent one form in which raw copper was transported around the Mediterranean during the Late Bronze Age.

Lead-isotope ratios for ingots from Crete, which date to the sixteenth century B.C. and are therefore some of the earliest ingots known, definitely do not match the ratios for copper ores from Laurion in Greece, from Cyprus or from any of the known ore sources in Anatolia. Two different ore sources appear to have been used. On the basis of the lead-isotope composition, one source dates to the Precambrian and therefore cannot be located in the Mediterranean region or in Anatolia. Instead, a location for the ore further east in Iran or Afghanistan is suggested.

For the later ingots, dating to the thirteenth and twelfth centuries B.C., Cyprus appears to have been the main source for the copper. The lead-isotope ratios for oxhide ingots found on Cyprus itself and on mainland Greece match those for the Cypriot ores (Fig. 15.6). However, many copper artifacts and other ingot types found on mainland Greece appear to have been made from copper from Laurion rather than from Cypriot copper. Again, the oxhide ingots found on Sardinia appear to have been made from Cypriot copper and not from the Sardinian copper ores that were being used to make local copper artifacts. Finally, of the 25 ingots (out of a total of about 240) from the two Late Bronze Age shipwrecks that have been analyzed, all but one fall within the lead-isotope field for Cypriot copper.

Having thus established the sources of the copper used to make the oxhide ingots, the next stage, in common with all provenance studies, is to attempt to interpret the results in terms of trade or exchange. This stage is often more difficult, principally because of the partial nature of the data available. First, there are only some four hundred known ingots spanning a period of about three to four hundred years, which must represent a very small proportion of the total produced. Second, our knowledge of the production centers for the ingots is very limited in that not all the ore sources have been located and none have been excavated to a sufficient extent to establish the scale of production. Third, and perhaps most important, copper oxhide ingots represent only one component in a very wide range of traded goods. For example, excavations of

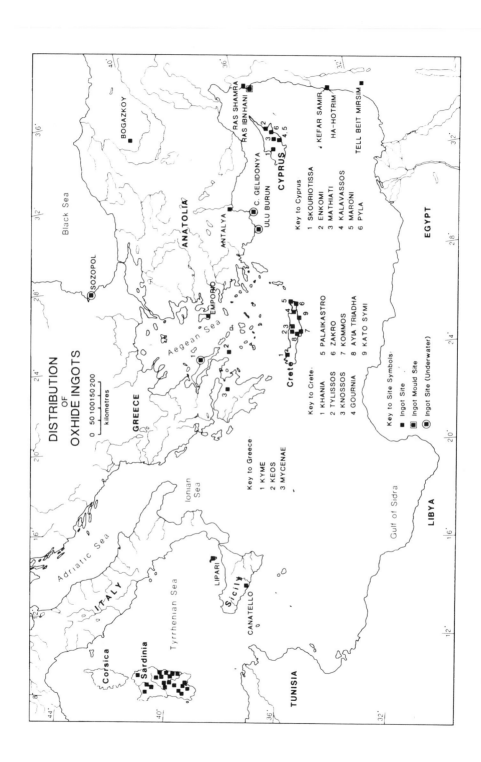

DISTRIBUTION
OF
OXHIDE INGOTS

0 50 100 150 200
kilometres

Key to Greece

1 KYME
2 KEOS
3 MYCENAE

Key to Crete

1 KHANIA   5 PALAIKASTRO
2 TYLISSOS   6 ZAKRO
3 KNOSSOS   7 KOMMOS
4 GOURNIA   8 AYIA TRIADHA
                9 KATO SYMI

Key to Cyprus

1 SKOURIOTISSA
2 ENKOMI
3 MATHIATI
4 KALAVASSOS
5 MARONI
6 PYLA

Key to Site Symbols:

■ Ingot Site
▣ Ingot Mould Site
◉ Ingot Site (Underwater)

GREECE

ANATOLIA

Black Sea

BOGAZKOY

SOZOPOL

EMPORIO

ANTALYA

C. GELIDONYA

ULU BURUN

CYPRUS

RAS SHAMRA
RAS IBNHANI

KEFAR SAMIR
HA-HOTRIM

TELL BEIT MIRSIM

Aegean Sea

Crete

EGYPT

Ionian Sea

Adriatic Sea

ITALY

Corsica

Sardinia

Tyrrhenian Sea

LIPARI

Sicily

CANATELLO

Gulf of Sidra

LIBYA

TUNISIA

the Late Bronze Age shipwreck at Ulu Burun have established that on board, in addition to the six tons of copper, were tin, glass, ebony, hippopotamus teeth, ivory, tortoise shell, and ostrich eggshells, as well as resin, spices, and foodstuffs (e.g., saffron, coriander, figs, pomegranates, olives, and grapes) together with amphorae and other pottery containers (Bass 1991). In addition, textiles of both wool and linen would have almost certainly have been traded.

Thus, one can visualize a complex network of exchange within the Mediterranean during the Late Bronze Age that provided the commodities for conspicuous consumption and display by emerging elite minorities (Sherratt and Sherratt 1991). The centers at which such commodities are found should not therefore be seen as market centers, because the commodities were more probably for the elites themselves, not for redistribution or marketing to the general population. Further, it has been hypothesized that metals provided a generally acceptable commodity that could be stored and used as required to balance exchanges within the network when reciprocity was not otherwise possible. Therefore, copper oxhide ingots, together with precious metals, can be tentatively regarded as a standard of value for exchange prior to the appearance of formal coinage.

Glass

Glass is typically produced from quartz sand plus a flux such as soda, potash, or lead oxide, added to lower the melting point, and stabilizers such as lime or alumina. The latter, often present as impurities in the sand, increase the durability of the glass. In addition, metallic compounds (e.g., copper, cobalt, manganese, tin, antimony) are often added as colorants and opacifiers.

Glass is therefore a multicomponent material and as a result, provenance studies to establish the sources of the various raw materials are rarely attempted. Instead, as for metals, bulk chemical analysis is used to study the development of and to distinguish between the different glass-making traditions (Sayre and Smith 1961; Henderson 1989). One can thus distinguish between glasses made using natron, soda-rich plant

Fig. 15.5. Map showing find spots for Late Bronze Age copper oxhide ingots from the Mediterranean region. (After Fig. 2, p. 200, of an article by N. H. Gale in Bronze Age Trade in the Mediterranean, SIMA XC [1991])

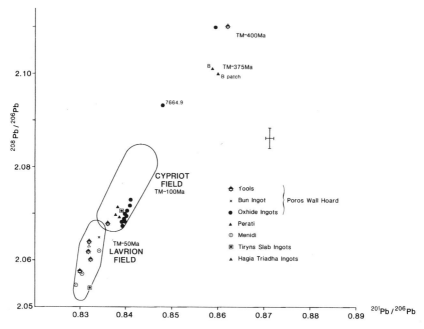

Fig. 15.6. Lead-isotope ratio diagram for Late Bronze Age ingots and artifacts from the Poros Wall Hoard, Mycenae, and other sites on mainland Greece. (Reprinted by permission of E. Hauptman, E. Pernicka, and G. A. Wagner, eds., Old World Archaeometallurgy, *Heidelberg, 1987, Fig. 29.16, p. 247)*

ash, or potash-rich plant ash as flux. Similarly, a distinction can be made between the use of tin-based and antimony-based opacifiers. On the basis of such essentially technological parameters, the general region of production of a group of glass can sometimes be suggested.

USAGE STUDIES

The investigation of the way in which artifacts were used has received far less scientific input than either technological or provenance studies. The first clue to the use of an artifact must come from a consideration of its visual appearance and, if known, the archaeological context in which it was found. Further information can sometimes come from the study of illustrations on contemporary wall paintings or pottery and from consideration of ethnographic parallels.

The scientific input to usage studies is essentially threefold. The first approach involves assessing the physical properties of an artifact, which determine its performance in use, and seeing whether these properties are appropriate to the hypothesized use of the artifact. The second approach involves inferring the use of an artifact from the wear or microwear pattern observed on the surface. The third, and perhaps most powerful, approach is to try to establish with what plant or animal products an artifact has been in contact by analyzing any organic residues absorbed by or adhering to its surface. Finally, any hypotheses regarding the use of an artifact should be tested experimentally by producing replica artifacts, using them in the way suggested, and then, as appropriate, examining them for wear and organic residues.

Usage studies are normally confined to stone artifacts and pottery, because microwear and organic residues rarely survive on metals and glass due to the corrosion or weathering of the surface, particularly during burial in the ground. Furthermore, because metals and glass are impermeable, organic residues cannot be absorbed into the surface of an artifact.

Stone

Microwear analysis of the surfaces of Paleolithic stone tools has been extensively undertaken in an attempt to identify the materials (e.g., wood, bone, hide, meat) on which the tools were used. Particular emphasis has been given to investigating the possibility of distinguishing between these different materials on the basis of the surface polish observed at magnifications of 400× under an optical microscope. Although blind tests have sometimes produced ambiguous results, it does seem that, if all aspects of the surface appearance (i.e., edge profile and damage, surface pitting and striations, and distribution and smoothness of polish) are considered, it is possible to obtain valid and useful information about the materials on which tools were used (Keeley 1980; Grace 1989). What is now needed is the examination of entire tool assemblages from particular sites in order to obtain an overall picture of the uses to which a site was put.

Careful examination using optical microscopy has established that a range of animal and plant residues can survive on stone tools (Loy 1991). These residues, which have been found on tools as old as 100,000 years, include blood, muscle tissue, hair, and bone from animals; and woody tissue, phytoliths, starch grains, and resin from plants.

In the case of blood residues, it has been claimed that the associated animal species can be identified using techniques such as immunological assay and haemoglobin crystallization. For example, Loy has reported finding blood from animals such as moose, caribou, grizzly bear, and sea lion on tools from sites in British Columbia dating from 1,000 to 6,000 B.P. Similarly, he reports the identification of human blood on a tool from a Paleolithic site in Iraq. In this case, because other evidence suggests that the tool was used for woodworking, the presence of human blood is more probably indicative of a cut finger than of cannibalism! In considering these results, it should be emphasized that other researchers have been less successful in identifying animal species from blood residues.

In the case of plant residues, the identification of starch grains on stone tools from the northern Solomon Islands is of particular interest (Loy, Spriggs, and Wickler 1992). On the basis of the grain morphology, the starch was shown to come from two taro genera. The results therefore provide direct evidence for the use in the Pacific region of root vegetables some twenty-eight thousand years ago.

Pottery

The physical properties of pottery vessels are sometimes helpful in providing a clue to the use to which the vessels might have been put (Ericson, Read, and Burke 1973; Bronitsky 1986). For example, one would expect that a vessel used to store water would have a high permeability, because the water was kept cool by evaporation from the outer surface of the vessel (Schiffer 1988). Similarly, vessels used for cooking are subjected to rapid changes in temperature and therefore should have high resistance to thermal shock. As a result, cooking pots tend to have a coarse and open fabric that allows them to accommodate the stresses associated with expansion and contraction. However, the proposal that coarse shell or limestone temper was specifically chosen for cooking pots in preference to coarse quartz sand remains unproven (Woods 1986).

The identification of surviving organic residues provides probably the most powerful method for establishing how pottery was used as well as for obtaining information on past diets (Biers and McGovern 1990; Evershed et al. 1992). The objective is to detect the food remnants or sealants adhering to the surface or absorbed into the porous body of pottery during use and to then relate their chemical composition to the original animal and plant species. The most useful organic compounds for this purpose are lipids, which are constituents of fats, oils, waxes, and resins. A particular advantage of lipids is that, because of their hydrophobic properties, migration of lipids from the burial soil into the pottery does not appear to be a serious source of interference.

Identification of lipids involves their extraction from a powdered sample of the pottery by solvent. The individual lipids are then separated by gas chromatography, and the mass spectra of each lipid, resulting from its breakdown by ionization, is recorded by mass spectrometry. Each lipid can then be identified by a combination of its retention time in gas chromatography and its mass spectra.

The identification of the originating animal or plant species from the lipid data is, however, more difficult, because the animal and plant materials will have been structurally and chemically altered during both culinary processes and subsequent burial in the ground. A first stage is to determine whether the lipids originate from an animal or plant source. This assignment can be made through the analysis of the trace sterol components, the presence of cholesterol indicating animal origin. Precise assignment of a residue to a particular animal species is rarely possible. However, dairy product residues can usually be recognized by the presence of short-chain fatty acids. In the case of plants residues, the long-chain alkyl compounds found in the epicuticular leaf waxes of plants can be used to distinguish between a range of leafy vegetables.

Until recently, organic-residue analysis has tended to be performed only on single vessels or small groups of vessels. A current, and more comprehensive, application involving the analysis of several hundred sherds is the study of Late Saxon/Early Medieval pottery from Raunds, Northamptonshire. One aspect of this project is the identification of the natural products used in association with the vessels from the analysis of the specific lipids composition. Thus, the presence of the appropriate epicuticular leaf-wax components (nonacosane, nonacosan-15-one, and nonacosan-15-ol) provided clear evidence that a brassica species, either cabbage or turnip leaves, was being cooked and formed a significant component of the diet of the community (Fig. 15.7). Similarly, evidence indicated the cooking and consumption of leeks.

A second aspect of the project was the investigation of the quantities of lipids that had accumulated in particular parts (i.e., rim, body, and base) of different types of vessels (Fig. 15.8), reconstructed vessels being used for this purpose (Charters et al. 1993). Various types of jar were found to have high concentrations of lipids surviving on the upper parts

Fig. 15.7. Partial gas chromatogram for (a) the total lipid extract of a potsherd from a Late Saxon/Early Medieval cooking vessel, which shows components similar to those in (b) the hexane-soluble fraction of the epicuticular leaf wax of the brassica species, cabbage. (Reprinted from Proceedings of the British Academy, *vol. 77,* New Developments in Archaeological Science, *Fig. 10, p. 204)*

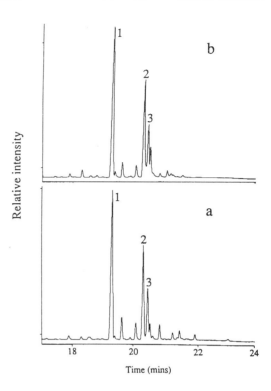

of their inner surfaces, and this distribution pattern could be the result of lipids rising to the surface when foodstuffs were boiled in water in these vessels. Conversely, lipids were distributed fairly uniformly across the inner surfaces of "top hat" vessels, which could reflect to use of these vessels for roasting meat, during which fat is likely to have coated all parts of the inner surface. Finally, the shallow bowls contained only low concentrations of lipids, which suggests that they were not used for cooking. The above interpretations of the use of vessels from the distribution of surviving lipids are inevitably tentative; what is now required are simulation cooking experiments using replica vessels.

CONCLUSIONS

In this chapter I have tried to show that scientific dating methods have provided archaeology with something approaching a worldwide absolute

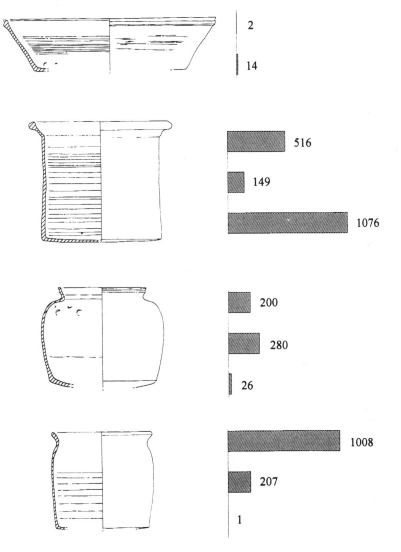

2

14

516

149

1076

200

280

26

1008

207

1

μg lipid g⁻¹ sherd

Fig. 15.8. Total lipid contents for rim, body, and base sherds from four reconstructed Early Medieval vessels, the vessel types being a shallow bowl, a "top hat" vessel, and two jars. (Reprinted by permission of Archaeometry. From S. C. Charters, R. P. Evershed, L. J. Goad, A. Leyden, P. W. Blinkhorn, and V. Denham, "Quantification and Distribution of Lipid in Archaeological Ceramics: Implications for Sampling Potsherds for Organic Residue Analysis and the Classification of Vessel Use," Fig. 2, Archaeometry 35 [1993])

chronology from man's beginnings some two million years ago through to modern times. Science-based artifact studies have similarly extended our knowledge of trade and exchange in antiquity; of the way in which stone tools and pottery were used; and, as discussed in previous chapters, of the technology of artifact production.

A general point that should be emphasized with regard to the study of past material culture is the importance of considering the whole system in a holistic manner rather than focusing on individual facets. Thus in studying a group of artifacts, it is essential to consider the complete cycle, from the selection of the raw materials through the production and distribution of the artifacts to their use and ultimate discard: that is, artifacts must be considered within their overall historical, cultural, social, and economic context as well as with respect to their associated natural environment. Only in this way is it possible to sensibly interpret the data obtained on technology, provenance, and usage and thus answer the question why a particular technology, provenance, or use.

Such a holistic approach requires close and effective collaboration between archaeologists and scientists. For such collaborations to be successful, both groups need to be trained at least to understand each other's aims and methodologies so that they can have meaningful dialogues. The aim of this chapter, and of this volume as a whole, is to contribute to increasing the effectiveness of such dialogues in the future.

REFERENCES

Aitken, M. J. 1985. *Thermoluminescence Dating*. London: Academic Press.
————. 1990. *Science Based Dating in Archaeology*. London: Longman.
Aitken, M. J., P. R. S. Moorey, and P. J. Ucko. 1971. "The Authenticity of Vessels and Figurines in the Hacilar Style." *Archaeometry* 13:89–141.
Baillie, M. G. L. 1982. *Tree-Ring Dating and Archaeology*. London: Croom Helm.
Bass, G. F. 1991. "Evidence of Trade from Bronze Age Shipwrecks." In *Bronze Age Trade in the Mediterranean*, edited by N. H. Gale, 69–82. Göteborg: P. Astroms Forlag.
Baugh, T. G., and J. E. Ericson, eds. 1994. *Prehistoric Exchange Systems in North America*. New York: Plenum Press.
Beck, C. W. 1986. "Spectroscopic Investigations of Amber." *Applied Spectroscopy Reviews* 22:57–110.
Biers, W. R., and P. E. McGovern. 1990. "Organic Contents of Ancient

Vessels." *MASCA Research Papers in Sciences and Archaeology*, vol. 7. Philadelphia.

Bonani, G., S. D. Ivy, Th. R. Niklaus, M. Suter, R. A. Housley, C. R. Bronk, G. J. van Klinken, and R. E. M. Hedges. 1992. "Altersbestimmung von Milligrammproben der Otztaler Gletscherleiche mit der Beschleuniger-massenspektometrie-Methode (AMS)." In *Der Mann im Eis, Band 1*, edited by F. Hopfel, W. Platzer, and K. Spindler, 108–16. Innsbruck: Veroffentlichungen der Universität.

Bowman, S. G. E. 1990. *Radiocarbon Dating*. London: British Museum Publications.

Brill, R. H., and H. P. Hood. 1961. "A New Method for Dating Ancient Glass." *Nature* 189:12–14.

Bronitsky, G. 1986. "The Use of Materials Science Techniques in the Study of Pottery Construction and Use." *Advances in Archaeological Method and Theory*, vol. 9, edited by M. Schiffer, 209–73. New York: Academic Press.

Charters, S., R. P. Evershed, L. J. Goad, A. Leyden, P. W. Blinkhorn, and V. Denham. 1993. "Quantification and Distribution of Lipid in Archaeological Ceramics: Implications for Sampling Potsherds for Organic Residue Analysis and the Classification of Vessel Use." *Archaeometry* 35:211–23.

Clough, T. H. McK., and W. A. Cummings, eds. 1988. *Stone Axe Studies*, vol. 2. CBA Research Reports 67. London.

Craddock, P. T. 1985. "Three Thousand Years of Copper Alloys: From the Bronze Age to the Industrial Revolution." In *Application of Science in Examination of Works of Art*, edited by P. A. England and L. van Zelst, 59–67. Boston: Museum of Fine Arts.

Craddock, P. T., M. R. Cowell, M. N. Leese, and M. J. Hughes. 1983. "The Trace Element Composition of Polished Flint Axes as an Indicator of Source." *Archaeometry* 25:135–64.

Cresswell, R. G. 1991. "The Radiocarbon Dating of Iron Artefacts Using Accelerator Mass Spectrometry." *Journal of the Historical Metallurgy Society* 25:78–85.

Damon et al. 1989. "Radiocarbon Dating of the Shroud of Turin." *Nature* 337:611–15.

Ericson, J. E. 1985. "Strontium Isotope Characterization in the Study of Prehistoric Human Ecology." *Journal of Human Evolution* 14:503–14.

———. 1989. "Some Problems and Potentials of Strontium Isotope Analysis for Human and Animal Ecology." In *Stable Isotopes in Ecological Research—Ecological Study Series*, vol. 68, edited by P. W. Rundel, J. R. Ehlenringer, and K. A. Nagy, 252–59. New York: Springer-Verlag.

Ericson, J. E., D. W. Read, and C. Burke. 1972. "Research Design: The Relationships between the Primary Functions and the Physical Properties of

Ceramic Vessels and Their Implications for Ceramic Distributions on an Archaeological Site." *Anthropology UCLA* 3:84–95.

Evershed, R. P., C. Heron, S. Charters, and L. J. Goad. 1992. "The Survival of Food Residues: New Methods of Analysis, Interpretation and Application." In *New Developments in Archaeological Science,* edited by A. M. Pollard, 187–208. Oxford: Oxford University Press.

Fant, J. C., ed. 1988. "Ancient Marble Quarrying and Trade." *British Archaeological Reports, International Series,* no. 453. Oxford.

Fleming, S. J. 1970. "Thermoluminescence Dating: Refinement of the Quartz Inclusion Method." *Archaeometry* 12:133–45.

Gale, N. H. 1991. "Copper Oxhide Ingots: Their Origin and Their Place in the Bronze Age Metals Trade in the Mediterranean." In *Bronze Age Trade in the Mediterranean,* edited by N. H. Gale, 197–239. Göteborg: P. Astroms Forlag.

Glascock, M. D., J. M. Elam, and K. Aoyama. 1991. "Provenience Analysis of Obsidian Artefacts from La Entrada Region, Honduras." In *Archaeometry '90,* edited by E. Pernicka and G. A. Wagner, 395–404. Basel: Birkhauser Verlag.

Gowlett, J. A. J., R. E. M. Hedges, and I. A. Law. 1989. "Radiocarbon Accelerator (AMS) Dating of Lindow Man." *Antiquity* 63:71–79.

Grace, R. 1989. "Interpreting the Function of Stone Tools." *British Archaeological Reports, International Series,* no. 474. Oxford.

Grun, R., and C. B. Stringer. 1991. "Electron Spin Resonance Dating and the Evolution of Modern Humans." *Archaeometry* 33:153–200.

Hedges, R. E. M. 1987. "Radiocarbon Dating by Accelerator Mass Spectrometry: Some Recent Results and Applications." *Philisophical Transactions of the Royal Society* 323:57–73.

———. 1990. "A Review of the Application of AMS-14C Dating to Archaeology." *Nuclear Instruments and Methods in Physics Research* B52:428–32.

Henderson, J. 1989. "Scientific Analysis of Ancient Glass." In *Scientific Analysis in Archaeology,* edited by J. Henderson, 30–60. Oxford University Committee for Archaeology Monograph, no. 19. Oxford.

———, ed. 1989. *Scientific Analysis in Archaeology.* Oxford University Committee for Archaeology Monograph, no. 19. Oxford.

Hughes, M. J., M. R. Cowell, and D. R. Hook, eds. 1991. *Neutron Activation and Plasma Emission Spectrometric Analysis in Archaeology.* London: British Museum, Occasional Paper 82.

Hughes, M. J., and A. G. Vince. 1986. "Neutron Activation Analysis and Petrology of Hispano-Moresque Pottery." In *Proceedings of the 24th International Archaeometry Symposium,* edited by J. S. Olin and M. J. Blackman, 353–67. Washington, D.C.: Smithsonian Institution Press.

Huntley, D. J., D. I. Godfrey-Smith, and M. L. W. Thewalt. 1985. "Optical Dating of Sediments." *Nature* 313:105–7.

Keeley, L. H. 1980. *Experimental Determination of Stone Tool Uses: A Micro-wear Analysis*. Chicago: University of Chicago Press.

Kempe, D. R. C., and A. P. Harvey, eds. 1983. *Petrology of Archaeological Artifacts*. Oxford: Oxford University Press.

Lanteigne, M. P. 1991. "Cation-Ratio Dating of Rock-Engravings: A Critical Appraisal." *Antiquity* 65:292–95.

Loy, T. H. 1991. "Prehistoric Organic Residues: Recent Advances in Identification, Dating, and Their Antiquity." In *Archaeometry '90*, edited by E. Pernicka and G. A. Wagner, 645–56. Basel: Birkhauser Verlag.

Loy, T. H., M. Spriggs, and S. Wickler. 1992. "Direct Evidence for Human Use of Plants 28,000 Years Ago: Starch Residues on Stone Artefacts from Northern Solomon Islands." *Antiquity* 66:898–912.

McDougall, I. 1981. "Ar^{40}/Ar^{39} Age Spectra from KBS Tuff, Koobi Fora Formation." *Nature* 294:120–24.

Mellars, P. A., M. J. Aitken, and C. B. Stringer. 1993. "Outlining the Problem." In *The Origin of Modern Humans and the Impact of Chronometric Dating*, edited by M. J. Aitken, C. B. Stringer, and P. A. Mellars, 3–11. Princeton, N.J.: Princeton University Press.

Middleton, A., and I. C. Freestone, eds. 1991. *Recent Developments in Ceramic Petrology*. London: British Museum, Occasional Paper 81.

Newton, R. G. 1971. "The Enigma of the Layered Crusts on Some Weathered Glasses, a Chronological Account of the Investigations." *Archaeometry* 13:1–9.

Northover, P. 1989. "Non-Ferrous Metallurgy." In *Scientific Analysis in Archaeology*, edited by J. Henderson, 213–36. Oxford University Committee for Archaeology Monograph, no. 19. Oxford.

Renfrew, C., J. E. Dixon, and J. R. Cann. 1966. "Obsidian and Early Cultural Contact in Near East." *Proceedings of the Prehistoric Society* 32:30–72.

Roberts, R., R. Jones, and M. A. Smith. 1990. "Thermoluminescence Dating of a 50,000-Year-Old Human Occupation Site in Northern Australia." *Nature* 345:153–56.

Sayre, E. V., and R. W. Smith. 1961. "Compositional Categories of Ancient Glass." *Science* 133:1824–26.

Scarre, C., and F. Healy. eds. 1993. *Trade and Exchange in Prehistoric Europe*. Oxbow Monograph, no. 33. Oxford.

Schiffer, M. B. 1988. "The Effects of Surface Treatment on Permeability and Evaporative Cooling Effectiveness of Pottery." In *Proceedings of the 26th International Archaeometry Symposium*, edited by R. M. Farquhar, R. G. V. Hancock, and L. A. Pavlish, 23–29. Toronto: University of Toronto.

Schwarcz, H. P. 1980. "Absolute Age Determination of Archaeological Sites by Uranium Series Dating of Travertines." *Archaeometry* 22:3–24.

Sherratt, A., and S. Sherratt. 1991. "From Luxuries to Commodities: The

Nature of the Mediterranean Bronze Age Trading Systems." In *Bronze Age Trade in the Mediterranean,* edited by N. H. Gale, 351–86. Göteborg: P. Astroms Forlag.

Smith, B. W., E. J. Rhodes, S. Stokes, N. A. Spooner, and M. J. Aitken. 1990. "Optical Dating of Sediments: Initial Quartz Results from Oxford." *Archaeometry* 32:19–31.

Stevenson, C. M., J. Carpenter, and B. E. Scheetz. 1989. "Obsidian Dating: Recent Advances in the Experimental Determination and Application of Hydration Rates." *Archaeometry* 31:193–206.

Stos-Gale. 1989. "Lead Isotope Studies." In *Scientific Analysis in Archaeology,* edited by J. Henderson, 274–301. Oxford University Committee for Archaeology Monograph, no. 19. Oxford.

Stulik, D. C., and D. J. Donahue. 1992. "AMS Radiocarbon Dating: Its Current and Future Role in Art Research." *Materials Research Society Bulletin* 27:53–60.

Thorpe, R. S., O. Williams-Thorpe, D. G. Jenkins, and J. S. Watson. 1991. "The Geological Sources and Transport of the Bluestones of Stonehenge, Wiltshire, UK." *Proceedings of the Prehistoric Society* 57 (2): 103–57.

Tite, M. S. 1972. *Methods of Physical Examination in Archaeology.* London: Seminar Press.

———. 1991. "Archaeological Science—Past Achievements and Future Prospects." *Archaeometry* 33:139–52.

Valladas, H., J. L. Joron, G. Valladas, B. Arensburg, O. Bar-Yosef, A. Belfer-Cohen, P. Goldberg, H. Laville, L. Meignen, and Y. Rak. 1987. "Thermoluminescence Dates for the Neanderthal Burial Site at Kebara in Israel." *Nature* 330:159–60.

Valladas, H., J. L. Reys, G. Valladas, O. Bar-Yosef, and B. Vandermeersch. 1988. "Thermoluminescence Dating of Mousterian Proto-Cro-Magnon Remains from Israel and the Origin of Modern Man." *Nature* 331:614–16.

van der Merwe, N. J., J. A. Lee-Thorp, J. F. Thackeray, A. Hall-Martin, F. J. Kruger, H. Coetzee, R. H. V. Bell, and M. Lindeque. 1990. "Source-Area Determination of Elephant Ivory by Isotopic Analysis." *Nature* 346:744–46.

Watchman, A. 1993. "Perspectives and Potentials for Absolute Dating Prehistoric Rock Paintings." *Antiquity* 67:58–65.

Woods, A. J. 1986. "Form and Function: Some Observations on the Cooking Pot in Antiquity." In *Ceramics and Civilization,* vol. 2, *Technology and Style,* edited by W. D. Kingery, 157–72. Westerville, Ohio: American Ceramic Society.

Zimmerman, D. W. 1971. "Thermoluminescent Dating Using Fine Grains from Pottery." *Archaeometry* 13:29–52.

Contributors

MAJORIE AKIN is assistant research anthropologist at the University of California–Riverside.

JOSEPH J. CORN is senior lecturer of history at Stanford University.

CATHERINE S. FOWLER is professor of anthropology at the University of Nevada–Reno.

DON D. FOWLER is professor and chair of anthropology at the University of Nevada–Reno.

DAVID KILLICK is assistant professor of anthropology and adjunct assistant professor of materials science and engineering at the University of Arizona–Tucson.

W. DAVID KINGERY is Regents Professor of Anthropology and Materials Science and Engineering at the University of Arizona–Tucson.

KRISTIAN KRISTIANSEN is professor of archaeology at the University of Gothenburg, Sweden.

STEVEN LUBAR is curator of engineering and industry at the National Museum of American History, Smithsonian Institution, Washington, D.C.

RUTH OLDENZIEL is associate professor at the Research Center, Belle van Zuylen Institute, University of Amsterdam, Netherlands.

NANCY J. PAREZO is curator of ethnology at Arizona State Museum at the University of Arizona–Tucson.

JULES D. PROWN is interim director of the Art Gallery and Paul Mellon Professor of the History of Art at Yale University.

MICHAEL B. SCHIFFER is professor of anthropology at the University of Arizona–Tucson.

MICHAEL S. TITE is director of the Research Laboratory for Archaeology and the History of Art and Edward Hall Professor of Archaeological Science at Oxford University, England.